Concepts and Strategies in International Human Rights

TEACHING TEXTS IN LAW AND POLITICS

David A. Schultz
General Editor

Vol. 5

PETER LANG
New York • Washington, D.C./Baltimore • Bern
Frankfurt am Main • Berlin • Brussels • Vienna • Oxford

Concepts and Strategies in International Human Rights

George J. Andreopoulos
EDITOR

PETER LANG
New York • Washington, D.C./Baltimore • Bern
Frankfurt am Main • Berlin • Brussels • Vienna • Oxford

Library of Congress Cataloging-in-Publication Data

Concepts and strategies in international human rights /
edited by George J. Andreopoulos.
p. cm. — (Teaching texts in law and politics; v. 5)
Includes bibliographical references and index.
1. Human rights. I. Andreopoulos, George J. II. Series.
JC571 .C6477   323—dc21   2002005219
ISBN 0-8204-5225-4
ISSN 1083-3447

Die Deutsche Bibliothek-CIP-Einheitsaufnahme

Concepts and strategies in international human rights /
ed. by: George J. Andreopoulos.
–New York; Washington, D.C./Baltimore; Bern;
Frankfurt am Main; Berlin; Brussels; Vienna; Oxford: Lang.
(Teaching texts in law and politics; Vol. 5)
ISBN 0-8204-5225-4

Cover art by Enis Selimovic
Cover design by Dutton & Sherman Design

© 2002 Peter Lang Publishing, Inc., New York

All rights reserved.
Reprint or reproduction, even partially, in all forms such as microfilm,
xerography, microfiche, microcard, and offset strictly prohibited.

TABLE OF CONTENTS

Acknowledgments vii

1   Introduction: A Half Century After the Universal Declaration
    George J. Andreopoulos 1

2   The Challenges of Humane Governance
    Richard Falk 21

3   Human Rights Standards and the Human Rights
    Movement in the Global South: The UDHR and Beyond
    Susan Waltz 51

4   Rescuing Human Rights: The Prospects
    for Humanitarian Intervention
    Tom Farer 73

5   On the Prevention of Genocide: Humanitarian
    Intervention and the Role of the United Nations
    George J. Andreopoulos 97

6   A Glass Half Full: The NAFTA Labor Agreement
    and Cross-Border Labor Action
    Lance Compa 139

7   The Right to Education and Human Rights Education
    Richard Pierre Claude 163

8   A Strategy for Human Rights: Five Internet Projects
    That Can Change the World
    Lloyd S. Etheredge 185

Appendix. Selective Overview of Major Developments
    in Human Rights 213

List of Contributors 221

Index 223

ACKNOWLEDGMENTS

The idea for this book began after a discussion with Dr. Basil Wilson, Provost of the John Jay College of Criminal Justice, on ways to celebrate the fiftieth anniversary of the Universal Declaration of Human Rights. Dr. Wilson strongly endorsed the idea of devoting his Fall 1998 Lecture Series to this topic.

Several of the chapters of this book were originally presented as lectures in the Series. The Provost's support and assistance throughout this project are deeply appreciated. In addition, I would like to thank Professor Peter Juviler of Columbia University for his permission to include in this volume two papers originally presented at Columbia University's Seminar on Human Rights, which we co-chair. The myriad of tasks associated with the edition of such a volume were rendered manageable due to the skills, dedication, and energy of my research assistant Isorys Dilone. Valuable research assistance was also provided by Andre Dowdie and Eugenia Coker. At Peter Lang, it was a great pleasure to work with Phyllis Korper, Acquisitions Editor; Jackie Pavlovic, Production Supervisor; and Bernadette Alfaro, Production Coordinator. Their encouragement and advice made my task easier than I could ever imagine. Last, but not least, I would like to thank my fellow contributors whose scholarly commitment made this book possible.

New York City, December 2001

CHAPTER ONE

Introduction:
A Half Century After the Universal Declaration

George J. Andreopoulos

The recent interest in the role of human rights norms and their impact on domestic and international politics often elicits an ambivalent reaction. This ambivalence was reflected in the varied commentaries to the Pinochet case that unfolded as the international community was preparing to celebrate the fiftieth anniversary of the Universal Declaration of Human Rights (UDHR). The decision by the British Home Secretary to sign an authority, on the eve of the anniversary, enabling the British courts to proceed with the Spanish Government's request for Senator Pinochet's extradition on charges of genocide, terrorism, and torture,[1] was indicative of both the promises and challenges that lie in the path of enforcing human rights norms.

As is well known by now, Pinochet was not extradited but the decision had nothing to do with the merits of the case. (After all, extradition is first and foremost a political act.) On the contrary, as the case moved through the British legal system, certain important norms were reaffirmed. Upon reading the arguments offered by those Law Lords who initially ruled in favor of the Spanish Government's request, one cannot help but appreciate the resilience of these norms. Lord Nicholls, for example, argued, in his opinion in favor of allowing the extradition request to go forward, that both the Charter of the Nuremberg Tribunal and the subsequent judgment had affirmed the basic principle that "certain types of conduct, including torture and hostage-taking, are not acceptable conduct on the part of anyone. This applies as much to heads of state, or even more so, as it does to everyone else; the contrary conclusion would make a mockery of international law."[2] And he concluded: "From this time on, no head of state could have been in any doubt about his potential personal liability if he participated in acts regarded by international law as crimes against humanity."[3]

Yet, at the same time, the tortuous path of the Pinochet case revealed the continuing tensions between the grounding of these norms by state-centrist notions of criminal jurisdiction, and the emerging global ethos of accountability manifested through the dynamic interplay of international and national justice options. To those who see the glass half full, the eventual narrowing of the list of charges against Pinochet constituted an eerie reminder of the constraining effects of territorially based jurisdictional initiatives. To those who see the glass half empty, the ensuing debate in Chile on Pinochet's legacy and the concomitant legal challenges against the aging dictator were a powerful testimony to an important development: *the mainstreaming of the domestic delegitimization of Pinochet*, which would have been inconceivable without his humiliating detention and subjection to court proceedings in Britain. Thus, the Pinochet saga confronted both optimists and pessimists with developments that could not be explained on the basis of their preconceived notions relating to the impact of human rights norms.

Despite the understandable frustrations that such a mixed record generates, even the skeptics would have to acknowledge that certain substantive developments have occurred since the immediate aftermath of World War II. At that time, the international community, shocked by the revelations concerning the abusive conduct of the Axis Powers against occupied populations, made the first concerted effort to take human rights seriously.[4] The framers of the two main international instruments of that period, the Charters of the International Military Tribunal (Nuremberg) and of the United Nations, had to maintain a delicate balance. On the one hand, they needed to demonstrate a commitment to the nonrecurrence of gross and systematic violations of human rights and fundamental freedoms. On the other hand, they needed to ensure that any proposed normative commitments would elicit a positive response from member states, always sensitive to any undue intrusion upon their sovereign prerogatives.[5]

These competing considerations can be found in both instruments. In the Nuremberg Charter, the most forward-looking provision on crimes against humanity was subsumed under the crimes against the peace and war crimes provisions. In the United Nations (U.N.) Charter, although the promotion and encouragement of respect for human rights was listed as one of the main purposes of the organization, it was hierarchically inferior to the maintenance of international peace and security. By linking the concern for human rights to interstate peace, these instruments delivered a consistent message: protection of human rights (including possible enforcement action in defense of human rights) would materialize in cases of violations resulting from the commission of interstate aggression (crimes against the peace—Nuremberg Charter/breach of the peace, acts of aggression—U. N. Charter).[6] In the absence of cross-border impact, the sovereign authority of the country in question would handle actions contributing to human rights violations. Any international action would be confined to advocacy to be conducted on a consensual basis, primarily in collaboration with the responsible authorities of the states concerned. Thus, the U.N. Charter employed the nonthreatening language of promotion, as opposed to protection, of human rights and posited a nonconfrontational strategy vis-à-vis member states.

To be sure, it was easy to make a mockery of such an undertaking. Skeptics could point to the structural constraints imposed by statist considerations and by the power asymmetries in the community of states. In addition, by allocating primary responsibility for human rights to the state, whose rulers were the main agents of potentially abusive conduct, it could be argued that the human rights provisions of the Charter rendered normative considerations as epiphenomena at best. While some of these critics do not deny the importance of norms, they believe that they are not determinative of state behavior for various reasons, including power asymmetries and the lack of mechanisms for deciding among competing norms.[7]

The normative "softness" of the human rights discourse was compounded by the decision of the Commission on Human Rights to proceed with a declaration, as opposed to a more comprehensive undertaking that would have included a declaration, a covenant, and provisions for their implementation. While the latter would have been consistent with the tenor of the Economic and Social Council's original request for an international bill of rights, geopolitical considerations, amplified by emerging Cold War tensions, were to doom such an undertaking and could have even threatened the adoption of the declaration.[8] Thus, despite the relative optimism of the early postwar years, what emerged was a normatively downsized human rights project, shadowed by an impending coup de grace. The bipolar configuration of Cold War politics did not augur well for its future prospects.

These obstacles notwithstanding, what is noteworthy about human rights norms is their resilience and transformational capacity. The very "subversive" nature of the human rights discourse,[9] even in its most innocuous of formulations, rendered the malleability of the UDHR a source of strength, not weakness. While hindsight undoubtedly helps here, it is important to stress that the essence of the dominant paradigm in human rights advocacy, premised on an antagonistic relationship between the individual/group and state authority structures, makes the use of the human rights language coextensive with the quest for change. Thus, rather than constraining, the declaratory nature of the document offered ample room for cutting-edge strategies of promotion and (to a lesser extent) protection. In addition, not being intertwined with any implementation mechanisms, the UDHR acquired from its inception "an independent moral status in world affairs and law,"[10] thus universalizing the notion of a fundamental baseline of human well-being.

Another positive outcome of the nonbinding nature of the Declaration was its eventual acceptance by states that were to emerge from colonial occupation. At the time of the UDHR's adoption, the majority of developing nations were under colonial rule. This presented delegates from the then newly independent states with a formidable task: to ensure the widest possible ownership with respect to the UDHR.[11] A truly participatory endeavor, coupled with the document's inherent flexibility, were key catalysts in the progressive legitimization of the declaration's norms in the era of decolonization.

Nothing exemplifies better the aforementioned transformational capacity of these norms than the increasing relevance of human rights considerations in international politics, a development initially nurtured within the framework of an aspirational initiative. This achievement goes beyond the still growing corpus of international human rights law, and encompasses— among other things—the catalytic role of non governmental organizations (NGOs). NGOs had already played a crucial role in the incorporation of human rights provisions in the U.N. Charter, and the Economic and Social Council had authorized their consultative status in the organization well before the adoption of the UDHR.[12] In just a few decades, NGOs have turned from marginal into vital transnational actors capable of mobilizing support for sustained scrutiny and pressure against governments in a variety of situational contexts.[13] Their enhanced profile carries a critical message: *the realization of humane outcomes is largely dependent on the creative uses of normative space, uses that should encompass but never be reduced to lawmaking.*

This growth in transnational activism reflects the convergence of several factors, two of which are of particular relevance here. The first relates to a more nuanced perception of the state that transcends the limitations of the prevailing human rights paradigm. While the paradigm's state-centered ness is the logical concomitant of the postwar legacy and of the fact that ruling authorities remain prime perpetrators of human rights violations, it has—until recently—failed to take seriously the array of nonstate actors capable of systematic violations, particularly (but not exclusively) in the socioeconomic sphere. The second is related to the first. By placing increasing emphasis on nonstate actors, the traditional Manichaean dichotomy between state and civil society is being replaced by a more complex reality that acknowledges the state's dual role as both promoter and abuser of human rights. Thus, the transformational capacity of human rights norms is being enhanced by the progressive incorporation of a more holistic understanding of state activism. For example, a recent study conducted by the Asian Development Bank (ADB) on legal empowerment and its role in good governance and poverty reduction, concluded that government can play a vital role in legal empowerment efforts. According to the study, a key feature of the enabling environment for successful legal empowerment work occurs "where government agencies and civil society work together as full-fledged partners, drawing on the resources and authority of the former and the flexibility, grassroots outreach, and goodwill of the latter." Consequently, one of the report's key recommendations relates to the need for international development agencies to support "the collaborative efforts of civil society organizations and government agencies."[14]

A critical corollary to this is the emergence of a more nuanced perception of civil society, its actors, and its institutions. For a long time, civil society was a residual and rather amorphous concept in which human rights activists would place all their hopes for grass roots initiatives in defense of humane values. Up to a certain point, this was justified by the manifest contributions of civil society actors in the area of monitoring and dissemination. In the process, these actors were also instrumental in the broadening of the policy space. Thus, what Higgott has termed as a site of "emancipatory counterhegemony" would denote a terrain on which challenges against established authority structures could be launched, and more ambitiously, in the context of a "global civil society," as the terrain of intersocietal issue networking for an alternative world order. However, the expanding agenda of civil society initiatives has also brought into sharper focus the dark side of counterhegemony's activism: the networking of forces converging on exclusivist, discriminatory, and inhumane practices.

In such a context, the evolving nature of both state and societal activism generates the potential and promise of new coalitions formed by transnational social movements and states to deal with a whole set of critical policy issues, including the protection of civilians in armed conflict, the employment and environmental implications of regional economic initiatives (like the North American Free Trade Agreement), the elimination of antipersonnel mines, and the establishment of an international criminal court, to name a few.[15] The changing parameters of the Westphalian landscape (originally bounded by a clearly defined correspondence among territory, people, institutions, and authority structures) coupled with more complex civil society configurations could generate new coalitions of state and nonstate actors challenging established policies in key issue areas. Thus, the crucial focus here is on the quest for an outcome consistent with a deepening adherence to human rights norms and the democratization of authority structures at all inter-and intrasocietal levels, rather than on the state/civil society dichotomy.

On the theoretical level, this quest reflects the growing emphasis on the role of ideas, norms, and transnational actors in international relations.[16] Going beyond the realist focus on material factors as determinants of political outcomes, several studies have challenged realist assumptions in several key issue areas, including that of security policy in both its domestic and international variants.[17] While material considerations remain relevant, this body of literature has been critical of the view that ideas should be considered as mere epiphenomena, nothing more than vehicles of legitimization of preexisting interests, with no causal role in policy outcomes.

For example, a recent study on the role of transnational networks in promoting ideas and policies that would lessen the danger of a superpower nuclear showdown during the Cold War, has found that transnational activism indeed had an impact on Soviet conduct. Soviet reformers used international norms conveyed by these networks (in particular norms relating to nuclear disarmament, common security, and nonoffensive defense) to promote and sustain Gorbachev's foreign policy initiatives. While material factors (economic situation, military needs, and the actions of the United States and its allies) were important, the solutions that "Gorbachev embraced in pursuit of foreign policy reform cannot be explained without acknowledging the normative commitments that he shared with his advisers and with their transnational colleagues: to nuclear disarmament and to integration of the Soviet Union as a "normal country" into the international political and economic community."[18]

In the human rights context, an ideational perspective would emphasize the staying power of human rights norms and their impact on policy outcomes, in situations where material interests or other "broader utility functions" would dictate a different course of action.[19] For example, in the case of Operation Restore Hope (Somalia), geostrategic or other material considerations cannot be considered as determinative of the initial decision to intervene. A more complete understanding of this decision, in light of President Bush's statement at the time,[20] would have to take into consideration certain normative developments of the early post–Cold War era. In particular, but not exclusively, the enhanced normative status of the rule of law and of collective security, and the growing awareness of the linkages between rights deprivations and threats to international peace and security.[21] A realist perspective on the Somali case is more helpful in explaining subsequent developments (like the Unified Task Force's (UNITAF) reluctance to engage in the disarming of the different Somali factions) rather than the decision to intervene in the first place.[22]

On the more practical level, this quest is consistent with an emphasis on innovative strategies. So far, the greatest achievements of the human rights movement have been in the area of standard-setting. The rather impressive body of international human rights law and the reaffirmation of the codified norms in subsequent declarations and resolutions have undoubtedly constituted the bedrock of the human rights revolution. This emphasis has also produced the main strategy of the movement: the articulation of legal strategies to hold states accountable to the standards already adhered to. The gap between formal adherence to these standards and actual state practice would provide the opening for public exposure and eventual compliance, known as shaming. While this remains an important weapon in the human rights arsenal, the evolving coordinates of social, economic, and political life generate the need for new instruments and approaches.

Up to a certain point, the need for a new strategic thinking is the product of rising expectations. These expectations have been embedded in varying references to human rights as the (near) universally accepted frame work for moral discourse.[23] Yet despite the accomplishments in the area of standard-setting and monitoring, human rights are continuously and massively violated throughout the world. Thus, the human rights movement is called upon to address a paradox: dissemination of information about abusive conduct, and subsequent denunciations do not seem to have much of an impact on key issue areas of human rights concern. In some instances, the generation of information, rather than serving as a call for action, seems to provide an excuse for inaction.

The gap between increasing awareness and effectiveness is troubling to many analysts and activists. According to the executive director of the American branch of Amnesty International, "...human rights groups had a great deal of success by setting in motion a process in which the human rights groups would inform the media, the media would inform the Government and then the Government would do something...but that model is breaking down."[24] How can the movement translate its moral authority into more effective compliance with international standards?

While there is no easy answer to such a complex question, the first step forward is an acknowledgment that human rights activism exhibits aspects of what might be termed as the military planners' syndrome: the tendency to plan for the last rather than the next war. In less militaristic language, this would translate into a proclivity to use dated strategies and tactics in confronting new challenges.

The issue of civilian protection is a good case in point. One of the unmistakable trends in recent conflicts has been the increasing victimization of civilians. As the latest report of the Secretary-General to the Security Council on this subject noted, civilian casualties constitute the principal aim, rather than the unintended consequence of otherwise legitimate military operations.[25] A contributing factor in the growing irrelevance of human rights/humanitarian standards is the prominence of nonstate armed groups.

Many of these groups operate within a gray area between semipolitically motivated acts of violence and outright banditry. A recent report by the International Committee of the Red Cross (ICRC) identified the fading away of the distinction between political action and organized crime as one of the most disturbing trends in nonstate armed group activity.[26] Very often, these groups exhibit a loose to nonexistent command structure, are undisciplined and, more ominously, demonstrate a lack of interest in any form of external recognition.[27]

All these elements pose a very serious challenge to the normative framework of the Geneva Conventions, a framework devised for conflict situations in which all parties (whether state or nonstate) share a minimum set of basic characteristics: they are under responsible command, and exercise such control over part of the territory in question so as to be able to "carry out sustained and concerted military operations"[28] among other things. However, there is an important premise here that directly relates to the earlier point about recognition. The 1977 adaptation of the Geneva Conventions (the Additional Protocols) was indicative of the international community's normative response to the challenges posed by national liberation movements. While many of these movements engaged in terrorist-related activities that violated basic human rights/humanitarian norms, these activities were controlled by and subsumed under a political agenda which aimed at international recognition. The prospects of becoming a legitimate member of the international community acted as a constraining factor that sought to ensure the ultimate primacy of politics over pure violence.

The landscape has clearly changed. Many nonstate armed groups do not care about recognition. Thus, it is becoming increasingly difficult to articulate a strategy of adherence to international standards when the main incentive (international legitimacy) carries very little weight. The solution does not lie in further codification, despite the fact that certain gaps exist in the protective regime shaped by the growing intersections between international humanitarian law (IHL) and international human rights law (IHRL). Too much energy devoted to filling these gaps would clearly echo the aforementioned military planners' syndrome. Given the appalling record of observance of already applicable standards, codification is not a promising path to adherence.

What are the relevant incentives? The international community is currently seeking to address this critical issue. In the aforementioned report on the protection of civilians, the Secretary-General proposed a "structured dialogue" with armed groups. This dialogue would be presumably facilitated by the development of "a manual of best practices for engagement" with these groups, a task to be entrusted—according to the report—to the U.N.'s Inter-Agency Standing Committee. One of the reasons for an engagement, as opposed to a codification and enforcement strategy, is the belated realization that "many armed groups *deliberately* operate outside the recognized normative and ethical framework in furtherance of their objectives."[29] While it is not clear—at the time of this writing—what the constitutive elements of an engagement strategy are, this path marks an unmistakable shift of emphasis away from the traditional codification and enforcement strategy.

Here an important clarification is in order. Placing the emphasis on nonlegal strategies does not mean that norms are becoming less relevant. On the contrary, this author would argue that no structured dialogue could have a chance of succeeding unless it relates to the relevant human rights/humanitarian framework. Within this framework, however, those engaged must make more creative use of the available normative space, including the mobilization of key constituencies affected by the outcome of the dialogue. A useful entry point for dialogue with armed groups could be to focus on particularly egregious violations that the groups themselves might consider as "indefensible, or...otherwise counter-productive to their cause," as a recent study on this subject has suggested.[30] For example, addressing the issue of abusive conduct vis-à-vis child soldiers might induce greater compliance with international standards than the issue of adult captives.[31] At the same time, a multifaceted strategy could encompass the targeting of key constituencies and sources of support (including local populations, diaspora communities, and private business) that could be mobilized to support an array of measures,[32] including—as a last resort—the imposition of appropriate enforcement action.[33]

This brings us to a point raised by some of the critics of the human rights movement. For the movement to keep its relevance in the new century, it has to reassert its political profile and mobilize key constituencies in critical issue areas around specific policies and preferred courses of action.[34] The standoffish attitude exhibited by many established human rights organizations, in which impartiality and objectivity very often become ends in themselves, robs the movement of its "subversive" capacity and alienates it from its rich and proud heritage.[35] It is in a sense ironic that some of the most promising initiatives are currently being explored by what was until recently considered a moribund labor rights movement. For example, as a result of the North American Agreement on Labor Cooperation (NAALC), unprecedented opportunities for the transnational mobilization of labor rights advocates have emerged that are slowly but steadily transforming the landscape of labor activism.[36]

At the dawn of the new century, the human rights movement can rightly lay claim to some remarkable achievements, but it must—at the same time—remain cognizant of a whole array of new and unprecedented challenges. Some of the challenges relate to effective new strategies that would make use of the "globally available...resources in combination with burgeoning international networking" to promote promising human rights

Introduction 11

initiatives, as in the area of human rights education.[37] For example, in its legal empowerment study report, the ADB highlighted the central role that knowledge of international human rights can have in raising legal awareness among the disadvantaged.[38] In any discussion of forward-looking strategies, the role of the emerging global Internet would be critical.[39] Other challenges relate to the conceptual framework within which the human rights movement has been operating, and the need to question some long-held assumptions on the role of normative considerations in international politics, as well as on the parameters and transformative potential of a reinvigorated human rights discourse.

The study of these achievements and challenges has been of primary concern to the contributors of this volume. From the global prospects for humane governance to the future of human rights activism in the developing world; from the risks and opportunities associated with humanitarian intervention, the international community's most controversial and blunt instrument in the service of human rights, to the prospects for the transnational networking of labor rights activists; and from the encouraging initiatives in human rights education to the liberating potential of the Internet, the continuing quest for human empowerment, as a key means of addressing political, social, and economic inequities, underscores the work of all the contributors.

Richard Falk's essay presents a comprehensive overview of the main achievements in human rights, as well as an assessment of some of the critical challenges that lie ahead. Any approach to evaluation should—according to the author—avoid the twin pitfalls of legalism and cynicism. For example, a strict legalist approach would be critical of the fact that the UDHR is not a legally binding instrument. Yet, as subsequent developments were to demonstrate, the very recommendatory nature of the UDHR proved to be a source of strength rather than weakness. Its adoption has provided a universal foundation for the human rights discourse, and has shaped the quest for humane governance which the author defines as the proposition that "the totality of authority at all levels of social order should be exercised in conformity with widely shared human values, as embodied in the main formulations of human rights." Falk surveys some of the main achievements, including the emergence of human rights activist organizations, the antiapartheid movement, and the human rights campaign in the Soviet Union and in Eastern Europe under the auspices of the Helsinki Accords. These remarkable achievements, however, should not make the human rights community lose sight of the formidable challenges that lie ahead, including globalization, the politics of identity, and the need for a "new internationalism" in the shape of new coalitions between civil society actors and states on global issues.

The origins of the UDHR and the question of its ownership are key issues addressed in Susan Waltz's essay. Over the years, many critics have seen this foundational document as a construct designed to universalize Western values and norms. Waltz argues that although the idea of human rights may be traced through Western intellectual developments, the UDHR "was a politically negotiated and constructed agreement." To understand the importance of the document and its global impact, an appreciation of the intellectual contributions of delegates from Lebanon, China, and several Latin American countries is imperative. The globalization of the document's origins is not only a much-needed corrective, but also a reaffirmation that human rights constitute "a compelling concept for many non-Western advocates of social justice." In the quest for social justice, human rights advocates in the global South face some major challenges: first and foremost, surviving threats to freedom and physical safety; developing organizational strength for effective action; and transcending rivalry with other human rights NGOs in the midst of an often resource-deprived environment. Yet, despite these difficulties, human rights activism continues to grow, its very existence being—according to Waltz—"a testimony to the universality of human rights."

Few issue areas have generated the level of controversy that has been associated with humanitarian intervention. As the two essays by Tom Farer and George Andreopoulos indicate, the series of operations that have come under that rubric have offered certain lessons; yet, it remains unclear what—if any—lessons have been learned in the process by the key actors involved.

As part of what are called "peace operations," humanitarian intervention faces—according to Tom Farer—some generic obstacles characteristic of all these operations. These obstacles include the United Nations itself with the perennial problems associated with the organization's two political organs (Security Council and General Assembly), as well as with the resistance of its operating agencies to any form of cooperation, let alone coordination; the easy access to small arms and light weapons for "any group with a violent impulse" that "immensely complicates the effort to halt fighting, deliver aid and build peace"; and problems relating to the relief-to-development continuum, in particular the weakness of the intermediate, but vital link of rehabilitation, or recovery assistance. Some of these issues are illustrated through a detailed study of the Somali case, which the author experienced from the inside. The troubled and uneven record of humanitarian intervention operations, argues Farer, offers various lessons, two of which are critical: the need for the creation of strategic planning units to work on "disaster scenarios and strategies of response," and—in the absence of iron rules in strategy and tactics—"the irreducible need for wise judgment."

The targeting of civilians in many of the recent crises has rekindled the debate over the uses of humanitarian intervention to prevent or stop genocidal killings. The latest controversy, as George Andreopoulos argues in his essay, followed the Secretary-General's opening remarks on the need for a forcible option in cases of gross and systematic violations of human rights, made at the 1999 annual session of the General Assembly. These remarks reflected a perspective that could be traced back to the euphoria of the early post–Cold War period, and to exultant references about a "new humanitarian order" with an emphasis on prevention. However, the operations undertaken in defense of human rights have reconfirmed the underlying tensions between their political and humanitarian objectives, thus undermining the effectiveness of the international community's response to genocidal situations. Andreopoulos surveys the options available for prompt and effective action, an issue "revisited with a vengeance ever since the Rwanda tragedy." While there is consensus on the need for a force as the ultimate instrument of prevention, recent initiatives and suggestions have left a lot to be desired. Ultimately, "any credible responsive action rests and will continue to do so with member states."

The promotion and protection of socioeconomic rights remains one of the most elusive goals on the human rights agenda. Progress is invariably slow and uneven. Yet, recent years have witnessed some encouraging developments in some unlikely quarters. According to Lance Compa, the NAALC, NAFTA's labor side agreement, "provides an opportunity for workers, trade unions and their allies...to work together concretely to defend workers' rights against abuses by corporations and governments." While commonly criticized as "toothless," the Labor Agreement has given rise to an impressive array of cases covering issues relating to minimum employment standards, worker organizing, migrant worker protection, and occupational safety and health, among others. Compa surveys some of the major cases and concludes that even in situations "where no immediate concrete results are apparent, the claims procedure and its public hearings...have dramatically increased public awareness and concern over labor standards in North America." Last, but not least, the NAALC has been a key catalyst in the "deepening of labor rights advocacy in North America," as trade union leaders and activists seek to cope with the effects of economic integration.

When the General Assembly declared the period 1995–2004 as the United Nations Decade for Human Rights Education, it identified human rights education (HRE) as "a comprehensive, life long process by which people...in all strata of society learn respect for the dignity of others and the means and methods of ensuring that respect in all societies."[40] Although HRE has a long history, it has only recently begun to realize its empowering potential. In his essay, Richard Claude reviews the origins of the article on the right to education in the UDHR, and then proceeds to discuss key goals of HRE by profiling creative programs that fit each of these Declaration goals. Whether one examines the "Law to the Villages" program launched by the Thongbai Thongpao Foundation in Thailand, the "Bringing CEDAW Home"[41] community-based program initiated by "Action Professionals for the People" in Ethiopia, or the "Diplomacy-Training for NGOs" program at the University of New South Wales in Australia, there is a vision shared by all those involved: the construction of a "universal culture of human rights." According to Claude, "this vision is no longer utopian"; rather, it is the manifestation of an obligation "at the international, national, local and personal levels to implement effective programs of human rights education."

The potential impact of the emerging global Internet constitutes a major intellectual and policy challenge to conventional notions of social change. To fully appreciate the contribution of these new capabilities to problem-solving, argues Lloyd Etheredge, we need to "recalibrate our imagination," given the perennially slow response of institutions to the opportunities offered by new technologies. Building upon earlier work in the social sciences, Etheredge offers four lessons to predict how these technologies "will partly shape our future." While welcoming the enhanced capacities for new networking and deepening collaboration in a whole array of key human rights issues, Etheredge is also mindful of the possibility of regression: "fragmentation, retribalization, and/or the option to use new technologies for political control and to reverse progress in human rights." The task here, however, is to harness these technologies for humane outcomes. In this vein, Etheredge uses a policy science–oriented framework to examine five cutting-edge Internet projects and "draw implications for system-level innovations to promote human rights." Taking these new technologies seriously increases—"at a surprisingly affordable cost"—the range of available strategies for their promotion.

Postscript

In a recent address at an international conference on accountability, former Finnish President Marti Ahtisaari reminded the audience that

> Crime and human rights violations emerge from causes deeply embedded in the structure of societies: poverty, deprivation, social injustice...The recent attention to developing a functioning international criminal justice system has to be warmly welcomed—but we should not forget that it should be accompanied by efficient international policies and structures that are intended to deal with those root causes. In this area, much remains to be done.[42]

Dealing with the root causes of human rights violations remains a formidable task. While the human rights community has every reason to be proud of its achievements, nothing will do greater justice to the cause than the continuing effort to refine our conceptual framework and devise new and effective strategies. The world is changing, but the commitment to a humane and just order is as relevant as ever. In this quest, the essence of the human rights discourse, subversion/transformation, is not simply a warning against the pitfalls of complacency. More than anything else, it is a clarion call for the creative uses of normative space on which the realization of humane outcomes rests.

Notes

1 Maria del Carmen Marquez Carrasco and Joaquin Alcaide Fernandez, "In Re Pinochet," *American Journal of International Law*, vol. 93(3), July 1999, pp. 690-696.

2 House of Lords, Judgments- *Regina v. Bartle and the Commissioner of Police for the Metropolis and others EX Parte Pinochet; Regina v. Evans and another and the Commissioner of Police for the Metropolis and others EX Parte Pinochet*, http://www.parliament.the-stationery-office.co.uk/pa/ld199899/ldjudgmt/jd981125/pino08.htm

3   Ibid.,http://www.parliament.the-stationery-office.co.uk/pa/ld199899/ldjudgmt/jd981125/pino09.htm

4   George Andreopoulos, *On the Fiftieth Anniversary of the Universal Declaration of Human Rights*. Keynote address, Teachers College, Columbia University, December 12, 1998 (on file with the author). Part of what follows reflects the remarks in that address.

5   The debate in the United States between those advocating human rights and those fearful of undermining the country's sovereignty, as reflected in the workings of the Advisory Committee on Postwar Foreign Policy, is discussed in Paul Gordon Lauren, *The Evolution of International Human Rights. Visions Seen*. (University of Pennsylvania Press, 1999), especially pp. 161-165.

6   George Andreopoulos, "Offenses Against the Laws of Humanity: International Action," in Neil J. Smelser and Paul B. Baltes (eds.), *International Encyclopedia of the Social and Behavioral Sciences*. (Pergamon, 2001); and Beth Van Schaack, "The Definition of Crimes Against Humanity: Resolving the Incoherence," *Columbia Journal of Transnational Law*, vol. 37(3), 1999, pp. 788-850.

7   For a recent realist perspective on the importance of human rights norms in understanding key attributes of sovereignty, see Stephen Krasner, *Sovereignty. Organized Hy pocrisy*. (Princeton University Press), 1999, pp. 105-126.

8   The ups and downs of the prospects for a convention and a declaration, as opposed to the eventual outcome, are well described in Johannes Morsink, *The Universal Declaration of Human Rights. Origins, Drafting &Intent*. (University of Pennsylvania Press), 1999, especially pp. 12-20.

9   As Richard Falk has aptly noted.

10 Johannes Morsink, supra note 8, p. 20. See also similar remarks in Richard Falk's chapter in this volume.

11 For a discussion on the importance of the variety of the document's sources, as well as of the role of delegates of smaller nations, see Mary Ann Glendon, *A World Made New. Eleanor Roosevelt and the Universal Declaration of Human Rights*. (Random House, 2001), pp. 143-171; Paul Gordon Lauren, supra note 5, pp. 219-240; see also relevant remarks in Susan Waltz's chapter in this volume.

12 Paul Gordon Lauren, supra note 5, pp. 188-190; Zehra Arat, *Looking Beyond the State but not Ignoring it: Non-State Actors and Human Rights,* University Seminar on Human Rights, Columbia University, October 10, 2000 (on file with the author).

13 David Weissbrodt, "The Contribution of Non-Governmental Organizations to the Protection of Human Rights," in Theodor Meron (ed.), *Human Rights in International Law: Legal and Policy Issues*. (Clarendon Press, 1984), pp. 403-437; Claude E. Welch, Jr., *Protecting Human Rights in Africa: Strategies and Roles of Non-Governmental Organizations*. (University of Pennsylvania Press), 1995, pp. 42-83; Richard Higgott, *Coming to Terms with Globalization: Non State Actors and Agenda for Justice and Governance in the Next Century*.

Institute for Globalization and the Human Condition, McMaster University (on file with the author); and Ann Marie Clark, *Diplomacy of Conscience. Amnesty International and Changing Human Rights Norms.* (Princeton University Press, 2001), pp. 37-123.

14 The study defines legal empowerment as "the use of law to increase the control that disadvantaged populations exercise over their lives"; Asian Development Bank, *Legal Empowerment: Advancing Good Governance and Poverty Reduction, Overview Report,* June 2001 (on file with the author). The quoted passages are from pages xiv and xix, respectively. The author wants to express his thanks to Mr. Kim McQuay of the Asia Foundation for a copy of the report.

15 See relevant remarks in the chapters by Lance Compa and Richard Falk in this volume.

16 Judith Goldstein and Robert Keohane, "Ideas and Foreign Policy: An Analytical Framework," in Judith Goldstein and Robert Keohane (eds.), *Ideas and Foreign Policy. Beliefs, Institutions, and Political Change.* (Cornell University Press, 1996), pp. 3-30; and Martha Finnemore, *National Interests in International Society.* (Cornell University Press, 1996).

17 Peter J. Katzenstein, "Coping with Terrorism: Norms and Internal Security in Germany and Japan," in Judith Goldstein and Robert Keohane (eds.), *Ideas and Foreign Policy,* ibid., pp. 265-295; and (ed.), *The Culture of National Security: Norms and Identity in World Politics.* (Columbia University Press, 1996); and Matthew Evangelista, *Unarmed Forces. The Transnational Movement to End the Cold War.* (Cornell University Press, 1999).

18 Evangelista, ibid., p. 388.

19 See the discussion in Goldstein and Keohane, supra note 16.

20 See the relevant discussion in this author's chapter in this volume.

21 On the aftermath of the first ever meeting held by the Security Council at the level of Heads of State and Government (January 1992), the United Nations issued a report on ways of strengthening its capacity for preventive diplomacy, peacemaking and peacekeeping. In it, the Secretary-General noted that one of the aims of the organization must be "...in the largest sense, to address the deepest causes of conflict: economic despair, social injustice and political oppression"; United Nations General Assembly, Report of the Secretary-General on the Work of the Organization, *An Agenda for Peace. Preventive diplomacy, peacemaking and peace-keeping,* UN Doc. A/47/277/S/24111, 17 June 1992.

22 On the relevant phrasing found in the enabling resolution, see Sean D. Murphy, *Humanitarian Intervention. The United Nations in an Evolving World Order.* (University of Pennsylvania Press, 1996), pp. 226-227. On the limits of the realist model re the Somali case, see George Andreopoulos, *Violations of International Humanitarian Law and Threats to International Peace and Security.* Paper presented at the UNU-SIM Conference *From a Culture of Impunity to a Culture of Accountability. International Criminal Tribunals, the Interna-*

tional Criminal Court, and Human Rights Protection. Utrecht, November 26-28, 2001. On the background to Operation Restore Hope, see Tom Farer's chapter.

23 David Rieff, for example, states that "In these post-Communist, post-modern times, human rights seems to have become the dominant moral narrative for thinking about world affairs; "The Precarious Triumph of Human Rights," *The New York Times Magazine,* August 8, 1999. In an effort to explain the universality of the human rights idea, Michael Ignatieff notes that "The doctrine of human rights is morally universal because it says that all human beings need certain specific freedoms "from"; it does not go on to define what their freedom "to" should comprise"; "The Attack on Human Rights," *Foreign Affairs,* vol. 80(6), November/December 2001, p. 113.

24 Quoted in David Rieff, ibid.

25 United Nations Security Council, *Report of the Secretary-General to the Security Council on the protection of civilians in armed conflict,* S/2001/331, 30 March 2001.

26 "Holding Armed Groups to International Standards." An ICRC view (on file with the author).

27 Ibid; see also International Council on Human Rights Policy, *Ends & means: human rights approaches to armed groups.* (Geneva, 2000), especially pp. 1-10.

28 This language is from the 1977 Geneva Protocol II Additional to the Geneva Conventions.

29 My emphasis; *Report of the Secretary-General to the Security Council on the protection of civilians in armed conflict,* supra note 25.

30 *Ends &means,* supra note 27, p. 48.

31 Ibid.

32 Ibid., pp. 44-45.

33 In his first report on civilian protection, the Secretary-General recommended—as a last resort—enforcement action "in the face of massive and ongoing abuses." His comments related to the activities of both state and nonstate actors; *Report of the Secretary-General to the Security Council on the protection of civilians in armed conflict,* S/1999/957, 8 September 1999.

34 See relevant remarks by David Rieff, supra note 23.

35 For example, the anticolonial and antiapartheid movements, and the CSCE process, among others.

36 See relevant remarks in Lance Compa's chapter in this volume.

37 See relevant remarks in Richard Claude's chapter in this volume.

Introduction

38 *Legal Empowerment: Advancing Good Governance and Poverty Reduction*, supra note 14, p. xvii.

39 See relevant remarks in Lloyd Etheredge's chapter in this volume.

40 United Nations General Assembly Resolution 49/184, *United Nations Decade for Human Rights Education*, A/RES/49/184, 23 December 1994.

41 CEDAW stands for the United Nations Convention on the Elimination of All Forms of Discrimination Against Women.

42 Marti Ahtisaari, *Justice and Accountability: local or international?* Keynote Address at the UNU-SIM Conference *From a Culture of Impunity to a Culture of Accountability. International Criminal Tribunals, the International Criminal Court, and Human Rights Protection.* Utrecht, November 26-28, 2001.

CHAPTER TWO

The Challenges of Humane Governance

Richard Falk

A Point of Departure

The recently celebrated fiftieth anniversary of the Universal Declaration of Human Rights (UDHR) presents an obvious and appropriate moment to rethink what has been achieved with respect to human rights over the last half century and what remains to be achieved in the future. It is very much an instance of the glass being either half full or half empty. It is natural to appreciate, even to celebrate, the extraordinary evolution of human rights on an international level that has occurred during this half century, essentially since the end of World War II. At the same time, it is plausible to lament the continuing failure to implement human rights more fully, especially if one understands human rights as they are specified in international law; that is, including economic, social, and cultural rights. These categories of rights are still not taken seriously by the liberal democracies in the North, despite their formally obligatory status.[1] To affirm what has been done without overlooking deficiencies of implementation depends upon adopting an approach to evaluation that is neither legalistic nor cynical.

It is also possible, I think, to acknowledge that the United Nations, which has provided the formal auspices under which international human rights has developed, has made a more lasting contribution to the quality of world order and the human condition in this domain than in relation to either peace and security or economic development, the two issue-areas to which the United Nations is most associated. Such an assessment is especially convincing if human rights is understood as including the positive role played by the United Nations in encouraging the processes of decolonization and self-determination, and in the successful waging of the antiapartheid campaign. If one considers the human rights record of the United

Nations, it is quite reasonable to believe that this is the issue area where the United Nations has achieved the most. This assertion may seem like a trivial observation, but it goes directly against what the people who set up the United Nations thought and said they were mainly doing—they were, in 1945, creating primarily a peace and security organization preoccupied with avoiding major warfare in the future. And even secondarily, these architects of the United Nations later thought, especially after many countries from the South entered the United Nations as members in the 1960s, that they were providing a forum for North-South dialogue and leading support to the demands from the South for a fairer, more equitable international economic order.

In my view (and this is admittedly a highly subjective interpretation) the United Nations has been generally unsuccessful with respect to deterring aggression or in its efforts to protect the victims of aggression.[2] And to the extent that victims of aggression have been protected, as arguably occurred when the sovereignty of Kuwait was restored through the mechanism of the Gulf War, such an outcome was essentially a geopolitical calculation that would have been achieved with or without the United Nations. The war against Iraq was waged because strategic interests were engaged: oil, the stability of the Middle East, the security of Israel, and a concern about the proliferation of nuclear weapons. The normative rationale associated with responding to aggression provided a convenient window dressing and, on a more practical level, helped weaken domestic opposition in the United States. When the strategic interests went the other way—as the case, for instance, in relation to Indonesia's 1975 invasion of East Timor—the United Nations remained passive, and limited its response to a muted resolution of censure.[3] When Iraq attacked Iran in 1980, at a time when it was very popular to destabilize the Khomeini government in Iran, the United Nations was eerily silent about this major instance of aggression, leading to prolonged and costly warfare, because the Soviet Union and the United States both felt strategically threatened by the Islamization of Iran. The bypassing of the United Nations and its Charter requirement that regional enforcement actions receive *prior* authorization by the Security Council was dramatically evident in the 1999 NATO War against Serbia (former Yugoslavia) with respect to Kosovo. In effect, the United States and its main allies made it clear that they did not have confidence in the capabilities or feel constrained to act within the legal framework of the United Nations in relation to peace and security challenges. Additionally, the avoidance of the United Nations was rationalized because of anticipated Chinese and Russian opposition to any proposed undertaking of "humanitarian intervention" on behalf of the besieged Kosovars.[4]

My point is this. The United Nations deserves a lot of credit in the human rights area for what it has achieved. An impressive normative architecture pertaining to human rights is now widely accepted throughout international society, although unevenly implemented. At the same time, despite some positive effects here and there, the United Nations has been disappointing with regard to peace and security, undertakings for which the organization was originally established and for which the majority of its members and the public are most deeply committed. Such a double assessment could quickly change in the years ahead on both fronts. The inability to move toward more evenhanded and comprehensive implementation of human rights standards could lead to disillusionment, or even a backlash involving a reassertion of the autonomy of the state and the applicability of a strictly interpreted duty by the U.N. to refrain from intervening in matters within "domestic jurisdiction." Similarly, a changed orientation of American global leadership could breathe new life into the United Nations, virtually overnight. In effect, assessments of the U.N. record must be treated as provisional, and subject to rapid upward and downward revisions in response to the rather volatile assessments of public opinion and the prevailing "spins" favored by the media.

The Emergence of the Universal Declaration of Human Rights

It is also, I think, interesting to take account of how important the Universal Declaration has become as a text, or almost a scripture, for those who are dedicated to the promotion of human rights. This prominence is surprising from a legalistic point of view because the UDHR is not even a treaty; it is not a binding legal instrument at least in the form in which it was originally adopted. The UDHR was set forth as a resolution of the U.N. General Assembly, which is supposed to be only recommendatory in character, or at most declaratory of a preexisting state of legal affairs. And yet, over time, the UDHR has provided the fundamental framework within which human rights has been conceived and continues to be conceived. Louis Henkin, one of the most influential jurists of this era, frequently refers to the Universal Declaration as the most important legal document in the history of international law. I have heard Professor Henkin argue that the UDHR was more important than the U.N. Charter itself in terms of its contribution to the humane development of international society.

It is noteworthy that when the Declaration was later transformed and restructured to assume the shape of a treaty, it was broken in two. In place of the Universal Declaration, international covenants on political and civil rights and on economic, social, and cultural rights were concluded in 1966, and opened for signature. These treaty instruments were promoted as a major advance over the Universal Declaration, but they have not had nearly its inspirational impact, and indeed have not replaced, nor even superseded the earlier document. The UDHR, it should be realized, has been incorporated as a totality into the constitutions of several African countries. Of course, such an impact is often symbolic and rhetorical. The formal endorsement of the UDHR does not ensure a serious willingness to accept the UDHR as a guide to policy and behavior, or to endow civil society with a watchdog role, ensuring the means to enforce its provisions. Such a constitutional embodiment is, as such, little more than a symbolic expression of the view that governments should conduct their affairs within the limits set by norms of international human rights, and that the UDHR is the best formulation of these norms.

So, we pose the question why has this Declaration become such a historic document with such a long life span? I think an important part of the answer is because the UDHR text has generally succeeded in providing a genuinely universal foundation for the discourse of human rights. In some respects, its declaratory status is an advantage. The authority of the UDHR exists independently of formal adherence. The UDHR in one sense transcends the positive international legal order, being situated in a realm of natural law, *jus cogens*, and meta-law. It provides a summary of how to conceive of humane governance with respect to state/society relations. Unlike the Covenants, the Universal Declaration combines civil, political, economic, social, and cultural rights in a single integral document, implying a more holistic view of the human condition. As such, it provides a comprehensive view of human rights with an especial appeal for countries in the South, particularly those with non-Western civilizational identities. The UDHR expresses human rights in a language that has a strong flavor of morality and aspiration that makes it seem potentially congenial to religious viewpoints.[5]

When adopted in 1948 the Universal Declaration was unanimously endorsed by the current membership of the U.N., although the Soviet bloc abstained. The Soviet Union did not oppose the UDHR but they chose to distance themselves from it at the time on the grounds that it represented too strong an endorsement of an individualist view of human rights. The Soviet posture was carefully formulated. It did not signify a Soviet repudiation of the human rights idea, but, according to their representatives at the time, their abstention was due to their view that the UDHR was not socialist enough in its orientation. In fact, some effort in drafting had been made to strike a compromise between socialist and Western liberal ideas about human rights. It is helpful to note, also, that Latin American jurists of a noncommunist persuasion, lent influential weight to the Soviet-led insistence that human rights be extended to embrace an ethos of societal solidarity, and hence embracing social, economic, and cultural matters.

The Soviet Union, under Stalinist rule in the years after World War II, was very sovereignty oriented. Moscow was very suspicious about vesting potential authority in an international institution to question what went on within the borders of a territorial state. Of course, such suspicions arose within a global setting that seemed to be moving toward a geopolitical confrontation between East and West, what later became the Cold War. In such a setting, the Soviet Union (and its allies and satellites) would be badly outnumbered if controversial issues were put to a vote in the main U.N. organs. Endowing the United Nations with the authority to judge the behavior of governments was undoubtedly correctly seen, by Soviet leaders as fashioning a weapon that could (and would) be used against them. In these circumstances, ideologically and prudentially, Soviet resistance to U.N. authority in the human rights sphere is both understandable and predictable. Indeed, it is somewhat odd that they went along with the exercise as much as they did. It is probable, although not yet documented by historical research, that Soviet opposition to the UDHR was confined to an abstention for three reasons: first, because the content of the document conformed in many of its aspects with their own *formal* views on the rights of people; second, because the declaratory and recommendatory character of the document rendered it rather ineffectual as a potential instrument of U.N. intervention; and third, because the Soviet Union was struggling to gain a firm foothold on the moral terrain of world politics so as to mount an appeal for the allegiance of people throughout the world to its ideals as ethically superior to those of the capitalist West.

The question of challenging sovereignty was not just of interest to the Soviet bloc. It was and remains the fundamental issue for all states. How much can one trust the organized international community to make assessments of the propriety of the behavior of a government toward its own citizens? This is a difficult issue in relation to human rights in general because the basis of international society, especially in the middle of the 20th century, was that sovereign states were the only significant political actors in international society, and that sovereignty essentially meant that there was no external accountability and certainty, no internal intrusion.[6] There was an agreement to maintain certain norms, but one of the elements of that agreement, as far as the United Nations was concerned, as set forth in Article 2 (7) of the Charter, was that the organization had no authority to intervene in matters that were essentially within the domestic jurisdiction of member states. This deference to sovereign rights was an integral aspect of the social contract between the members and the nascent organization, and was explicitly affirmed as a guiding principle in the U.N. organic law, the Charter. The way a government treats its own citizens is clearly something that was supposed to fall within domestic jurisdiction, and yet, the whole burden of international human rights claims is to posit some sort of duty to treat such matters as objects of legitimate international concern.

This kind of tension was implicit since the beginnings of U.N. efforts, and it should be remembered that geopolitically grounded claims to protect human rights had preceded by several centuries the rights-based claims. Ever since Westphalia such claims have challenged the internal sovereignty of weaker states. Initially, these claims were asserted on behalf of an ethos of religious tolerance or diversity, especially as against Ottoman rule in Greece, while later on, the main pattern of assertion was in defense of ethnic and religious minorities, although understood as protecting *individuals* rather than *groups*. Such international claims could, after the adoption of the UDHR, be reformulated as efforts to provide protection against the abuse of human rights standards. This tension between international human rights and sovereignty is unavoidably present as long as the state remains the paramount international actor.[7] It is helpful to appreciate that this tension is deeper than the Cold War expressions associated with the Soviet Union. Indeed, the *internationalizing* of human rights, even if only as a normative set of standards and guidelines, poses a challenge to the coherence of the Westphalian (black box) image of world order.

Ever since the French and American Revolutions, and before with respect to religious liberty, there was widespread support for the idea that governments should uphold these rights. This idea is something that confers on international, or external, authority some right of humanitarian intervention or even the authority to pass judgment. In this sense, the whole human rights tradition as part of international law is subversive of state sovereignty. A disquieting question presents itself: Why did governments agree to the creation of such a subversive creature? Human rights is a kind of subversive and wild creature that was let out of the zoo, so to speak, by those keepers who would be most likely subject to its hostile attention.[8]

It seems clear from the historical record that this subversive principle was only accepted in 1948 by states, especially those with strong sovereignty views, because they were convinced that the adoption of the Universal Declaration would have no behavioral consequences. It was at the time very much of a sideshow. It was a matter of governments giving lip service to some moral abstractions in response to pressures that came from civil society to do something symbolic in light of the failure of international society to address the 1930's challenge of Hitler as constituted by domestic patterns of persecution, especially of the Jews. The original impulse to enunciate human rights within the United Nations was a rather painless way to acknowledge the failures of the past, without really taking substantive steps to correct them, and ensure against their repetition. It is important to remember and realize that the liberal democracies had stood by as virtually mute spectators, or worse, while Hitler went forward with the Nazi program of action. These countries, despite their own liberal identities, had denied access to refugees; they had participated in the Berlin Olympic games in 1936, and they acted as if as long as the Nazi party and the Nazi movement only persecuted its own people within its borders the harm done was nothing for international society to worry about. This posture of indifference was difficult to maintain once the magnitude of Nazi genocide was revealed. In fact, nothing by way of concrete commitments was embedded in the UDHR with respect to what might happen when and if the next Hitler emerged. At least, however, the general spirit of the UDHR suggested that if a government abused its own people it could be treated as a matter that engaged some kind of international responsibility.[9]

The whole process by which the Declaration was drafted reinforced this understanding that it was not given any political weight at the time of its adoption. The main development was entrusted to Eleanor Roosevelt, the controversial wife of a President who was an outstanding public figure but was considered a do-gooder by the people that ran the world at the time, not a figure to be taken seriously in the realist domain of geopolitics or a person to be entrusted with a major policy mission. I think a preliminary task of inquiry is to ask why did this Declaration that started so inauspiciously begin to gather momentum over the last half century, and has managed, contrary to all expectations at the point of origin, to change the manner in which a significant portion of international politics is conducted. That is an achievement that could not have been reasonably anticipated. Instead of being a barely noticed sideshow, human rights has become one of the main acts, it has become a challenge to leaders and, more recently, even to the corporate and financial world. Human rights are being treated as if important in many foreign policy and private sector settings.[10]

Against this background, this chapter considers the role of civil society. Such a concern would have been inconceivable in 1945. The emergence of human rights nongovernmental organizations (NGOs) was unanticipated and nonexistent in relation to international human rights, and virtually no one thought about it in the years following World War II. What brought the Universal Declaration off the shelf initially was the emergence at the grassroots level of human rights activist organizations that did take seriously the standards of behavior enunciated, and were of the view that world peace could not be preserved unless minimum standards of human rights were observed. Amnesty International, Human Rights Watch, and a host of other transnational human rights organizations used information very effectively and in a manner that could not be easily dismissed either by the media or governments as propaganda, as merely a partisan condemnation from a hostile ideological source. These efforts mobilized a variety of pressures that were awkward for the target governments that, despite their behavior at home; increasingly sought a positive image and reputation in international society. One of the techniques that Amnesty, for instance, used very effectively was to show government officials a report on a confidential basis before it was released, giving the government that was being criticized an opportunity within time limits to alter the practices in exchange for not publishing the report. This leverage was used to achieve dramatic effects in several countries. The reports if and when issued were often very helpful to oppositional forces in countries that refused to alter violative practices, particularly because many governments generally did, although not in all instances, move toward compliance.

Two other developments were important in reinforcing the impact of human rights. The first, earlier referred to in a different context, was associated with the universal mobilization around antiapartheid issues and the degree to which that mobilization included important grassroots efforts, especially in the United Kingdom and the United States. The antiapartheid campaign rested on widespread support for the norm of racial equality. This consensus led to a repudiation of apartheid by the U.N. General Assembly as "criminal," a form of governance that deliberately involved systematic racial persecution and discrimination. This antiapartheid struggle demonstrated that there could be a global politics of human rights of an extraordinarily influential character under certain circumstances, admittedly of a limited scope with special features. The campaign also showed that the United Nations was very important in legitimating such a politics of human rights. The subsequent peaceful abandonment of apartheid by South Africa adds to this impression of a successful human rights campaign that contributed greatly to a process of repudiating an entrenched unjust social and political arrangement that very few people at the time anticipated could be ended without sustained violence. Most observers believed that apartheid could be challenged only by large-scale collective violence in the form of an ugly ethnic civil war. Almost everyone, including myself, believed that it was a utopian project to envisage the voluntary renunciation of apartheid by the South African elites who were then firmly in control of the country, and seemed ready to go to extremes to retain their position of privilege and power. Human rights were not, by any means, the whole of this remarkable story of transformation. The inspirational role of the African National Congress (ANC), epitomized by the leadership of Nelson Mandela, played a major role in the latter stages. But the stigmatization of the apartheid government played a major part in encouraging the white power structure to finally consider favorably the option of a multiracial democracy. It is easy, in retrospect, to overlook the magnitude of this achievement. It is an outcome that societies with seemingly far less severe cleavages have not managed. One need only think of Ireland, the Philippines, Indonesia, former Yugoslavia, and a series of sub-Saharan countries where ethnic or religious conflict has only been overcome, if at all, by prolonged civil strife and where efforts at international mediation failed for years.

This positive experience relating to South Africa was reinforced further by the perceived contributions that human rights made during the same period to the emancipation of the countries of Eastern Europe and to the collapse of the Soviet Union itself. In the 1980s, groups like Charter 77, Solidarity, and the Moscow Trust Group, all justified their militant opposition to the established governments of Czechoslovakia, Poland, and the Soviet Union on the legal commitment that those governments had made to uphold international human rights norms. They legitimated their own resistance on this basis, thereby challenging and undermining the legitimacy of the governing elite. When other conditions began to change, especially the emergence of Mikhail Gorbachev as a reformist leader of the Soviet Union adopting a new set of policies centered upon improving East/West relations, these opponents of Communist regimes gained in credibility and boldness.

Here again, as in South Africa, a combination of factors that included human rights led to an unexpected series of developments that produced a peaceful transformation of historical proportions that caught even the most respected commentators on the Cold War by surprise. Again, human rights were by no means the only element, and were probably not the effective cause of change, but the acknowledgment of rights was one dimension of the struggle from below, the struggle of long-oppressed peoples against these regimes. Such a struggle had already been formally validated by the Helsinki Accords, the treaty arrangement negotiated in the mid-1970s that recognized as valid the boundaries in Eastern Europe established after World War II. At the time this result was widely criticized in the West as a political victory for Moscow.

The fact that the Soviet Union had accepted, in exchange for stabilizing boundaries, an obligation by the governments of Eastern Europe to participate in annual inquiries under international auspices of their observance of human rights obligations was viewed with extreme skepticism as a meaningless gesture. For this reason, many people, especially political conservatives in the United States, attacked the Helsinki Accords as a give-away, a second Yalta. With exquisite irony, the subversive impact of the human rights part of the Helsinki Accords actually contributed to a reversal of Yalta within a decade or so. In other words, the obligation of the East European governments to respond formally to complaints directed at their human rights records was a means used by Western media and others to highlight the illegitimacy of these regimes due to their refusal to abide by widely endorsed norms relating to civil and political rights. When other conditions changed, the elites themselves substantially lost their will to rule, and were pushed aside far more effortlessly than could have been anticipated given the harshness of their methods of governance.

Something had happened historically that could not have been anticipated. This peaceful transformation of Eastern Europe and the Soviet Union, and the achievement of political self-determination for these peoples long subject to direct and indirect Soviet control, was dismissed as too dangerous even to contemplate. Fears of provoking World War III were prevalent. This record, I think, creates a very powerful claim that human rights has influenced the course of international relations in a dramatic way during this last half century. It is much more widely understood that civil society can be a potent democratizing force under certain conditions, and that such movements offer an alternative approach to transformative politics to those revolutionary outlooks that suppose that only violence and armed struggle can be successful.

Of course, not all human rights and democracy movements are triumphant. During the turbulent 1980s there were several notable failures, most prominently in China and Myanmar. In both of these countries, comparable movements to what had worked so well in East Europe emerged, but were eventually crushed by militaristic responses that reestablished effective structures of oppression. Furthermore, civil society should not be romanticized. In some circumstances, civil society can also foster extremely antidemocratic and abusive movements that later engage in repressive behavior when and if control over state power is gained. The Nazi movement is, of course, paradigmatic. More recently, the rise to power of religious and ethnic extremists in several countries has been based upon the backing of civil society. Backlash politics involving resistance to "globalization" and "Americanization" can generate chauvinistic and extreme forms of nationalism, which lead to the denial of basic human rights to immigrants and unwanted outsiders.

One need also to qualify this enthusiasm for the contributions of the human rights tradition by careful reference to what has not yet been accomplished, giving the half-empty glass its due. One of the critical factors is that humane governance as a comprehensive realization of human rights has, as I said at the outset, not been achieved in most, if not in any part, of the world. And even where there has been substantial realization at the level of the state, there is a long way to go in extending humane governance to regional and global arenas of authority. The idea of humane governance is something broader than government.[11] It is not addressing only the desirability of humane government, but it is proposing that the totality of authority at all levels of social order should be exercised in conformity with widely shared human values, as embodied in the main formulations of human rights. Such a framework that aspires to provide a global cartography of authority is dedicated to achieving a fulfilling life experience for all peoples on the planet, while taking due account of civilizational, religious, and geographical differences.

In this respect, I think the Western ideas of the Enlightenment are foundational for our understanding of humane governance, although not necessarily for its realization under current conditions. The West articulated most clearly the idea that only through the gradual embodiment of reason and reasonableness in human affairs could a just society be achieved and sustained. And further, that such goals could not be reached for humanity without the abandonment of truth claims for any particular view of how society should be organized and life lived. I think there is a very important commitment present: the commitment to respect differences, and even to celebrate diversity as enriching for the overall human experience. This is, in effect, an embodiment of the ethos of tolerance, but it is more than "mere toleration," as it understands that learning from others is valuable and that diversity makes any failure in one societal space less systemic. This celebration of difference as a positive and inevitable aspect of human experience presupposes a renunciation of any claim that a particular way of presenting reality or perceiving the sacred is applicable to those who hold contrary beliefs and values. The psychological and political abandonment of truth claims is integral to the promotion of tolerance, although it need not challenge the clarity of personal beliefs as to the nature of truth, beauty, and goodness.

The monotheistic religions of Christianity, Islam, and Judaism are all at risk, as their practices and ethical claims rest on unconditional truth claims as applicable to nonadherents. At the very least, the outlook of these religions has been and can be interpreted as bastions of intolerance. With the recent resurgence of religion as a political force in the public sector, this issue of tolerance assumes a very crucial role in relation to upholding fundamental human rights on the ground. Extremist tendencies associated with these monotheistic traditions often are at odds with what is perceived to be the wishy washy ethical and metaphysical positions embodied in "secularism."[12]

Ironically, Hinduism and the other main Asian religions provide better foundation for the Enlightenment ideas of reason and tolerance than what comes from the more familiar Western traditions. There is a kind of paradox present that is quite illuminating. Part of the importance of encouraging the public abandonment of truth claims and the related acknowledging of tolerance and mutual respect has to do with limiting to the extent possible the domain of justifiable violence. To the extent that a given line of belief or action is seen as "untrue" or "unacceptable," especially on matters of great importance, violence seems justifiable to limit the influence of such dangerous outlooks. In contrast, to encourage a politics of nonviolence, or that minimizes violence, it seems most helpful to confirm a condition of fundamental doubt and contingency about the nature of shared or public reality.

I think it is not surprising that the most powerful formulation and practice of nonviolence came out of Indian civilization, and that Gandhi remains the most compelling figure for this kind of perspective.[13] There is the potentiality for a strange East-West collaboration, grounding humane governance on a series of philosophical assumptions about human solidarity and civilizational diversity. Of course, the recent rise of Hindu nationalism has manifested intolerant and violent facets of Hinduism based on claims of racial exclusivity and superiority. All the world religions have these contradictory predispositions in relation to tolerance of difference and violence, but Western religions have been more easily drawn into crusading postures that rest on ideas of exclusivity.[14] At the same time, in the West these ideas have been more fundamentally challenged for several centuries by a secular ethos that limits the truth claims of religion to matters of personal belief.

Limitations of the Universal Declaration

As argued, the UDHR represents a major step forward in articulating a globally acceptable framework for the promotion of human well-being by way of specifying basic rights. At the same time, it embodies the limitations of understanding and empathy that shaped the consciousness of those who drafted the document back in the 1940s, and of those who have interpreted its meanings over the years. It seems appropriate to identify some of these limitations of the UDHR, partly to set an agenda for the future and to appreciate better some of the disappointments of the past. These limitations pertain both to conception and implementation.

As remarkable as has been the influence of the UDHR, it certainly possesses some of the marks of its mode of creation. Among the most obvious of these is the degree to which its provisions are formulated in the patriarchal discourse of its time. The UDHR is extraordinarily gendered in its language of formulation. There is a pervasive tendency to confuse "human rights" and "the rights of men." This usage is evident even in the preamble: "*Whereas* it is essential, if man is not to be compelled to have recourse, as a last resort, to rebellion against tyranny and oppression, that human rights should be protected by the rule of law."[15] Or consider Article 13 (2): "Every one has the right to leave any country, including his own, and to return to his country." Or, "No one shall be arbitrarily deprived of his property" (Art. 17). Even when reference is made to standard of living, the right is articulated from the perspective of men only: "Everyone has the right to a standard of living adequate for the health and well being of himself and of his family…" (Art. 25).

It is inconceivable that such a discourse would be relied upon in a redraft of the UDHR. It would be so self-evidently unacceptable as to not even be an issue. Remember that it was Eleanor Roosevelt, perhaps the leading feminist of her day, then renowned as a champion of human rights and of women's issues, who led the drafting group that produced the UDHR. In retrospect, it seems quite remarkable that she was so socialized into the language habits of a patriarchal world that she would not have insisted on a less gendered text. The fact that there was no objection to the patriarchal phrasing suggests how far we have moved away from a crudely patriarchal discourse. Of course, the use of more gender-neutral language is no assurance that patriarchal behavior has altered to a comparable degree. Indeed, the evidence suggests that behaviorally progress has often been disappointing. Even in societies where women seem most influential, gendered abuses and patterns of exploitation and discrimination persist.

A second quite extraordinary oversight embedded in the UDHR is the total neglect of the distinctive outlooks of indigenous peoples. The Universal Declaration had no participation by Native Americans or other representatives of the 300 million or so indigenous peoples around the world. These peoples cover a spectrum of perspective, but most share a commitment to the preservation of their traditions and traditional rights. The UDHR presupposes that all individuals seek participation in the modern world. But what of communities emphasizing group identities, and intent on practicing traditional patterns of living? The UDHR is utterly insensitive to this type of demand that subsequently in many arenas has come to be associated with a very different approach to human rights as they have been enunciated by representatives of indigenous people. It has taken several decades of activism and struggle for indigenous peoples to set forth their idea of human rights in an authoritative document called The Rights of Indigenous Peoples. This document has been scrutinized within the U.N. system for several years. Whether it will finally be accepted in whole or in part by the U.N. General Assembly remains in doubt, as does its impact on the substance of international human rights.

Aside from the substantive neglect of the concerns of indigenous peoples, serious issues of process and participation are also raised. The absence of genuine participation makes it far more difficult for actors to bond with the outcome of a norm-creating process even in the absence of substantive objections. But there are also reasons to believe that distinctive substantive claims will be ignored, or inadequately represented, if their assertion is not made by those whose identities are at stake. Certainly, this has been the experience and perception of indigenous peoples, as well as of non-Western cultures, in relation to the formation and enunciation of human rights standards.

If you are not there in the process, others with fundamentally different identities are unlikely to speak for you. And if they speak they are likely to speak falsely. I think we understand again the ethics and politics of participation much better in 1999 than we did in 1948. In the 1940s there existed stronger convictions that human rights could be specified simply by applying universal reason to the human condition. And thus the fact that the perspectives of indigenous people or Islam, or those of others were not reflected, or reflected insufficiently, was of no consequence because the process of articulating universal truths supposedly made cultural differences irrelevant.[16] I think many of us are now aware that this is an important deficiency in the development of a human rights tradition of maximal acceptability to all the peoples of the world. How to address this deficiency brings other tensions to the surface. Those who argue on behalf of "universality" tend to view the criticism of the tradition as "Western" and "biased" as a pretext relied upon by non-Western authoritarian governments and their apologists to divert attention from abusive behavior. While granting this misappropriation of the cultural argument occurs, it does not overcome the critique. To the extent that human rights are more likely to be respected by their voluntary implementation, it remains relevant to note that the minimal influence of non-Western participation upon the norm-creating process weakens the *legitimacy* of the human rights tradition, as well as its substantive *acceptability*.

There are ways of belatedly addressing this matter of non-Western civilizational outlooks. Indigenous peoples in recent decades have mounted a major campaign to recast human rights to reflect more closely the civilizational values they hold in common, and distinguishing themselves from the tradition embodied in the UDHR. Such an exercise has also disclosed the diversity on human rights *within* the framework of indigenous peoples. As is evident, intracivilizational diversity covering a wide spectrum is to be expected, and certainly also exists within the context of Western thought and practice about human rights.

The main effort of indigenous peoples has been within the U.N. system, taking advantage of the arena provided annually by the subcommittee of the Human Rights Commission that is dedicated to problems of racial discrimination and persecution. The Informal Working Group of Indigenous Population drafted, in the course of a decade of tough negotiations, a text entitled the Declaration of the Rights of Indigenous Peoples. In effect, the representatives of indigenous peoples were united in their deep dissatisfaction with the Universal Declaration to make the creation of an alternative document their main joint undertaking. Their objective was to produce a document that adequately reflects distinctive indigenous peoples' values, perspectives, interests, concerns, and aspirations. It is being reviewed by representatives of member states within the U.N. system before being allowed to be brought before the U.N. General Assembly. The most controversial aspect of their approach, as might be anticipated, is an insistence on claiming a full right to self-determination for indigenous people, implicitly including the option to secede from the state in which a given indigenous people is located. For many reasons such a demand has predictably met with resistance from many governments of sovereign states. The prospect, however remote in reality, of numerous separatist movements and claims is threatening to existing territorial governments that rest their sovereignty on a multiethnic base. There are 700 Indian tribes in Canada alone, and most of them are not content to accept a second-class right of self-determination involving limited internal autonomy, but insist on a first-class right of self-determination comparable to that enjoyed by colonized peoples.[17] Indigenous peoples have had some notable successes in this period. Their status has been much more widely acknowledged and many more of their claims upheld in local settings. In some instances, their claim to be "nations" and "sovereign nations" has received support within the domestic constitutional system of important countries, especially members of the Commonwealth. The core claim of "self-determination" continues to be widely resisted, and viewed as potentially explosive. However understandable is this political reaction, the juridical argument on behalf of indigenous peoples is strong. The Covenants (and other authoritative instruments in international law) use the referent "peoples," not "nation" or "state," to identify those qualified to enjoy a right of self-determination. The U.N. system tried to interdict the claim of right by referring to indigenous communities as "populations," not "peoples," but such a labeling did not confront the issue of identity very persuasively. We must still face the question—if all "peoples" are entitled to self-determination, why not indigenous peoples? It is a hard argument to resist in terms of its normative logic.

A third difficulty, which is less obvious than the first two, is that the Universal Declaration is a secular document that arises directly from the Western liberal tradition of separating church and state, and regarding religion as essentially confined to individual conscience and private domain. But for many civilizations and an increasing number of countries in the world such a sharp distinction does not make sense, lacks legitimacy, and in some instances, appears perverse. The approach to religion contained in the UDHR is not resonant with the perspectives of many non-Western peoples. Their representatives again did not participate very actively in the formulation of the Universal Declaration and successor documents, and to the extent they did, their views were either unheeded or were themselves artificially "Westernized." As argued with reference to indigenous peoples, without a full sense of participation, not only is the outcome and phrasing likely to be affected, but the result does not generate a sense of obligation. This psychic level of incorporation is particularly important as the international human rights regime retains a largely "voluntary" character, effectiveness normally depending essentially on "self-enforcement."[18]

This unresponsiveness to non-Western religious orientations should not be overstated, especially as many religiously minded individuals and groups search for dialogue about divergencies, and accept the UDHR as the best available starting point. Increasingly, non-Western religious leaders, including those associated with moderate versions of "political Islam," are favorably encouraging a shared dialogic approach to the West based on responding to the UDHR and other widely accepted human rights texts. In other words, although theological objections may be present, still these texts are acceptable broadly enough on an intercivilizational basis to enable a useful conversation, and to provide a constructive alternative to contentions that the peoples of the world are enmeshed in a harsh period of "clash" among the great world civilizations.

The fourth and final possible shortcoming of the Universal Declaration in relation to present attitudes is that it offers a static view of the world. It depicts the world as essentially constituted by states and individuals, and therefore it does not have much place for the role of civil society, for regional and global arenas, and for cultural emphases on community solidarity. In this regard, norms about responsibilities as well as permissive rights should be part of what is expressed under the rubric of "human rights." The argument, again capable of self-serving distortions, is that an acceptable Universal Declaration would set forth a balance between the rights of an individual and his/her duties to wider human communities, ranging from family to planet. As is well known, and a theme of confrontation between South Asia and the West (especially, the United States), is the issue of cultural context. Leaders in Singapore, for instance, allege that Western permissiveness toward the individual produces decadent and criminalized societies. The Western retort is that efforts at regulating behavior within the social sphere stifles human creativity and tends to validate in authoritarian styles of governance. The controversy about whether Asian values are relevant to the content of human rights turns on this issue of whether "human rights" should also take direct account of "human responsibilities," as well as on the allegation that invoking Asian values is merely a diversionary move to deflect criticism of oppressive practices by some Asian governments.

These areas of deficiency raise serious concerns about the viability of the UDHR as a global framework in the next century. These issues need to be addressed to achieve an improved basis for establishing a globally effective regime for human rights in the future.

In addition, accounts need to be taken of two sets of failures with respect to implementation. First, it is important to note that the actual response to the Universal Declaration is highly selective in relation to the spectrum of norms specified. The overwhelming focus of the human rights community has been on gross governmental abuse in the area of political behavior. Such abuse takes various forms: denying individuals their basic political rights, the practice of torture, arbitrary execution, death squads, and disappearances. Most concern is directed at the most ugly things that governments do to their citizens, and encompassing in its reach, authoritarian practices of government. But what has received very little attention so far is comparable treatment for denials of rights arising from poverty, homelessness, social inequity, abuses, accumulations of wealth, and oppressive social and cultural practices that are not connected with the state. In India, for instance, a great deal of brutal behavior is culturally sanctioned rather than governmentally directed. The exploitation and mistreatment of women is very much associated with deeply embedded cultural practices. There are similar problems as well in Africa.

There is an extreme selectivity in the implementation, including on the part of NGOs. NGOs, particularly those based in the North, have been generally unwilling to treat human rights comprehensively as including economic, social, and cultural rights.[19] Human rights NGOs have devoted almost all of their budgets to political and civil rights, and more recently to some of the worst ravages of war, particularly antipersonnel landmines. Such a pattern of selectivity reinforces the accusation of the UDHR as essentially a Western project with Western priorities.

There is another dimension to selectivity of implementation that bothers Third World commentators on human rights. Efforts at censure and implementation appear to be subordinate to central geopolitical goals. International institutions, most governments, and even NGOs are very uneven in their scrutinizing role with respect to states. Favorite instances in the West of "a blind eye" are Israel and Turkey, while examples of exaggerated attention include Cuba and Nicaragua during Sandinista rule.

The Neglected Promise of Humane Governance

Embedded in the Universal Declaration is a neglected commitment to a future world order in which every person has an entitlement to all the specific rights set forth. This entitlement is specifically extended to cover the material needs of individuals and families. There is also a recognition that the global setting must be shaped in a manner that is supportive of this normative promise to uphold the panoply of human rights for everyone. At the same time, there is no indication in the UDHR whether the existing world order made up of sovereign states possesses even the potentiality to realize such expectations.

The two most far-reaching provisions of the UDHR are Articles 25 and 28. Article 25, although phrased in patriarchal language, addresses the fundamental question of material subsistence:

> Article 25 (1). Everyone has the right to a standard of living adequate for the health and well-being of himself and of his family, including food, clothing, housing and medical care and necessary social services, and the right to security in the event of unemployment, sickness, disability, widowhood, old age or other lack of livelihood in circumstances beyond his control.

It needs to be recalled that such a right was confirmed despite the pervasiveness of mass poverty in the 1940s throughout the non-Western world.[20] It was also adopted despite the prevalence of a capitalist ethos of individualism in the United States, the dominant state at the time. Such sentiments partially reflected the influence of Latin American socialism on the drafting process, a point well developed by Johannes Morsink in his comprehensive study of the Universal Declaration.[21]

Even more drastic in its implications, given the makeup of the world after 1945, was Article 28:

> Article 28. Everyone is entitled to a social and international order in which the rights and freedoms set forth in this Declaration can be fully realized.

Such a commitment, if seriously implemented, would seem to imply the establishment of democratic government in state/society relations, a substantial move toward social democracy with respect to political economy, and an unprecedented degree of cooperativeness at the international level so as to be able to devote the material resources of the planet to the promotion of human well-being.

These radical aspirations, formulated in the potentially mobilizing language of rights, realistically proposed major modifications of world order. As Ken Booth (and others) has shown, the Westphalian system of states has for 350 years endured "human wrongs" of great magnitude.[22] It would be naïve to suppose that sovereign states committed to the maximization of relative gains for their own citizenry would voluntarily accept obligations to transfer resources and benefits to alleviate the economic distress of distant strangers. The unevenness of resource endowments and degrees of modernization has meant great disparity in living standards between rich and poor, and globalization has steadily widened this gap.[23]

Some optimistic assessments of economic globalization envision a raising of world living standards as a consequence of this new era of economic integration premised on information technology.[24] In a sense, the productive energies of globalization are establishing the material foundations for the fulfillment of the most ambitious promises of the Universal Declaration.

The annual volumes of the Human Development Report prepared under the auspices of the United Nations Development Program support the view that with a somewhat greater commitment to social goals, globalization could provide a context for satisfying the basic human needs of all persons. The 1999 volume, for instance, asserts that globalization "...offers enormous potential to eradicate poverty in the 21st century—to continue the unprecedented progress in the 20th century. We have more wealth and technology—and more commitment to a global community—than ever before."[25] Such hopeful assessments of globalization seem to overlook its neoliberal ideational content that subordinates human well-being to the efficiency of capital as *a matter of principle*, as well as its tendency to make the rich richer and the poor poorer. As the *Human Development Report 1999* indicates, the inequality gap between the richest one fifth and the poorest one fifth has been steadily increasing under the impact of globalization. According to their calculations this gap was 30:1 in 1960, 60:1 in 1990, and 74:1 in 1997. It is also evident that globalization has the effect of virtually overlooking the circumstances of entire distressed regions, as has been the case for sub-Saharan Africa, and unprofitable sectors of the most advanced economies. Such impacts aggravate cleavages among states, regions, and social classes.[26] Given these impacts, as well as the ideas dominating global economic policy, it seems highly unlikely that globalization will have such a positive effect, at least on the attainment of economic and social rights.[27]

At least it can be argued that, globalization (along with other developments in this period) has encouraged the spread of democracy. The empirical trend strongly supports the perception of democratization of state/society relations, and this trend is reinforced by the ideological pressures associated with "the new geopolitics." The United States has led the way in interpreting the outcome of the Cold War as showing the superiority of market-oriented constitutionalism; that is, "globalization with a demo cratic (but not necessarily a human) face."²⁸ Granting the importance of these trends toward democratization, much remains to be achieved both in state/society settings and with regard to extending democratic values and practices to encompass regional and global arenas of authority and decision.²⁹

Unquestionably, Articles 25 and 28 depict normative horizons that seem almost as distant from the world of 2001 as they did from the world of 1948. Arguably, such ideals are even more remote, despite this impressive spread of democracy, due to the collapse of a socialist alternative to capitalism and as a consequence of the severe weakening of organized labor as a counterweight to business and financial interests. How, then, should these provisions be understood in relation to the onset of the 21st century?

Clearly, in the past, human rights NGOs have generally ignored these provisions, concentrating their energies exclusively on the specific duties of states to terminate gross abuses of their own citizens. These articles have been effectively "buried," even as international human rights have flourished in a manner exceeding all reasonable expectations a half-century ago. Such an emphasis on these specifics seemed both "practical" and a response to the most urgent concerns.

But what of the future? The material capabilities definitely exist to create a world without poverty. Further, globalization "internationalizes" the state, giving it more of a stake in the nonterritorial realities of global finance compared to its traditional spatial rootedness with respect to the well-being of its citizens living within territorial boundaries.³⁰ Yet, as argued, this prevailing economistic outlook leads to an erosion of support for those who are being victimized by the impact of globalization. The market ethos has been critical of pro-poor public sector activism of the sort associated with "the welfare state." Only if this ethos is modified can we expect this era of globalization to give life and meaning to the goals of Articles 25 and 28.

Considered abstractly, such goals seem "utopian" and are directly challenged ideologically from the perspectives of neoliberalism. The best hope for a serious commitment to Articles 25 and 28, as political undertakings, depends on the continuing emergence of transnational social forces as a new source of progressive agency in relation to global policy.³¹ In the course of promoting a more people-oriented globalization, Articles 25 and 28 give a legitimacy to the restructuring demands of transnational social forces that resembles, to some degree, the positive impact of human rights on the legitimacy of domestic civil society challenges mounted so successfully in the 1980s against a variety of oppressive regimes, most notably in Eastern Europe, South Asia, and the Philippines.

Perhaps the early years of this century will exhibit a growing interest in the normative horizons depicted within the Universal Declaration. At least, it seems likely that Articles 25 and 28 will be rescued from the oblivion of the first fifty years, and find a place in the political consciousness of future global reformers.

Concluding Observations

The idea of "humane governance" is taking hold of the political imagination. Even if not in these words, it is the implicit vision of those many individuals and groups that are currently dedicated to constructing a peaceful, sustainable, and equitable future for the peoples of the world. The growth of the international human rights tradition and institutional infrastructure over the past several decades gives these expectations a solid ethical foundation and widespread political backing. This development has been called "a human rights culture" by Richard Rorty, and "an ethos of human solidarity" by others.[32] The following three challenges seem likely to form the agenda for international human rights in coming years.

Responding to Globalization
As suggested, the human deprivations arising from the differential gains and losses arising from economic globalization give prominence and urgency to economic and social rights. Such a shift in emphasis away from political and civil rights reflects both the relative success of democratization of state/society relations and the existence of material capabilities to overcome poverty due to the dynamics of global economic growth. This shift in emphasis is not meant to suggest that the political and civil dimensions of human rights should or will be taken for granted. There remains much work to do, but this aspect of the normative challenge is now widely supported, and pressures and procedures exist for implementation.

Responding to the Politics of Identity
It is evident that there has been a growing emphasis on intercivilizational relations and the bearing of cultural values on the interpretation of human rights standards. The human rights tradition was overwhelmingly shaped by

Westerners rooted in the orientation of the European Enlightenment that fostered the growth of the modern secular state. To give human rights a truly universal character requires much work in overcoming the perception and reality of this Western heritage, including a greater effort to incorporate the perspective of the world religions into the interpretation of norms, and the relations between religion and politics.[33] Despite the limitations resulting from this Western heritage, the language of human rights still provides the best available universal discourse within which to build intercivilization trust, understanding, and mutual respect, including in relation to indigenous peoples.

The antagonistic views that surfaced around the publication of Salmon Rushdie's *Satanic Verses* are expressive of tensions and misunderstandings arising from intercivilizational diversity of conditions as well as values. I am not referring to the infamous death sentence imposed by Ayatollah Khomeini's *fatwa*, but rather to the question of whether a book deemed offensive to Muslims should be allowed to circulate freely in society. At issue was a collision of values relating to the balance between upholding literary freedom of expression and respecting community sentiments about matters of religious belief. Also at stake were societal settings in which the distribution of such a book would likely lead to civic turbulence, including riots that cause death. The wave of hate-related violent crimes in the United States since the mid-1990s has raised uncertainties about whether even a Western democratic society can (or should) continue to uphold its virtually unconditional commitment to freedom of expression. Especially given migratory patterns mixing civilizations within the same political and geographic space to a greater extent than ever before, it becomes more important to establish an intercivilizational normative framework. Such a context should condition the interpretation and application of human rights standards.

There are other aspects of this search for universality amid the realities of civilizational diversity. Some cruel caste practices of India or the persistence of tribal rituals resulting in the genital mutilation of young girls in parts of Africa raise difficult issues of cultural practice versus universal standards of dignity. First, practices embedded in custom and culture may persist most rigidly in the rural hinterlands of states, which are beyond the reach of a "modern" government even if the political will exists to suppress such behavior.[34] Second, the cruelty is being practiced in a manner that does offend a universal conscience, including that of the civilization within which it persists. Third, the perpetrators are often among those who have been historically victimized by Western power, making alleged Western concern seem hypocritical in the extreme. Fourth, the maintenance of customary practices is closely linked to traditional local power structures.

Responding to the Quest for Humane Governance
As argued in relation to Articles 25 and 28 of the UDHR, to achieve human rights for everyone in the world seems to require a post-Westphalian world order. It is arguable that globalization is moving in such a post-Westphalian direction, but without a guiding notion of "human community." The challenge is, then, to provide guidelines for human development that condition the play of global market forces. Since 1997 when the Asian financial crisis first hit the world economy and raised doubts about whether neo-liberalism was a reliable basis for global stability, there has been some mainstream criticism of the ideological dimensions of globalization and of its antiregulatory bias. The World Economic Forum at Davos adopted "responsible globality" as its theme. George Soros issued a series of warnings against "market fundamentalism."[35] Even such previously strong proponents of neoliberal policies as the World Bank and International Monetary Fund began to qualify their economic outlook and acknowledged that it could be a mistake to make some governments swallow the medicine of "fiscal discipline" all at once. There were many proposals for what was generally referred to as "a new financial architecture" appropriate to this emergent global economy.

There are new signs of a search for new political guidelines at the level of the state that depart from neoliberal orthodoxy. Anthony Giddens has proposed "the third way," the Copenhagen "social summit" in 1995 sought to revive the social agenda of world leaders, and the electorate of several countries has sent a social democratic message to its government. At the same time, as the German experience of social democracy during the past few years has exemplified, a mandate from the citizenry is impossible to implement if it collides with the priorities and views of the business community. The resignation of the reform-minded Finance Minister Oskar LaFontaine after only a few weeks in office and Schroeder's moves to affirm global market policies support the view that democracy within a state cannot successfully challenge global market forces at this time.

Perhaps, frameworks of action other than state/society relations may be more effective. One possibility would be the emergence of "compassionate regionalism" in Europe. If, indeed, Europe manages to gain the economic advantages of globalization, while upholding its deep commitment to the full spectrum of human rights, then it will have set a strong precedent for other regions to emulate.

Also supportive are various moves of collaboration between elements of global civil society and receptive governments. These coalitions have been very effective in relation to the campaign against antipersonnel land mines and on behalf of establishing an international criminal court. In effect, this linkage between civil society and states on global issues is generating a new form of world politics, which I have called "the new internationalism." Whether such coalitions are able to reshape global policy on crucial issues is dubious, even in relation to land mines and the international criminal court, the mere nonparticipation (let alone the opposition) of the United States (and China) raises serious questions about whether the treaties agreed upon will prove to be of much relevance to the behavior addressed. Such initiatives seem currently incapable of challenging the dominating relationship between geopolitical actors (mainly the United States) and the transnational private sector, but may be important indications of the birth of a new type of international politics.

The 21st century begins with an unquestioned salience for international human rights as an essential underpinning for legitimate government at the level of the territorial state. The idea of sovereignty is no longer a secure shield against international claims of accountability with respect to human rights.[36] Such claims are also reinforced by the trends toward "humanitarian intervention" in response to humanitarian catastrophes within a given state. The global responses to such catastrophes during the 1990s, as in sub-Saharan Africa and the Balkans, presents a mixed picture, but overall, exhibit a definite willingness to challenge the rights of a territorial sovereign to carry its authority to the extremes of genocide and "ethnic cleansing."[37]

Similarly reinforcing human rights is the emergent movement to punish political leaders believed responsible for the perpetration of crimes against humanity. The establishment of a special tribunal under U.N. authority in the Hague to address the crimes associated with the breakup of Yugoslavia and the 1994 Rwanda genocide was expressive of renewed intergovernmental support for imposing criminal liability on responsible leaders.[38] The Pinochet detention by the United Kingdom in response to an extradition request from a Spanish court in relation to crimes committed in Chile during the late 1970s is a further move toward restricting territorial sovereignty and imposing outer limits on tolerable behavior by governing elites. In one respect, these initiatives and others suggest support for global humane governance as an overriding project of reform. Such an undertaking is reconcilable with globalization conceived of by reference to technological innovation and business practice, but not if globalization is understood to imply adherence to neoliberal economics. The prospect of humane governance is also not at odds with the persistence of the territorial state as a primary political actor, provided states are not dominated by militarist notions of security and are able to accept more autonomous roles for regional and global institutional structures. Such acceptance would mean that effective action could be undertaken by multilateral institutions without the degree of dependence on geopolitical support as is presently the case. This geopolitical support is particularly evident in the 1990's controversies about humanitarian intervention and relates to the role of the United States as key to the action taken or the failure to act at all.

Human rights are available to provide the normative architecture for various aspects of "global humane governance," but the relevance of such an architecture will depend heavily on mounting pressures for implementation through concerted action by transnational social forces. Such a dynamic implementation would also tend to weaken the discrediting link that now exists between the foreign policy priorities of leading governments and the selective attention given to patterns of violative behavior.

Notes

1   Of course, this status is itself controversial and ambiguous. It seems widely accepted that the economic, social, and cultural dimensions of the Universal Declaration have passed into customary international law. At the same time, the nonratification of the 1966 Covenant on Economic, Social, and Cultural Rights by the United States casts a shadow of doubt over the whole subject matter.

2   It is correct that relatively few instances of major aggression have occurred since the United Nations was established. However, the generally accepted explanation for this achievement is usually credited to "deterrence," especially as reinforced by nuclear weapons. This explanation was persuasive in the Cold War era of bipolarity. See one standard account in John Lewis Gaddis, *The Long Peace* (New York: Oxford University Press, 1987).

3   Of course, when the geopolitical climate changed, as it did in 1999, the illegitimate means used in 1975 to gain control over East Timor was used to exert pressure on the Indonesian government to take steps toward respecting the rights of self-determination of the East Timorese people.

4   For an assessment of the policy dilemma posed by ethnic cleansing, on the one side, and the obstacles to legalized intervention on the other, see Richard Falk, *Kosovo, World Order, and the Future of Internationl Law,* American Journal of International Law, (http://www.asil.org/kosovo.htm#ed5).

5   See, for example, the invocation of the UDHR by Hans Küng, the prominent theologian, as supportive of his strong effort to identify a global ethical foundation for political and economic behavior in an era of globalization. Hans Küng, *A Global Ethic for Global Politics and Economics* (New York: Oxford University Press, 1998).

6   For a useful effort to disentangle various expressions of sovereignty and to suggest that the Westphalian affirmation of sovereign rights was never descriptive of international practice, see Stephen D. Krasner, "Globalization and Sovereignty," in David A. Smith, Dorothy J. Solinger, and Steven C. Topik, eds., *States and Sovereignty in the Global Economy* (New York: Routledge, 1999), pp. 34-52.

7   In Europe, of course, this paramountcy of the state has been voluntarily compromised within the setting of the European Union. Regional human rights take precedence over the sovereign rights of member states.

8   See Richard Falk, *Australian Journal of International Affairs,* vol. 52(3), 1998, pp. 255-272.

9   And, of course, this spirit of responsibility was carried much further by the adoption of the Genocide Convention and by the criminal proceedings of the war crimes trials at Nuremberg and Tokyo. See Richard Falk, "Telford Taylor and the Legacy of Nuremberg," *Columbia Journal of Transnational Law,* vol. 37 (3), 1999, pp. 693-723.

10 Of course, it is difficult to assess the motivations and depth of this rather recent surge of private sector acknowledgments of responsibility to avoid contributing to patterns of behavior that encroach upon human rights. Undoubtedly, public relations are a factor, as is the effectiveness of prior activist campaigns that have supported boycotts of corporations associated with specific human rights abuses.

11 For an interpretation, see Richard Falk, *On Humane Governance: Toward a New Global Politics* (University Park, PA: Penn State University Press, 1995).

12 For views on this issue, see Richard Falk, "Rethinking Secularism," unpublished paper presented at Bellagio Conference on secularism, May 1999; also Fred Dallmyer paper presented at the Annual Meeting of the APSA, Atlanta 1999, also with title "Rethinking Secularism."

13 Such an assertion is not meant to minimize the historic importance of such figures as Henry Thoreau, Leo Tolstoy, and Martin Luther King. Jesus, as an engaged person, also models nonviolence in an exemplary form.

14 This Western tendency also has been abetted by expansionist technologies and ideas that culminated in the colonial empires of the leading European states.

15 In defense, apologists would argue that "man" as used was intended to encompass men and women, and was not understood as excluding or demeaning women.

16 There was some prominent non-Western participants in the drafting process of the UDHR, but their education and social backgrounds made them "Western" in sensibility and outlook.

17 Many representatives of indigenous peoples speak of their peoples as extreme victims of European colonization, and regard their claims of nationhood to be fully justified.

18 Instances of international enforcement of human rights standards are limited to situations of extreme deprivation, and then only selectively. Kosovo is such a rare instance.

19 A notable welcomed exception is the relatively recently constituted Center for Economic and Social Rights in New York City.

20 It is also reinforced by Article 22.

21 Johannes Morsink, *The Universal Declaration of Human Rights: Origins, Drafting, Intent* (Philadelphia, PA: University of Pennsylvania, 1999).

22 Ken Booth, "Human Wrongs and International Relations," *International Affairs*, Vol. 71 (1995), pp. 103-126; on a possible reformed architecture of world order capable of fulfilling such promises, see Richard Falk, *A Study of Future Worlds* (New York: Free Press, 1975).

23 In their proposals for a transformed world order, although mainly preoccupied with the avoidance of large-scale warfare, Grenville Clark and Louis Sohn establish an equity fund that would address to some extent the problems of mass poverty and inequality. See Grenville Clark and Louis B. Sohn, *World Peace Through World Law* (Cambridge, MA: Harvard University Press, 3rd rev. ed., 1966).

24 See Thomas Friedman, *The Lexus and the Olive Tree* (New York: Farrar, Straus, and Giroux, 1999).

25 *Human Development Report 1999* (New York: Oxford University Press, 1999), p. 1.

26 Ibid., p. 3.

27 For skeptical accounts of the normative impacts of globalization, see John Gray, *False Dawn: The Delusions of Global Capitalism* (New York: New Press, 1998); Richard Falk, *Predatory Globalization: A Critique* (Cambridge, UK: Polity Press, 1999).

28 Undoubtedly, the most famous interpretation along these lines is that of Francis Fukuyama, *The End of History and the New Man* (New York: The Free Press, 1992); it is also the main theme of *The Economist* cover story "Reflections on the 20th Century," Sept. 11, 1999, pp. 19-20, and "A Survey of the 20th Century," pp. 1-44.

29 See David Held, *Democracy and the Global Order: From the Modern State to Cosmopolitan Governance* (Cambridge, UK: Polity Press, 1995), esp. pp. 219-286.

30 On this pattern of internationalization of the state, see Yoshikazu Sakamoto, ed., *Global Transformation: Challenges to the State System* (Tokyo, Japan: United Nations University Press, 1994).

31 For broad outlook, see Richard Falk, *Law in an Emerging Global Village: A Post-Westphalian Perspective* (Ardsley, NY: Transnational Publishers, 1998); a more specific goal-oriented proposal is set forth in Richard Falk and Andrew Strauss, "On the Creation of a Global People Assembly: Legitimacy and the Power of Popular Sovereignty," unpublished paper, Sept. 1999, p. 38.

32 See Richard Rorty, "Human Rights, Rationality, and Sentimentality," in Stephen Shute and Susan Hurley, eds., *On Human Rights: The Oxford Amnesty Lectures 1993* (New York: Basic Books, 1993), pp. 111-134.

33 Hans Küng has been leading an effort to clarify a global ethos that is sensitive to religious diversity without compromising the commitment to tolerance and the respect for difference. See Hans Küng, supra note 5.

34 See, for instance, the graphic account of caste cruelties in Rohinton Mistry's novel *A Fine Balance* (New York: Random House, 1995); on the complexity of condemning genital mutilation, see Alice Walker's fictional account, *Possessing the Secret of Joy* (New York: Harcourt, Brace, 1992).

35 George Soros, *The Crisis of Global Capitalism* (Public Affairs, 1998).

36 See, e.g., Kofi Annan, "Two concepts of sovereignty," *The Economist*, Sept. 18, 1999, pp. 49-50.

37 For skeptical assessment of this trend toward humanitarian intervention under U.N. auspices, see David Rieff, "Wars Without End?" *NY Times*, Sept. 23, 1999, p. A29.

38 For background here, see Roger S. Clark and Madeleine Sann, eds., *The Prosecution of International Crimes* (New Brunswick, NJ: Transaction, 1996).

CHAPTER THREE

Human Rights Standards and
the Human Rights Movement
in the Global South:
The UDHR and Beyond

Susan Waltz

On November 12, 1948, the U.N. General Assembly's Third Committee (the Committee on Social, Humanitarian, and Cultural Questions) held its 58th meeting in Paris at the Palais de Chaillot. Delegates from 58 countries turned attention to the agenda that had been before them every day since September 30: the UDHR draft. Line by line, phrase by phrase, they considered the text initially produced under U.N. auspices[1] and negotiated over the two previous years by a drafting party of eight state representatives.[2] The actual text under consideration by the Third Committee had been polished up as a working draft by noted French legal scholar Rene Cassin. This was the final review, leading up to the historic vote by the full General Assembly on December 10, 1948.

On November 12, the General Assembly's Third Committee happened to be considering what would become Article 21. That rather lengthy article is comprised of three parts and now reads:

1. Everyone has the right to take part in the government of his country, directly or through freely chosen representatives.
2. Everyone has the right of equal access to public service in his country.
3. The will of the people shall be the basis of the authority of government; this shall be expressed in periodic and genuine elections which shall be by universal and equal suffrage and shall be held by secret vote or by equivalent free voting procedure.

Discussion and debate on Article 21 had opened at 8:30 PM on November 11, and would extend over three separate sessions. The debate on this single article is covered in 15 pages of the official record. Charles Malik of Lebanon chaired these sessions, as he did each of the ninety-odd debates between September 30 and December 7. The committee had before it written amendments proposed by Sweden, the U.S.S.R., Egypt, Uruguay, Cuba, France, and a joint amendment from Colombia and Costa Rica.

During the proceedings, 28 delegates from a wide range of countries variously addressed matters of content and form. These included Belgium, Uruguay, the United States, Greece, Brazil, Venezuela, Iraq, China, Haiti, Cuba, Sweden, the U.S.S.R., Lebanon, the Philippines, and Saudi Arabia.[3] Haiti, for example, opposed inclusion of the idea of secret ballots—and ultimately voted against the article—on the grounds that secret balloting is only valid when voters are literate. The Ukraine delegate expressed regret that despite constitutional guarantees to electoral participation, some countries excluded many people on the basis of race, color, sex, political opinion, property, or birth. He pointed out that of 547 million subjects in the British Empire, 499 million were not represented in the British Parliament. He further contested the example of Switzerland—presented by the French delegate as a standard to emulate—reminding delegates that Swiss women were not permitted to vote. The Chilean delegate rose, in turn, to note that in some countries "one and the same government remains in office for years," and it cannot be presumed that such governments truly reflect the will of the people. U.S. commentary focused on access to civil service. On the eve of the McCarthy era, legislation had been enacted to require loyalty oaths from civil servants, and the United States contended that while access to civil service should be open to all, concerns about loyalty could not be compromised. The Belgian delegate insisted—to no avail—that the article include reference to "multiple lists of candidates." France argued, at some length, that the word "shall" was preferable to "is" in the phrase "the will of the people *shall* be the basis of the authority of government." And to resolve differences that appeared at various junctures throughout the debate, the Chinese delegate, Peng-chen Chang, offered an amendment to rearrange and rewrite paragraphs to alter the emphasis—essentially proposing what would become the final text. At the close of the session, the delegate from the Dominican Republic—Minerva Bernardino—noted her satisfaction with the final wording, which now referred to "everyone" rather than "every citizen," as some countries continued to deny the status of *citizen* to women.

With the distance of fifty years, the range of participants and the degree of engagement may seem extraordinary, but as the U.N. record attests, the debate over Article 21 was rather unexceptional. At the opening of the U.N. Third

Committee proceedings several weeks earlier, the U.S. delegation had hoped that the Third Committee would simply endorse the work of the initial drafting committee, but Latin American and other non-European delegates took umbrage at the idea of rubber-stamping the document that U Thant would eventually proclaim the "Magna Carta of Mankind."[4] Delegates finally haggled over more than 150 proposed amendments, and much of the daily debate on the UDHR was pedantic and pedestrian. There were occasional lofty references to 18th century European Enlightenment philosophy and Jeffersonian ideals (by speakers from various quarters of the world), but the most compelling examples were drawn from the experience of colonialism, racial discrimination in the United States, the new apartheid regime in South Africa, and, of course, the Nazi Holocaust. While the Third Committee held its debate in the fall of 1948, the International Military Tribunal for the Far East was concluding trials of Japanese war criminals involved in the Rape of Nanking and other atrocities,[5] and Chilean diplomats were exercised over the untimely refusal of Soviet officials to issue an exit visa to the Soviet wife of the Chilean ambassador in Moscow.[6] The only matter of substance to interrupt the formal discussion of the UDHR draft was the report from a U.N. envoy on the displacement of Palestinians, and delegates readily drew the linkage between the plight of those refugees and the broad question of human rights. Behind the veil of diplomacy delegates pursued the politics of an emerging East-West conflict and hinted of rising tensions between South and North, but they nevertheless kept in close focus the meaning and the significance of the task before them.

Viewed from up close, the construction and agreement of the UDHR was an international affair that engaged representatives of governments from all over the world. It was also a largely consensual affair. Disputes of real substance were rare. Most articles were adopted by the Third Committee by overwhelming majorities that crossed various political divides and, in the end, the finalized text of 30 articles was adopted by the General Assembly in a vote of 48-0 (with Honduras and Yemen absent). Although eight countries abstained from the vote—Byelorussia, Czechoslovakia, Poland, Saudi Arabia, South Africa, Soviet Union, Ukraine, and Yugoslavia—no country chose to oppose the historic Declaration.

The Question of Ownership

For many years the Universal Declaration and its story provoked little interest, but recognition of the political value of human rights discourse in recent times has served to refocus attention on this foundational text. Increasing sensitivity to multicultural perspectives, political rhetoric about "Asian values," and postmodern admonitions to examine the origin of ideas have all contributed to renewed interest in the political ownership of human rights in general, and the UDHR in particular. The question arises: is the Universal Declaration truly universal? Put bluntly, is the UDHR only a Western construct designed to universalize Western norms? To what extent can non-Western peoples claim ownership of the UDHR? To what extent does the UDHR meet its own hortatory claim to set a "common standard of achievement for all peoples and all nations"?

As a point of departure for addressing these questions, it is important to recall that the Universal Declaration was a politically negotiated and constructed agreement. The description of negotiations over Article 21 is illustrative. The UDHR is not a philosophical treatise. The text was certainly informed by intellectual traditions and cultural practices, but its contents were agreed through an elaborate political process involving pressures from many sources, and its birth was nothing less than a political event. The idea of human rights may be traced primarily through Western philosophy, but the legitimacy of the UDHR as a standard for good behavior by states derives not so much from its intellectual lineage as from the political recognition of its birth. Questions about ownership of the UDHR are answered through examination of the process that brought it into being.

Because the world in 1948 was dominated by the United States, it comes as no surprise that the international human rights project was introduced by Franklin Roosevelt. The appointment of Roosevelt's widow to chair the U.N. commission charged to produce an initial draft text is commonly seen as a further sign of U.S. hegemonic interest and influence. It is obvious that the United States had a vested interest in the outcome of the UDHR negotiations. Less obvious is the degree to which U.S. interests shaped and dominated the debate, and the extent to which non-Western states were seriously engaged with the process and the content of the UDHR. Did the U.S. and the U.S.S.R. in pursuit of their various political objectives leave enough space for meaningful participation by other states?

Before turning to questions about the contribution of small powers to the construction of the UDHR, the role of the U.S. and the U.S.S.R. requires some examination. Eleanor Roosevelt provided much-valued political leadership to the Commission that saw the UDHR through its initial draft, and it was largely through her efforts that the UDHR was not stalled by the Soviet Union's tactical maneuvers. The fact of her leadership, however, supports fewer inferences than are sometimes made. Americans did not author the text, and long before the UDHR was presented to the General Assembly for final vote, U.S. support had wavered. Indeed, without clever political work by Eleanor Roosevelt and her supporters, the United States might well have rejected the document its former president had helped inspire.

From the distance of five decades, Eleanor Roosevelt appears a heroine, and it is easy to look past many controversies over her role and her views. In her own time, however, many Americans disapproved of the First Lady, and by the time that work on the UDHR had commenced, even the projects and programs of the enormously popular FDR had come under fierce attack at home. Both U.S. and international politics shifted considerably over the course of the 1940s: by 1946, Harry Truman was in the White House, states' rights opponents of Roosevelt's New Deal were gaining strength, and the Cold War was taking shape. As debate over the UDHR progressed, Eleanor Roosevelt was frequently at odds with the U.S. State Department over the issue of socioeconomic rights,[7] and it was not uncommon for her to show some sympathy for representatives from other parts of the world who opposed certain U.S. positions.[8] Truman at the time was being drawn into battle with the right wing "Old Guard," and the State Department's own major worry was that some clause in the UDHR text might have direct and adverse impact on law and politics in the United States.[9] The Old Guard, which included Senator Joseph McCarthy, Senator John Bricker, and American Bar Association president Frank Holman, was adamantly opposed to expansion of federal power, particularly in the area of foreign affairs. Many states' rights advocates of the day feared that a human rights treaty would lead to federal legislation against lynching, and Holman, in particular, shamelessly aroused racist ire with incendiary pamphlets and public speeches. Holman and Bricker collaborated in their opposition to "treaty law," and Bricker nearly succeeded in winning Senate approval for a constitutional amendment to limit executive powers to enter legally binding international agreements.[10] The Bricker amendment ultimately failed, but the Old Guard did succeed in depriving the international human rights project of its American support.

As ironic as it may be, by the late 1940s the U.S. political climate was such that government officials sought to contain the doctrine of human rights nearly as vigorously as they were trying to contain communism. U.S. State Department records establish that the main U.S. concern during the final debate on the UDHR was to keep the human rights idea from getting out of hand.[11] As the 1950s opened, Eleanor Roosevelt was increasingly isolated in her support of the human rights project. To placate emergent conservative forces, the Eisenhower regime that succeeded Truman in 1952 put the international human rights project on a shelf, and there it remained for many years. It took the United States over 30 years to ratify the Genocide Convention, and it was not until 1992 that the U.S. Senate approved ratification of the International Covenant on Civil and Political Rights.

If the United States was a half-hearted champion of the human rights cause in 1948, its chief adversary showed little more enthusiasm. The Soviet Union had joined in the project only with some reluctance. In early phases of the debate, and again as the final vote on the UDHR approached, the Soviet bloc contended that rights could not be dissociated from the prerogatives of the state, and they argued that the UDHR should also establish, and elaborate, a citizen's duty to the state. To this end, Soviet bloc delegates criticized many of the draft articles as superfluous or beyond the powers of the United Nations. They systematically objected to the way the discussion was framed, but—contrary to popular impressions—they did not attack the standards advanced in the draft text nor did they defend abusive practices by those in power. (To the contrary, they lost few opportunities to point out the human rights failings of the United States, its Western allies, and South Africa.) The Soviets used several tactical ploys to prolong debate and ultimately abstained from the General Assembly vote, but the record of their contribution to the debates indicates support for most of the broad provisions of the UDHR. Unlike most of the participants in the Third Committee debates, however, Soviet bloc delegates were combative in pressing their points. Most participants cloaked critical comments in the oblique language of diplomacy, but Soviet bloc delegates were more often blunt in their criticism of other countries' human rights practices. On several occasions contentious Eastern bloc comments provoked angry rebuttals—particularly from South Africa. Their abrasive stance no doubt deprived them of some support they might otherwise have gained. As it was, amendments proposed by the Soviet bloc often involved small changes that in some way needled the United States or some other country, and most failed to win majority support. Some accommodation was made to Soviet concerns and objections,[12] however, and despite its abstention on the historic UDHR vote, the U.S.S.R. ultimately chose not to remain outside the international human rights regime. In 1973 it ratified the two major human rights covenants based on the UDHR.

The uncomfortable conclusion, nevertheless, is that by 1948 there was no hegemonic power behind the UDHR or the idea of human rights. U.S. distance from the international human rights project was so great in 1951 that as the peace treaty between Japan and the Allies was being concluded, the U.S. State Department formally discouraged Japan from including reference to its commitment to UDHR principles.[13] Some have argued that the absence of hegemonic enthusiasm stunted the development of a potent human rights regime.[14] No doubt it did. The U.S. and U.S.S.R. readily put human rights to the service of the Cold War but found no other useful purpose for it. The U.S.S.R. ratified the international human rights treaties but paid them little mind. The U.S. deliberately shelved the same treaties, fearful that if ratified they would have to be taken seriously.

For want of a hegemonic sponsor, the task of salvaging the international human rights project fell largely to the small and medium powers.[15] John Humphrey, the U.N.'s first Director of Human Rights, reports in his memoir that some of the most ardent support and innovative contributions to the process of constructing the UDHR came from individual delegates, and from nongovernment organizations lobbying behind the scenes.[16] While the NGOs were primarily from Western, industrialized countries, many of the individuals who made the greatest mark on deliberations were from Latin America and other regions that two decades later would be recognized as "the Third World."

Among them were Peng-chen Chang of China, one of the two men identified by Humphrey as outstanding intellectual forces.[17] Chang had studied Asian culture and held a doctorate from Columbia University; he was well versed in Western philosophy, but he also frequently introduced what he identified as Confucian perspectives. Consistently, he offered the editorial solutions that moved the Commission, and the General Assembly's Third Committee, beyond impasses where they were mired.[18]

Charles Malik of Lebanon was the second towering figure identified by Humphrey. His dogmatic attachment to the doctrine of natural rights provoked arguments with several delegates, including Chang and British delegate Charles Duke,[19] but it did not diminish the wide respect for his command of parliamentary procedure and his ability to steer the debates through some difficult moments. As Chair of the Third Committee proceedings, Malik was responsible for ensuring that proposed amendments were debated and decided openly and fairly, and to him must go much of the credit for establishing collective ownership and political legitimacy of the UDHR.

Malik and Chang, along with Eleanor Roosevelt, were among the best-known delegates at the fall 1948 hearings because they were the three individuals named to the Human Rights Commission established by the U.N. in 1946. They were not alone as delegates of the lesser powers to make an impact, however. Hernan Santa Cruz (Chile) had also served on the initial drafting committee and was recognized and respected as an advocate for the economically developing countries[20]; Minerva Bernardino (Dominican Republic) had served on the women's commission and championed equality for women. With the intermittent support of other Latin American states, Guy Perez Cisneros (Cuba) fervently defended an alternative to the Third Committee draft text, which arose from the ninth hemispheric meeting of American states in Bogota earlier in 1948. Saudi Arabia offered arguments to limit the right to marry; these were swiftly rebutted by Pakistani delegate, Mrs. Ikramullah.[21] In closing speeches in the U.N. Third Committee, Carlos Romulo of the Philippines asserted that "a bill of rights [has] long been needed by mankind, and [is] necessary for the founding of a common world order."[22] Of the world's major geographic regions, only Africa was not represented at the UDHR hearings (excluding, of course, South Africa, then under white separatist rule). As if to compensate for their exclusion, however, more than 15 African countries incorporated reference to the UDHR into their national constitutions as they gained independence in the 1960s.[23] Unfortunately, they have done no better than states elsewhere in honoring and upholding the standards to which they are pledged.

It is relatively easy to trace the Western philosophical heritage through the text of the UDHR, but philosophical contributions of the "developing world" are less transparent. Reasoning counterfactually, however, one may argue that some important ideas would likely have been omitted from the UDHR without Third World support. In particular, Third World delegations were adamant in their defense of the notion of socioeconomic rights. Mexico, for example, proposed to showcase socioeconomic rights by inserting into Article 1 a claim that the rights of sustenance, health, education, and work are essential for social justice. Argentina's delegation was strongly attached to the notion of social security for the aged, and devoted an impassioned speech to those concerns. Saudi Arabia and Iraq both criticized the draft text of Article 20 as too weak in its reference to social security, preferring explicit reference to social justice. The Saudi delegate pointed out that whereas social security was a recent political concept in the West, a system of social security—in the form of *zakat* and *waqf*[24]— had been in place in the Muslim world for almost fourteen centuries.

In the little-disguised tension between U.S. and Soviet perspectives on this issue, Third World attachment to socioeconomic rights can be said to have tipped the balance.

Third World delegates are also responsible for the UDHR's strongest statement on universality, reflected in the second article of the Declaration. The second paragraph of that article establishes that "no distinction shall be made on the basis of political, jurisdictional, or international status of the country or territory to which a person belongs, whether it be independent, non-self-governing, or under any other limitation of sovereignty," and it was incorporated in the Declaration only after much debate. The concern was introduced by Yugoslavia, and was no doubt intended to pique the European imperial powers. It did. But more importantly, it harnessed the political energies of delegates from countries such as India and Haiti who saw in this clause an instrument for advancing the process of decolonization.[25]

By the elaborate process of its construction, the UDHR engaged the commitment of all members of the United Nations. That commitment was reaffirmed by U.N. members in Teheran in 1969, and again in Vienna in 1993, following three separate and independent regional conferences convened to reexamine the Universal Declaration and progress in implementing human rights standards. At the 1993 World Conference on Human Rights (Vienna), some non-Western states took the opportunity to assert the primacy of state sovereignty; others pressed to elevate socioeconomic rights and the right to development. In final sessions at Vienna, U.N. members (greatly swollen in number since 1948) reaffirmed the unchanged text of the Universal Declaration, and further asserted the indivisibility of all the rights it enshrines.

Given U.S. detachment from the international human rights project at the time when support was most needed, it is somewhat ironic that human rights today are often presumed to be a projection of American political culture. Western philosophy and Western legal traditions, of course, lent considerable substance to the text of the UDHR and presumptions of hegemonic influence have been helped along in recent decades by the prominence of human rights concerns in U.S. foreign policy rhetoric. Human rights activists in the United States have likewise contributed to the perception by focusing on civil and political rights and presenting them as comfortably American. The historical record, unfortunately, attests to as much popular resistance to the idea of universal human rights in the United States as elsewhere, and the ugly traditions of slavery and xenophobia are as much a part of the U.S. heritage as free expression and individual liberty.

It is useful to be reminded that what one finds is at least partially determined by what one seeks. The Western contribution to the UDHR is incontestable, but the West can neither claim nor accept exclusive ownership of the negotiated text; it requires an ahistorical perspective to argue that human rights was a Western construct imposed unwillingly on the rest of the world. The concept of rights belonging to all peoples is a political construction as much as it is an intellectual one, and it is one of the important heritages of World War II. Non-Western statesmen (of both genders) participated in and contributed to the creation of the document that sets a worldwide benchmark and standard for human rights practice. Indeed, remembering the world of 1948, it is plausible that without the participation of countries outside the Soviet and Western blocs, the human rights project would have foundered on the shoals of the burgeoning East-West conflict. At the very least, without their participation, there would have been differences in the final text. It remains, now, for the world community of states, international institutions, and human rights activists to muster the will and devise the means to implement the neglected provisions of the UDHR that in 1948 were championed by the lesser powers.

From Promotion to Protection:
Human Rights Activism in the "Developing World"

The framers of the UDHR were conscious of the responsibility inherent in the task of setting international standards for the future behavior of governments. They suffered few illusions about the past performance of some governments, and many delegations registered concerns at one point or another about their own governments' ability to live up to the newly created expectations. Those who drafted and those who finally approved the UDHR were also conscious of the limited ability of the United Nations or any other external body to secure full adherence to the agreed human rights standards. In the end, respect for human rights norms depended on the voluntary self-restraint of governments. The fact that no enforcement mechanisms were envisioned, and the Declaration itself was not even a legally binding document, led some legal experts to doubt openly whether it would ever be honored by anything more than lip service. More optimistic observers noted the important steps of standard setting and promotional activities but nevertheless recognized that full protection of human rights depended upon implementation and effective enforcement.

Momentum for securing the implementation of human rights standards has been built and sustained by an international human rights movement comprised of numerous national and international nongovernmental organizations. Such groups have proliferated around the world in recent years. In 1981, a human rights clearinghouse listed several hundred organizations worldwide that addressed questions of human rights. The 1997 edition of the directory lists over 4000 organizations, more than 700 of which are African. The International Federation of Human Rights, based in Paris, has over 100 local affiliates around the world, 5 in Asia, 30 in Africa, 15 in Eastern Europe, 15 in Latin America, and 15 in the Middle East. Amnesty International has some 55 national sections, 8 in Asia, 8 in Africa, 3 in the Middle East, and 11 in Latin America.

Activists from around the world, working locally for social change, often acknowledge that the idea of "rights" is poorly understood in their society. Many likewise acknowledge the place of rights in Western philosophy. Few would agree, however, that representatives of their governments were unaware of their role and responsibility in approving the UDHR, or somehow naively believed that those international human rights standards were not intended to apply at home. Law is a well-represented profession within the human rights movement, and many regard the Universal Declaration as a secret guarded too well and too long. Within the body of international law, the UDHR is recognized as the foundational text. Just as national governments from all parts of the world participated in early deliberations about its content, U.N. members participated in subsequent international conferences convened to assess progress, and in the international human rights apparatus overseen by the United Nations. Viewed in this way, human rights is no less legitimate an area of international concern, and no more controversial, than other issues regularly appearing on the global agenda, including population and environment. There are indeed pockets of political resistance to the idea of human rights in the global South, but it is arguable whether such resistance effectively differentiates them from Western society, where resistance and unawareness also exist. International collaboration in creating and expanding a global framework has made human rights a compelling concept for many non-Western advocates of social justice, and there is now a sturdy base of support for human rights in areas of the world where the notion of universality is most seriously challenged. The expansion of the human rights movement in the global South offers important opportunities to advocates of human rights everywhere, but human rights defenders in the South also face important challenges. In numerous countries human rights defenders face threats to their physical safety, and ensuring their own survival is the first challenge. The most critical of these includes staying alive—literally, developing organizational strength, and transcending rivalry with other human rights NGOs. Each of these is discussed in turn.

Surviving Threats to Freedom and Physical Safety

In many countries the defense of human rights is a high-risk business. For rhetorical purposes, the notion of "human rights" is often separated from politics. Human rights may be presented as a moral issue of vital concern to those with humanitarian or idealistic interests, and only marginally related to the world of politics, where interest in order, security, and power prevails. That approach is misleading and, of course, it fails to explain why so many human rights activists around the world live in danger. Fundamentally, human rights activists are political actors. They have an interest in the way power is used and abused, and their message in many instances offers a direct challenge to vested authority. As Jack Donnelly puts it, "Respecting human rights is extremely inconvenient for a government, even in the best of circumstances. And the less pure the motives of those in power, the more irksome human rights appear."[26] In some countries, the readiness of human rights defenders to criticize political practice places them in danger.

Human rights groups, however, are not adversaries of the state or of those who govern. They tend to prefer reform over revolution. Their efforts are intended to support the rule of law, and government measures to curtail arbitrary and abusive exercise of power are usually applauded. Human rights activists are drawn disproportionately from among lawyers, health professionals, educators, and clergy—individuals whose professional lives have brought them uncomfortable knowledge of power gone awry. They are perhaps unusual in their sensitivity to issues of social injustice, but few social indicators distinguish them from the governing classes.[27]

Most human rights activists have some stake in the system, and most are careful to work within the law. Nevertheless, staying alive is a task. The point was driven home for me in 1994 as I was completing a book on human rights activism in North Africa. In 1991 I had interviewed Youssef Fathellah, then president of the Algerian League of Human Rights (Ligue Algerien des Droits de l'Homme, LADH). Fathellah at the time was aware that many were criticizing him for his low-key and nonconfrontational approach to human rights concerns already emergent in Algeria, and he quietly confessed his own misgivings about the strategy he had adopted. The political balance in the country was delicate, and he wanted to preserve the possibility of quiet talks with government authorities. That was 1991. Three years later, much had changed in Algeria: elections had been interrupted by the military, Islamists had been rounded up and taken to camps in the Sahara, and dissident groups waged a terrorist campaign that claimed the lives of many prominent journalists and political figures. Fathellah had seen and heard too much. Like others, he readily condemned the actions of so-called Islamic groups who had taken up arms, but in an international conference in Berlin, he went an important step further, charging the government, too, with its share of human rights atrocities. Two days later, back in Algeria, he was assassinated by gunmen in the stairwell leading to his office.

For many human rights defenders in the South, joining a human rights group and becoming active is no casual affair. Recruitment is often done circumspectly so that local groups are not infiltrated by security forces or paramilitary groups, and tactics intended to help promote and protect human rights may be carefully reviewed with an eye to political risk. Researchers have recognized that social movements are not fueled by socioeconomic grievance as they once thought but depend rather on socially constructed meaning.[28] The "collective action frame" of human rights has become a clarion call for social justice, and it inspires many whose lives are not mired in social injustice.

The work of those striving for change in the global South is made more difficult, and more dangerous, by the fact that some of the most pressing problems they confront lie outside the international framework that has established legal parameters for pursuit of human rights concerns. These problems include abuses committed by soldiers in a context of war and abuses committed by private actors but condoned by a state unwilling or unable to pursue an effective remedy. Wartime abuses that have received attention as human rights concerns only in the last decade include rape, pillage, and targeting civilians, often on a massive scale.[29] Less extraordinary but no less outrageous for the victims are privately perpetrated abuses that go unpunished by the state, even where protective legislation exists. The death of Samia Sarwar in Pakistan in 1999 is illustrative. Samia was murdered by her own family, in her lawyer's office, during the course of her efforts to obtain a divorce from her abusive husband. Legal provisions, numerous witnesses, and the efforts of her lawyer notwithstanding, state agents made no arrests. Religious authorities vigorously defended the family's action as in keeping with tribal law, and the local chamber of commerce issued a statement in support of its president, Samia's father. An indictment issued by Muslim clerics threatens Samia's lawyer, Hina Jilani, who with her sister runs the legal aid and human rights center in Lahore.

Just as in another epoch lynchings in the American South generally went unpunished, government authorities in various countries today tolerate the intolerable through complicity or inaction. Contemporary practices fought by human rights activists include sexual slavery and the trade of women and children, debt bondage and enslavement, bride burnings and honor killings, female genital mutilation, and domestic assault. Some of these practices have deep roots in local cultural traditions, and they may be promoted or defended by actors with considerable prestige, power, and financial resources.

Under the best of circumstances, local human rights defenders face an arduous struggle. In many cases their efforts constitute a direct assault on local power structures, and the population whose rights and welfare they defend may not understand or sympathize with actions perceived to undermine or supplant local traditions, even if supported by national law. Some victims may not recognize the injustice done them or, fearful of reprisals, may be unwilling to prosecute or even publicize their plight.

Local activists are further handicapped in their efforts to curtail abusive practices by traditions surrounding international human rights law, which makes states, not private actors, its subject. Human rights law has in fact been applied unevenly in this domain. Government responsibility to control the actions of paramilitary groups—such as the death squads that operated freely in Central America two decades ago—has generally been recognized, whether or not government authorities are openly complicitous with such groups. Torture, political killings, and "disappearances" carried out by such groups are subject to investigation and condemnation by various U.N. and other international bodies, and international censure provides indirect support to human rights advocates working locally. The international community, however, has been slow to recognize the responsibility of government authorities to punish and prevent many of the abusive practices directed toward women, children, minorities, and the poor in many countries. International investigatory mechanisms in this domain are relatively new, and relatively weak, and the hesitation to incorporate concerns about private perpetrators into the existing framework of international human rights reduces the moral force that might otherwise attach to the efforts of those working for change. By extension, it increases the danger they face.

Building an Organization for Effective Action

Fortunately, not all human rights groups in the global South must operate in such difficult circumstances. Yet even under politically benign circumstances, the task of building an effective human rights organization in the South can be daunting. This challenge may appear mundane, but an organizational base is crucial to sustain effective action. In many countries, the immediate reason for creating or joining a human rights organization is a protest motivation of one sort or another. Rosa Nair Amuedo is one of the *madres* who in their simple white head scarves made the Plaza de Mayo famous with their silent marches every Thursday morning, placards held high proclaiming the names of their sons and daughters who "disappeared" during Argentina's dirty war. Rosa's 20-year old daughter was arrested by security agents and held for a nightmarish year before she finally "disappeared," never to be seen again. The event changed Rosa's life, and she takes meaning from relentless work for the truth to be known. Most human rights activists have not suffered such devastation personally, but they are no strangers to passion.

Few set out calmly and deliberately to build an organization, recruiting members and laying in place the requisite organizational structures to sustain work. Many human rights advocates initially act alone, founding a group only when it becomes clear that collective action is required to sustain or enhance their efforts. Dankwart Rustow several years ago observed that the conditions necessary to establish democracy were not necessarily the same required to sustain democratic structures.[30] A similar observation can be made with respect to human rights organizations. Raising funds and creating a stable financial base, recruiting and replacing leadership, or building organizational structures rarely inspire charismatic human rights activists. But they are necessary if an organization is to sustain itself over the long haul.

Such challenges are all the more daunting where civil society is weak and activists have little experience organizing and mobilizing supporters, and they are often compounded when financial resources are limited and physical infrastructure is lacking. The Nigerian section of Amnesty International, for example, has some 5000 dues-paying members, and a seven-member board of directors. Board members outside of Lagos must travel several hours by dusty bus to attend meetings, often held in heat and humidity, without benefit of electricity to turn an overhead fan. Such circumstances are discouraging, to say the least, and sometimes lead to organizational collapse.

Transcending Rivalry and Competition

The proliferation of local human rights groups around the world has multiplied the number of participants working to promote and protect human rights, but unfortunately, it has not necessarily amplified their voices or increased their effectiveness. In many instances a new group is created not because there is a particular niche waiting to be filled, but as a fractious result of internal disputes.

Human rights groups are susceptible to the phenomenon that James Rosenau has labeled the "autonomy dilemma."[31] Many small nongovernmental groups face an organizational conundrum when group unity is threatened by dissident perspectives from strong and possibly charismatic leaders. The term "autonomy dilemma" captures the inherent tension between the organizational requirement of some minimal level of group cohesion and unity on one hand, and, on the other hand, the opportunity for individual expression that makes membership in such organizations attractive.

In countries where political systems are relatively closed, human rights groups may present an alternative to political parties as a means of participating in national politics. Frequently, those drawn to such groups have rejected the possibility of working with political institutions or civic organizations considered too staid, unresponsive, slow, bureaucratic, compromised, corrupt, or otherwise incompatible with personal drives and values. Individuals who affiliate themselves with a human rights group are usually willing to tolerate some political or social risk in exchange for increased opportunity to defend deeply held beliefs or pursue personal concerns for social justice. Personal commitment accounts for much of the success of the human rights movement, but fervent personal commitment may also lead to organizational tensions and fissures. Individual activists led by a strong desire for autonomous, effective action may consider an organizational split to be preferable to compromise on policy, principle, or tactics. Organizations heavily influenced by such members find themselves prone to splinter, and the tendency may be most pronounced in societies where opportunities for effective participation are limited. The risk to the human rights movement in the global South is that as groups split and multiply they will divide and dissipate the energies and the resources of the necessarily small core of people in a given country whose primary commitment is to advance the cause of human rights.

Partisan politics pose a particular challenge for the cohesion and effectiveness of human rights groups where a tradition of civil society is not deeply rooted. As suggested earlier, activists committed directly to the purpose of promoting and protecting human rights occupy political space just outside the main arena. They are concerned more with the apportionment and use of power than with the division of political spoils. Although many local variations are possible, in a broad sense the international human rights principles set the bounds for what is considered fair in political play—including free elections, right to association and speech, guarantees of due process, and prohibition of torture. The most central political role of human rights groups is to promote the rule of law and to denounce the arbitrary and abusive exercise of power, and such functions are most cleanly exercised at a distance from local political contests. Human rights advocacy presumes a freedom to exercise independent judgment, even if that sometimes entails criticism of natural allies. The credibility and effectiveness of human rights groups often depend upon political impartiality, and problems quickly arise where such impartiality cannot be assured. In some countries, political parties have found it expedient to establish human rights affiliates, and even where that is not the case, some who join human rights groups may pursue political ambitions of their own relative to a political party or other established political organization. Human rights groups in many contexts must actively guard against being compromised by political rivalries and partisan politics, for related tensions often split groups or diminish their effectiveness.

Any one of these challenges might prove overwhelming, but many groups in the global South must face all of them simultaneously. Civil society is weak; competition is rife; political dangers abound; and resources are few. It is no small wonder that many groups collapse or become moribund after a first bloom of activity. Yet despite the risks, costs, and challenges, human rights activists in the global South continue to grow. Activists derive motivation and inspiration from two apparent truths. First is the recognition that human rights are best defended at home. *Nunca mas* was the popular chant that swept across Latin America as the dirty wars finally came to an end, one after another, but without effective domestic safeguards, no echo of "Never More" really rings true. Human rights groups are the front line defense.

Human rights advocates in the global South are also aware that their very existence is a testimony to the universality of human rights, and no one has more at stake than they when universality is contested. For the benefit of their government delegates meeting to consider the Universal Declaration in preparation for the 1993 Vienna conference, nongovernmental organizations from Asia made clear their own attachment to international standards:

> Universal human rights standards are rooted in many cultures. We affirm the basis of universality of human rights which afford protection to all of humanity, including special groups such as women, children, minorities and indigenous peoples, workers, refugees and displaced persons, the disabled and the elderly. While advocating cultural pluralism, those cultural practices, which derogate from universally accepted human rights, including women's rights, must not be tolerated. As human rights are of universal concern and are universal in value, the advocacy of human rights cannot be considered to be an encroachment upon national sovereignty.[32]

Human rights advocates in the global South understand that the legitimacy of their own work depends upon international recognition of a set of commonly agreed and universally applicable standards of good governance. Carrying forward the work of delegates to the 1948 U.N. General Assembly, their commitment today is to make respect of those standards a universal political reality.

Notes

1   John Humphrey was the U.N.'s first Director of Human Rights, and it was under his direction that the first draft declaration was prepared. With the assistance of Egon Schwelb, Czechoslovakian scholar and legal advisor to the War Crimes Commission, he reviewed a number of documents—including one widely circulated text drafted by H. G. Wells and another submitted by Gutierrez Guzman. Humphrey reports that he relied most heavily on the document that had been prepared under the aegis of the American Institute of Law by an international group of lawyers that included the prominent Chilean jurist Alvaro Alvarez. Panama had unsuccessfully sponsored an earlier version of the document at the 1945 conference in San Francisco that chartered the United Nations. See John Humphrey, *Human Rights and the United Nations: A Great Adventure* (Dobbs Ferry, NY: Transnational Publishers, 1984), p. 32. Humphrey asserts that his decision to include socioeconomic rights in the first draft was a matter of personal conviction (pp. 2, 32, and 40).

2   These included Australia, Chile, China, France, Lebanon, the U.S., the U.K., and the U.S.S.R.

3   United Nations, *Official Records of the Third Session of the General Assembly, Part 1. Third Committee, Summary Records of Meetings, 21 September -8 December 1948* (Lake Success, New York, 1948), pp. 435-450.

4   "Human Rights Questions at the Third Regular Session of the General Assembly: The United States Position," in *Foreign Relations of the United States 1948*, Vol. 1 (U.S. Government Printing Office, 1975), p. 290. Also see John Humphrey, supra note 1, pp. 65-66.

5   Iris Chang, *The Rape of Nanking* (New York: Penguin Books, 1997), pp. 170-180.

6   "Human Rights Questions at the Third Regular Session of the General Assembly," supra note 4, pp. 293-295.

7   William Korey, "Eleanor Roosevelt and the Universal Declaration of Human Rights," in David A. Gurewitsch, *Eleanor Roosevelt: Her Day* (New York: Interchange Foundation, 1973), p. 21.

8   "Memorandum of Conversation," in *Foreign Relations of the United States 1951*, Vol. 2 (U.S. Government Printing Office, 1979), pp. 740-741.

9   "Human Rights Questions at the Third Regular Session of the General Assembly," supra note 4, p. 291.

10 Richard O. Davies, *Defender of the Old Guard: John Bricker and American Politics* (Columbus, Ohio: Ohio State University Press, 1993). Also see Natalie H. Kaufman and David Whiteman, "Opposition to Human Rights Treaties in the United States Senate: The Legacy of the Bricker Amendment," *Human Rights Quarterly*, vol. 10 (Number 3, August 1988), pp. 312-321.

11 Supra note 6, pp. 289-290.

12 The reference to slave trade included in the final draft of the UDHR, for example, was a Soviet proposal that was accepted despite U.S. objections (*U.N. Third Committee Summary Records*, 1948), p. 221.

13 Egon Schwelb, *Human Rights and the International Community* (Chicago: Quadrangle Books, 1965, pp. 48-49).

14 Tony Evans, *U.S. Hegemony and the Project of Universal Human Rights* (London: Macmillan Press, 1996), p. 41, and David Forsythe, *The Internationalization of Human Rights* (Lexington, MA: Lexington Books, 1991), pp. 108-112.

15 I have explored the role and contribution of these states more fully in "Universalizing Human Rights: The Role of Small States in the Construction of the Universal Declaration of Human Rights" *Human Rights Quarterly*, vol. 23 (1), February 2001, pp. 44-72.

16 John Humphrey, supra note 1, p. 13 and p. 17 and *passim*. There was considerable variation in the degree of formal instruction across the 58 delegations. Indeed, one of the early,

vigorous debates over the UDHR was about the extent to which delegates were free to represent their own opinions, as opposed to representing the official position of their government. The Soviet Union, in particular, objected to contributions made by uninstructed delegates, and ECOSOC eventually confirmed that the decision would be left to the choice of individual states. For the role played by nongovernment organizations, see William Korey, *NGOs and the Universal Declaration of Human Rights: A Curious Grapevine* (New York: St. Martin's Press, 1998).

17 John Humphrey, supra note 1, p. 23.

18 See Johannes Morsink, "The Philosophy of the Universal Declaration," *Human Rights Quarterly*, vol. 6 (3), August 1984, p. 330.

19 John Humphrey, supra note 1, p. 24 and William Korey, supra note 7, p. 16.

20 John Humphrey, supra note 1, p. 37 and p. 65.

21 Supra note 12, p. 374.

22 Ibid., p. 888.

23 Egon Schwelb, supra note 13, p. 51.

24 Saudi delegate Jamil Baroody informed the Third Committee of two Islamic institutions, *zakat* and *waqf*, that had stood the test of fourteen centuries. Baroody described *zakat* as a tax levied for the purpose of assisting the poor and unemployed, and noted that it is one of the five pillars of Islam. He also noted that income from property placed in trust, *waqf*, was frequently used for the relief of the poor or the unemployed (supra note 12, p. 515).

25 Ibid., pp. 740-747.

26 Jack Donnelly, "International Human Rights: A Regime Analysis," *International Organization*, vol. 40 (1986), p. 617.

27 This personal observation is indirectly substantiated in a number of published works, including Egon Larsen, *A Flame in Barbed Wire: The Story of Amnesty International* (New York: W. W. Norton and Co, 1979), passim, and Laurie S. Wiseberg, "Protecting Human Rights Activists and NGOs: What More Can Be Done?" *Human Rights Quarterly*, vol. 13 (1991), pp. 526-528. Also see Margaret E. Keck and Kathryn Sikkink, *Activists Beyond Borders* (Ithaca, NY: Cornell University Press, 1998), pp. 91-101; Claude E. Welch, Jr., *Protecting Human Rights in Africa: Roles and Strategies of Non-Governmental Organizations* (Philadelphia: University of Pennsylvania Press, 1995), pp. 50-69, and Susan E. Waltz, *Human Rights and Reform: Changing the Face of North African Politics* (Berkeley: University of California Press, 1995), pp. 156-166.

28 Carol McClurg Mueller, "Building Social Movement Theory," in Aldon O. Morris and Carol McClurg Mueller, eds., *Frontiers in Social Movement Theory* (New Haven, CT: Yale University Press, 1992), pp. 9-11.

29 The legal corpus known as humanitarian law (including the Geneva Conventions) initially pertained primarily to international war, and for many years the standards were rarely invoked during civil conflict. (Civil conflict, taking place within the bounds of a sovereign state, was generally viewed as outside the purview of international law.) That practice evolved over the course of the Yugoslav conflict, which did not easily fall into the category of either civil or international war, but which clearly involved the perpetration of heinous crimes. The U.N. Security Council's decision to establish a Tribunal for Investigation of War Crimes in the former Yugoslavia, followed by its decision to set up a second tribunal for Rwanda, has effectively expanded the applicability of humanitarian law to civil conflict. The gradual development of the concept of universal jurisdiction and innovative prosecution of "crimes against humanity" have likewise brought human rights law and humanitarian law closer together. See, for example, M. Cherif Bassiouni, *Crimes Against Humanity in International Law* (Dordrecht, Netherlands: Nijhoff, 1992), pp. 147-165, and Theodor Meron, "The Humanization of Humanitarian Law," *American Journal of International Law*, vol. 94 (April 2000), pp. 268-269. On the concept of universal jurisdiction, see International Law Association, Committee on International Human Rights Law and Practice, "Final Report on the Exercise of Universal Jurisdiction in Respect of Gross Human Rights Offenses," London Conference (2000), at www.ila-hq.org.

30 Dankwart Rustow, "Transitions to Democracy," *Comparative Politics*, vol. 2 (April 1970), pp. 337-363.

31 James Rosenau, *Turbulence in World Politics: A Theory of Change and Continuity* (Princeton, NJ: Princeton University Press, 1990), pp. 98-102.

32 Quoted in Peter R. Baehr, Fried Van Hoof, Liu Nanlai, and Tao Zhenghua, *Human Rights: Chinese and Dutch Perspectives* (The Hague: Martinus Nijhoff Publishers, 1996), p. 28.

CHAPTER FOUR

Rescuing Human Rights:
The Prospects for Humanitarian Intervention

Tom Farer

In the late spring of 1993, almost thirty years to the month from the time I left Somalia, I returned as legal consultant to the United Nations Intervention Force known as UNOSOM II with a mandate to help rebuild the police along with the rest of the justice system. By the time I reached East Africa, however, conflict had erupted between U.N. forces and the clan militia led by General Mohammed Farah Aideed. That conflict, within whose bitter heart I lived for almost two months, led quickly to a transformation of my task and more slowly to a series of disasters that prostrated the mission and culminated in its dispirited withdrawal.

"Humanitarian intervention" is a term often used loosely to describe practically any foreign intervention that has a military dimension and is motivated, allegedly, by a desire to protect the civilian population of the target state. But within the research and practitioner communities, it is in general used more narrowly to describe a particular species of the genus called "peace operations." The other species are traditional peacekeeping, multidimensional peace operations, and peace enforcement.

Traditional peacekeeping evolved during the Cold War. It amounted to the insertion, usually under a U.N. flag, of relatively small, lightly armed units of national forces to monitor a cease-fire usually agreed upon under pressure from the U.S. and the U.S.S.R. in cases where they feared being drawn into confrontation and where the status quo at the time of the cease-fire was deemed consistent with their respective interests. The intervention was for an indefinite period. The troops, invariably drawn from small countries, preferably neutral like Sweden, were expected to function as observers of the cease-fire and a symbolic trip-wire for international community response to renewal of the conflict. They were neither armed nor, for the most part, trained as an effective fighting force and correspondingly operated under extremely inhibiting rules of engagement. They could defend themselves if attacked, but they could not preempt or punish. Cyprus and Sinai were classic instances, the former still in place after twenty-five years.

Multidimensional peace operations are largely a post–Cold War phenomenon and began largely as a means of bringing that war's many vicious little proxy conflicts to a close. Support for closure flowed naturally from one superpower's loss of interest in "winning" and the other's disappearance. Civil conflicts like the one in El Salvador—which in the early eighties had gobbled up time and energy and conscience in Washington—became redundant nuisances once they could no longer be seen as tests of American credibility to bear any burden whatever the costs in other peoples' lives. Angola, Mozambique, Cambodia, Somalia, and Guatemala were prominent among the cases where the Cold War's passing did not immediately separate the local actors' homicidal embrace, and it appeared that only through international action could they be induced to let go.

Other man-made catastrophes had a somewhat different genealogy. Some stemmed from the general loosening of restraint on parochial actors' violent pursuit of strictly local interests which followed once one superpower had left the scene and the other had consequently lost its chief incentive to impose order with force or seduce it with dollars. Released from the discipline instinct when living in the shadow of robust and powerful states, political entrepreneurs within much weaker states could activate latent ethnic feuds often aided by shrinking economies hitherto sustained by largesse from the superpowers' respective treasuries. Bosnia is a case in point. And still others, like Liberia and Rwanda, were accidents waiting to happen, having been set in motion by Western intrusions long preceding the Cold War, and happening to coincide with the post–Cold War era.

Like traditional peacekeeping, the multidimensional form is initiated with at least the nominal and often the grudging if not partially coerced consent of the belligerents. But rather than arriving under the auspices of a simple cease-fire, the multidimensional operation usually rests on a peace accord, often provisional, containing a vision, often hazy, of the terms of a final political settlement. One reason for that difference—and another distinguishing feature of these missions—is that the belligerents are not rival states but rather political factions within a country, one of whom might occupy the capital and enjoy some degree of international recognition as the legitimate government. Consistent with that distinction is a mission goal that goes well beyond maintaining a ceasefire. Because, in addition, the intervenors intend directly to assist the belligerents in addressing the underlying causes of conflict and achieving a political solution with some capacity to survive the international mission's departure. In other words, they combine cease-fire maintenance with the building of what it is hoped will be a real peace. To that end, the U.N. mission marries a civilian with a military component and even the latter will often find itself employing skills more normally associated with civilians.

Transforming cease-fire into peace implies a broad continuum of non-military activities and associated skills. They include: mediating implementation of the details of the peace accord; distributing relief and initiating rehabilitation, administering civil government and elections; informing the public about the intervention's ends and means; facilitating grass roots organization; protecting refugees and internally displaced persons; monitoring human rights and assisting in the reconstruction of the legal order. Complexity and associated expense, together with the existence of an agenda for peace, encourage, although they do not compel, missions with a definite time line and are in that respect also unlike the traditional open-ended peacekeeping operations. What has served as something akin to compulsion is the insistence of some countries, most notably the United States, on a timed exit scenario that has sometimes appeared more imperative than successful.

Yet another distinction between the new and the old peacekeeping is a less anemic view of the military as an instrument of coercion. While still enjoined to maintain strict neutrality—that is to do everything possible to avoid affecting the political-military balance between the contending parties—international forces have sometimes been authorized to go beyond immediate self-defense and to take positive measures to maintain a secure environment for the civil functions of the mission. Since the mission originates in an accord, in theory it should not encounter armed resistance. But mandates sometimes fail to incorporate the commonsense view that local commanders of the target state's warring factions may either be entirely indifferent to agreements between their leaders, comfortably ensconced in a five-star hotel, or may insist on their own, possibly quite idiosyncratic interpretation of those agreements. Moreover, once peace begins to break out, the rank and file of rival armed factions may turn to outright banditry to maintain their standard of living and self-esteem.

This species of peace operation has a sibling identical in all civilian aspects but distinguishable by the absence of a military dimension. In order to consolidate a peace process, a government and its hitherto armed rival may invite in a multinational civilian mission—organized by the United Nations or a regional organization or by the two of them in a joint venture exemplified by the cases of El Salvador and Guatemala where the Organization of American States has been a decidedly junior partner. At this point in time, regional organizations outside Europe have little to contribute in terms of human and material resources. But despite the added complexity their presence brings to an operation, their inclusion may be useful to the extent that some institutional learning occurs, since they may be needed where the Security Council is paralyzed by a veto.

Humanitarian intervention in the peace operations idiom is distinguished by the absence of consent or of a ceasefire and by its notionally narrow albeit very tricky mission to help the population survive even as fighting continues. Incidentally, however, it may encourage or facilitate maintenance of a ceasefire and thereby create the space for a provisional political accord. Thus, as in the case of Somalia (and, more arguably, Bosnia), what begins as a strictly humanitarian intervention may transition to a multidimensional peace operation. The term might also be seen as embracing a case like Haiti where intense human rights violations coincide with the overthrow of a democratic regime. In that case, the forceful restoration of democracy—a legitimate end in itself at least in regions that have incorporated democratic norms in mutually binding treaties—was also the occasion for executing the protective mission.

Finally, there is *peace enforcement*, illustrated by the North Atlantic Treaty Organization's (NATO) Bosnia operations in defense of the Dayton accords. It is by definition an exercise in coercion, one designed to deter and repress renewal of the conflict and to impose and maintain a cease-fire that protects the civilian population and fosters political settlement. What begins as humanitarian intervention can therefore morph openly into unambiguous peace enforcement leading in its turn to multidimensional peacekeeping.

Obstacles to Success in Peace Operations

As I can attest, however clear the distinctions among these missions may appear on the written page, they can become practically indistinguishable in the muddy scrum of a real operation in very hostile territory. Taking peace operations as a whole, what are the generic obstacles to their successful completion? Some should have been apparent at the outset of the peace operations era, which began less than fifteen years ago. Others became grimly evident in the form of lessons learned from a mix of cases ranging, on an achievement continuum, from bloody awful failures to varying degrees of at least short-term success.

The United Nations (U.N.)
With very few exceptions, these have been U.N. operations. So the first obstacle, not surprisingly, is the United Nations itself. That self is actually plural selves, which is a large part of the problem. We have the two political organs—the Security Council and the General Assembly (GA). In this era, only the former has claimed authority to commission a peace operation, but the latter retains the power of the purse strings. It approves the U.N. budget and in doing so determines the programmatic ambit of the assessments that U.N. members are legally obligated to pay, possibly even the United States as the world's foremost exponent of law and order. Peacekeeping expenses, as defined by the GA, are paid out of a discrete part of the assessed revenues. Unfortunately, the GA definition of legitimate expenses does not now encompass relief, rehabilitation, and development, activities most observers deem critical constituents of successful multidimensional peacekeeping.

Along with the two political organs, we have the secretariat, the more-or-less permanent bureaucracy rising hierarchically to the Secretary-General who is impermanent. Numbering about 50,000 with a budget substantially less than that of New York City, and with a mandate encompassing the entire agenda of international concerns, it is about the size of the civil service that runs the state of Wyoming with its population of about 550,000. Political intervention in appointment and promotion has been endemic. Merit has often played fourth fiddle to the other overarching criterion for entry and advancement, namely broad geographic representation; yet tenure, once achieved, rivals the academic version as a bar to termination for mere incompetence or sloth. Still, the remarkable thing about the U.N. is the actual number of able and dedicated men and women the secretariat nevertheless includes, perhaps the most extraordinary of whom is the current Secretary-General.

For the first forty years of its life, the Secretariat was rarely asked to do anything more terminally risky than collecting data, drafting resolutions and treaties, and supporting countless meetings conducted by a just barely countable number of committees, commissions, and other bodies of diplomats (and, occasionally, experts) sometimes deliberating seriously and sometimes consuming time, space, trees, and water to no very apparent end other than the pleasures of consumption. On the other hand, it has been said that unlike many lawyers, polluters, and sundry others, they did little apparent harm. What is very often overlooked is the U.N.'s role over those first forty years in consolidating the revolutionary postwar prohibition of aggression and, more generally, vastly elaborating the rule of law in such areas as maritime jurisdiction, space, the environment, and cross-border commercial transactions. In addition, the endless meetings provided a backdrop for informal bilateral diplomacy often at high levels and often between countries prevented by old and popular antagonism from normal diplomatic intercourse much less periodic summits. In short, this Secretariat had virtues, but a refined capacity to oversee complex peace operations was not one of them. It had to learn on the run.

In one respect the directing brain at the top of the Secretariat, the Secretary-General (and his—or at some future time her—immediate assistants) is at the same time a separate actor in the drama of international governance. Drawing on their authority under the Charter, Secretaries-General have initiated good offices and mediation in conflicts, including those mixing domestic and foreign elements, and have recommended action to the Security Council. In the event of a Security Council resolution authorizing a U.N. peace operation, the Secretary-General selects senior mission personnel, not necessarily members of the Secretariat, who translate the mandate's inevitable generalities into operational facts. The Secretary-General's role is more peripheral where the Council authorizes another organization, like NATO in Bosnia, to execute its decisions.

Another important dimension of the Hydra-headed thing we call the United Nations consists of the operating agencies: The U.N. High Commissioner for Refugees (UNHCR), the U.N. International Children's Emergency Fund (UNICEF), the U.N. Development Program (UNDP) and the World Food Program (WFP), all better known by their respective acronyms. The latter three have development-related functions and all four play roles in relief and rehabilitation and are on the scene in every complex international emergency. In theory their activities are coordinated by the Secretary-General or his designee. To assist him in this task, the GA authorized the creation of a Department of Humanitarian Affairs (DHA) headed by an Under-Secretary-General. In January 1998, the DHA was renamed the Office for the Coordination of Humanitarian Affairs (OCHA). In the field, whether during complex emergencies or during the ordinary course of events, the local UNDP chief has normally been given the coordination function. For all the mandates and the fact that the entire U.N. relief, rehabilitation, and development effort falls under the directing power of another political organ, the Economic and Social Council, each of these agencies has exercised an autonomy reminiscent of the Duke of Burgundy during the low tide of French royal power, or of the local government of Washington, D.C., for much of the tenure of its former Mayor, Marion Barry, in relation to its Congressional suzerain. To be fair, as Jonathan Moore, a leading authority on complex emergencies has written, "The resistance of the U.N.'s operating agencies to co-ordination and even cooperation with each other comes from their headquarters....The separatism and turf-fighting...is least prevalent on the ground, where there is an urgent job to be done, where the instinct is to seek reinforcement, complementarity and collaboration, and where common sense has a better chance to prevail. The problem lies more at the top, where internecine politics have a richer tradition, bureaucrats abound, and fund raising and media battles are waged."[1]

Autonomy is, of course, relative. Compared to the so-called "specialized agencies" like the Food and Agricultural (FAO) and World Health Organizations (WHO), each with its own board, budget, and agenda, the operating agencies are docile instruments of the Secretary-General's will. Fortunately, for the latter's sanity and the coherence of peace operations, their resources and capacities are of marginal potential value to peace operations.

The same cannot, however, be said about another set of actors that fall, nominally, within the U.N. system, namely the Bretton Woods institutions, the World Bank, and the International Monetary Fund. There are those who feel that the latter's main role in connection with complex emergencies has been to help incite them by imposing austerities that in shrinking the domestic pie, set off a murderous scramble among groups for whatever is left. While I think that is a considerable oversimplification and to some degree amounts to accusing surgeons of drawing blood, it is a topic that would carry us far beyond the bounds of this relatively brief survey. On the negative side, it suffices to echo Jonathan Moore when he writes that the Bank and Fund "ascribe little relevance to rehabilitation...have poor relationships with U.N. entities generally [and] even though they are technically specialized agencies of the United Nations...they prefer to regard themselves as outside the U.N. system, and 'co-ordination' with it is anathema."[2] Is it necessary to add that the Bank and Fund could not maintain their attitude if the world's leading financial powers, the United States preeminent among them, decided it was dysfunctional?

The Global Arms Bazaar
The second generic obstacle that needs to be noted is the lush availability of

small arms and light weapons to any group with a violent impulse. By small and light I refer primarily to automatic weapons, light machine guns and mortars, and grenade launchers, although you could also include handheld antitank and surface-to-air missile launchers. A recent study by a leading German think tank conservatively estimates the number in uncontrolled circulation as 100 million and concludes that they have killed more civilians than the antipersonnel landmines recently outlawed by the international community.[3] Aside from helping to precipitate violence, the availability of small and light weapons immensely complicates the effort to halt fighting, deliver aid, and build peace. Almost all of these weapons began life licitly; that is, they were produced consistent with national law and, in many but by no means all cases, their first export was licensed. The great majority flow from stocks declared surplus by original purchasers after which they entered the vast sprawling global arms bazaar, one of the true, equal opportunity areas of international commerce. This was illustrated by a recent case where an arms shipment destined for a country in Africa originated in an Eastern European factory, was brokered by a private military security company based in Western Europe, and financed by an Asian national who is an entrepreneur in North America.[4]

The Separation of Operational Responsibility and Economic Means
Once antagonists in civil armed conflicts achieve a cease-fire and political accord, the outbreak of real peace depends crucially on the demobilization, rehabilitation, and reintegration of the young men in the contending forces now threatened with redundancy. The grunts in these conflicts, many of them adolescents and some even younger, often have no skills other than fighting and no tools other than a kalashnikov. Any peace process must, therefore, have an answer to their inevitable question, namely "What's in it for me?" Efforts to disarm and demobilize before answering that question are a recipe for renewed war or, at the very least, metastasized banditry.

This reality leads to a circular dilemma for peace operations. Relief and particularly rehabilitation and development agencies, much less investors, want to operate in a secure environment. A landscape strewn with volatile armed men is not secure. But only by committing funds and personnel to a process of rehabilitation and development can international institutions create conditions in which troops will have an incentive to demobilize. For the reasons I have already suggested, neither the Secretary-General nor the Security Council can square that circle. Neither has the effective power to command. The reality is that an organization politically and culturally disposed to treat force as the absolute last resort, if that, finds it much easier to deploy troops in a war-wracked country than to offer economic assistance. The troops are paid after the fact and payment is underwritten by the U.N.'s compulsory assessment system. Economic and technical assistance are not. Although the Special Representative of the Secretary General can develop plans for relief and rehabilitation, he or she can implement them only by wandering about the world with a begging bowl. Meanwhile, back in the bush, a tense cease-fire begins to crack along with the political will from which it stemmed.

Yet another facet of this problem is an allocation and interpretation of institutional mandates that tends to leave out of the peace process a critical link, namely rehabilitation. Humanitarian assistance and development agencies speak of a relief-to-development continuum. At the relief end, intergovernmental agencies and NGOs deliver food, medicine, and shelter to save people from imminent death. Pictures of starving, shelterless people will generally bring a flood of support from NGOs (who today often serve as vehicles for delivering aid actually supplied by governmental and intergovernmental agencies) and official agencies like UNHCR and UNICEF and the World Food Program. The world and regional development banks and various national aid agencies provide support for long-term development.

It is the intermediate link of rehabilitation or "recovery assistance" that often sags. To the humanitarian relief actors it seems less imperative, whereas to the developers it is something that should happen before they arrive. While not wholly unconnected to practice and prudence, the continuum image on balance is flawed. It is too neat and too linear. The purpose of recovery assistance is "to restore victims to self-sufficiency, to draw the society away from dependency and vulnerability toward viability and sustainability."[5] Conventional programs at this stage would include the following: (1) repair and upgrading of basic infrastructure such as secondary roads and bridges, well and irrigation systems, schools and clinics; (2) restoration of basic water, health, and education services; (3) refurbishing agricultural production, livestock, and fisheries (assuming any fish are left after the Japanese, Russian, Polish, and other large, long distance fishing fleets are finished vacuuming the seas); (4) renovation of markets, increase of trade, and creation of jobs; and (5) rebuilding capacity in local authorities and institutions of civil society.[6]

Action at the relief stage can make restarting local life more difficult. The straightforward, unconditioned delivery of food and shelter tends to create a mood of dependency which beneficiaries, already dazed and demoralized by loss of home and loved ones, and by all the traumas of intramural violence, may then have difficulty shaking. Moreover, decisions about which local actors to use as conduits and organizers and which to appease and from which to rent cars and guards and guides and houses can either facilitate or obstruct the move to rebuilding local authority and fostering civil society. In short, there ought to be a plan, a grand strategy of peacebuilding, which identifies linkages at the outset. But in order to develop much less execute credible strategies, one needs some assured access to funds. When the great powers impose on the Secretary-General the obligation to launch a peace operation, they do not tell him where to find the funds. Indeed they rarely say anything of substance about the operation's rehabilitation facet. The world and regional banks have the funds but the Secretary-General has no authority to demand that they join in the planning process much less fund its product.

Rehabilitation activities funded and under way can facilitate demobilization in at least two ways: their start conveys some sense that the society has a future; their existence provides a setting for compensating combatants and re-integrating them into the larger society by having them work with persons who were not engaged in the fighting. However, the opportunities stemming from conventional rehabilitation programs may not present themselves to fighters as an improvement on their position before the cease-fire. For officers and the more sociopathically inclined among ordinary soldiers, building schools may not have quite the same buzz as confiscating at gunpoint truckloads of supplies or striding through a village with absolute assurance that you can take whatever is there. Moreover, since civil conflicts generally end when the insurgents give up the gun in return for a promised share of power or participation in fair elections, where insurgents believe they have some chance to win, peace builders need to provide for those called upon to give up their weapons effective guarantees that demobilization will not prove suicidal and to provide for the government some assurance that the insurgents are not simply regrouping.

In the circumstances of a devastated society that has been passing through the inferno of armed conflict, the atmosphere is tense, volatile, and paranoid, and disarmament must be terrifying. Even for top leaders, much less for officers and men in the field, there are many incentives to change one's mind about disarmament agreements. Therefore, chances of success will be greatest when rehabilitation and income-sustaining projects for the about-to-be ex-combatants are conspicuously in place, the settlement agreement precisely details the sequential steps of demobilization, and external supporters of the accord trusted by both sides are willing and ready first to deploy strong forces manifestly able to enforce the agreement and then to keep them in place until the political settlement has taken hold.

Rebuilding Civil and Political Society and the Economy: The Post-Cold War Experience

I think it fair to say that not a single one of the post–Cold War peace operations has come close to satisfying those optimal conditions. Liberia, where the U.N., playing a generally supplementary role to a West African peace force, was supposed to play the key disarmament role, is one of the grossest cases in point. Requested vehicles arrived one week after the official close of the disarmament and demobilization process. Medium-lift helicopters, also essential equipment, also arrived after the event.[7] One result of the failed disarmament program was an exodus of armed bands from Liberia to neighboring Sierra Leone where they contributed to the generalized mayhem. The inability to deploy sufficient troops to provide a secure environment and also coercively to encourage compliance with disarmament provisions certainly was a factor in the failure of the first U.N. peace operation in Angola, which was succeeded by a new round of the civil war between the government and the National Union for the Total Independence of Angola (UNITA) insurgency of Jonah Savimbi.

In large part because it has lacked financial resources and sufficient expertise, rather than destroying arms following their surrender, U.N. commanders and officials have usually stored them near the demobilization point and generally under a two-key system which did not always succeed in preventing recovery of the arms by unreconstructed warriors. But that is a minor matter compared to the brevity of peace operations and hence the security guarantees that are so essential for successful demobilization. The temporal parameters of most operations have been set in terms of the period required for bringing the country to the point where it can hold elections. In other words, elections[8] have been a proxy for performance of all key functions including demobilization and reintegration of fighters and their leaders.

At the discursive level of life, certain important U.N. members, such as Saudi Arabia and China, have resisted the claim that elections equal legitimacy, or are otherwise necessary for effective governments ruling with at least the generalized acquiescence of their people. Nevertheless, the international facilitators and guarantors of internal political accords formally treat elections as the capstone of the peacemaking process. Behind the scenes, however, a more nuance reality normally prevails. For as noted earlier (and as the Northern Ireland peace accord nicely illustrates), settlement normally involves a commitment by one party to disarm in return for a share of power. Hence, to the extent elections denote majority rule inhibited only by the imperative of individual human rights, they are inconsistent with the rationale of settlement strategies, which often guarantee to both parties a share of power, economic opportunity, and other social goods. The need to cement in that allocation is especially evident where the contending factions are ethnic, religious, or racial identity groups and one is a permanent minority. For permanent minorities who have taken up the gun precisely to get a proportionate share of power, wealth, and prestige, a proposal that they submit to the unrestrained arbitrament of elections is largely indistinguishable from a proposal for unconditional surrender.

Somalia
These cool analytical points come to hot life in the maelstrom of a real peace operation. I decided to illustrate them through the Somali case because I experienced it from the inside. First let me sketch the context.[9] The country was formed in 1960 through the consensual merger at the moment of their simultaneous birth of the former British Somaliland and the Italian colony and later trust territory of Somalia. Texas-sized but stretching a bit thinly along the Indian Ocean from just opposite the southern tip of the Arabian peninsula all the way to Kenya, much of the country most of the time is a vista of parched bushland dotted with umbrella trees. Its people, largely nomadic for most of their ancient history, had reputations in East Africa as warriors with a taste for poetry and distaste for authority. Over 99 percent Sunni Muslim, they are a bridge between the Arab and sub-Saharan African cultural worlds. Beyond the immediate family, their loyalty has been to concentric circles of kinship culminating in a few huge clan families numbering up to half a million or more people. Wider even than the clan family was a sense of nationhood unusual in Africa, a sense of a Somali people united by religion, culture, and history. The locus of loyalty varied with the circumstances across a spectrum from sub-subclan groups to the Somali people as a whole.

The merged entity spent nine years under elected governments marked by the delicate balancing of clan and subclan coalitions and unashamed corruption. Corruption even of the electoral process stripped legitimacy from the electoral system. Meanwhile, an ill-advised arms and training agreement with the Soviet Union converted the national army from a lightly armed decidedly rag-tag affair into a modestly professional fighting force with the esprit and confidence to seize power, which it did in 1969 led by General Siad Barre. He purported to impose a regime of scientific socialism; however, clan connections continued to structure loyalties. With few other targets of opportunity in the region and liking its proximity to the Persian Gulf, the Soviet Union poured in economic and military aid and technical assistance particularly from the more ruthlessly competent security services of Warsaw Bloc allies like East Germany. For a time, Siad Barre leavened repression with cooption, scattering Soviet largesse to leaders from the various clan and subclan groups. He also exploited nationalist feeling, building up the armed forces for an envisioned showdown with Ethiopia that would recapture the Somali-ethnic lands incorporated into Ethiopia in the 19th century.

The props under his regime other than naked force began to collapse when the Soviets shifted their support to Ethiopia following that country's revolution in 1975. Defeat in the war finally launched against Ethiopia in the late 1970s, just after the Soviet allegiance shift, accelerated dissent. Governments routed in wars they initiate are likely to experience a legitimacy meltdown. Moreover, defeat promotes dissent within the armed forces coincident with the competitive flight from responsibility. The rest of the 1980s was a cycle of ever more ferocious repression carried out by forces reduced progressively to Siad Barre's clan and then subclan which led in turn to more ferocious resistance. Finally, in 1989, with clan militias converging on the capital and the local population in revolt, Siad Barre took the remnants of his armed forces and subclan supporters and launched a fighting retreat to new bases in the south on both sides of the Kenyan border pursued by perhaps the toughest clan militia, the warriors of the Habr Gedir led by former General Mohammed Farah Aideed.

Hardly had Siad Barre been ousted than his opponents fell into a harsh dispute about the division of power, a dispute aggravated by the meddling of external actors including the Egyptians, Saudis, and Italians. Seeing their opponents preoccupied, Siad Barre's forces surged up from the south only to be blocked within 100 miles of Mogadishu by Aideed's improvised, Mad Max mobile units. During an 18-month period stretching from 1990 to 1992, the tide of battle ebbed and flowed over an area southwest of the capital that happened to be the only part of the country with year-round water and hence a sedentary farming population. In wrestling with each other, the opposing forces flattened the local economy, consuming everything down to the very seed for the following year's crop and leaving the resident population destitute.

Drought, added to the crushing weight of the rapacious little armies, opened the door to famine.

Word of the gathering famine reached Western NGOs and U.N. agencies before its victims appeared on CNN. Both tried getting food into the most affected areas as early as 1991. Mogadishu, far and away the country's largest city, the seaside point of departure for the paved road to the stricken area, with its big port and airfield and million-plus population, was the natural gateway for this effort. But from the moment of their arrival at Mogadishu's port or airfield, relief supplies had to run the gauntlet of hungry clan armies and bandits. In addition, during part of 1991, when the tensions between Aideed's subclan based in the city's southern half and his subclan opponents in the northern area burst into furious combat that completed the destruction of the city's core, aid deliverers could not function at all.

By 1992 Boutros Boutros-Ghali was announcing a holocaust in Somalia and CNN was televising it directly from the famine region, since it was proving easier to get film out than food in. Both within and outside the United States a growing number of people and humanitarian organizations called for military intervention to establish a secure environment for relief operations. Colin Powell, the very public chair of the Joint Chiefs of Staff, helped lead the resistance to these calls. U.S. troops, he insisted, should be placed in harms way only when the United States was prepared to deploy overwhelming force to achieve decisive results on behalf of well-defined objectives of high importance to the national interest.

Pentagon hostility to peacekeeping missions stemmed also from the conviction that they erode the combat readiness of U.S. forces. In part, officers argued, erosion would result from failure to use specific skills such as battalion-level fire coordination, large-scale synchronization of battlefield forces, employment of antitank weapons and tank-against-tank maneuvers. Of course many of these skills are difficult to maintain at a high level even in the regular course of peacetime service. Because they intensely consume material and to some degree human resources, combat training exercises are episodic. Moreover, common sense and available evidence, including post-peace operations assessments conducted by the army itself, suggest that peace operations actually enhance some combat skills such as rapid mobilization, force-protection techniques, construction of fighting positions, small unit operations, intelligence collection and analysis, communications, and almost all logistic operations.[10]

Another line of thought, springing from the service culture and probably strongest in the Marines, claims that the restrained use of force native to peace operations and the tendency to avoid demonization of any party, to seek political settlement rather than victory, degrades the warrior spirit essential to winning real wars. Not all students of military affairs are persuaded. Some argue that, on the contrary, "exposure to the complexities of peace operations develops...capability to respond more nimbly to any situation [including] combat."[11]

To avoid intervention, the Bush administration tried various palliatives including airdropping supplies on a large scale. Very little of the food actually got into the bellies of the starving. Finally, in late fall 1992, with the Secretary-General threatening to pull all U.N. agencies out of the country because of the dangerous environment—although by this time Mogadishu itself was quiet, the benefit of a cease-fire between Aideed and his enemies—and announcing that over a million people were on the edge of starvation, President Bush, having already lost his bid for reelection, decided in favor of action. Probably something over 100,000 Somalis had already died of famine-related causes. The Security Council authorized a U.S.-led coalition to use all means necessary to establish a secure environment for the delivery of aid.

It landed on December 2, 1992, preceded by what seemed like half the world's press and, more importantly, by U.S. Ambassador Robert Oakley, who was sent to assure General Aideed and other militia leaders that the U.S.-led force would do nothing to affect the existing balance of power—it would oversee feeding and then, within several months, would leave. However, in carrying out its mandate from the Security Council, it would not tolerate threats and, unlike classical U.N. peacekeeping forces, it had the means and the will to preempt and to punish.

The coalition force built quickly to 38,000 troops with powerful air cover and offshore fire power. General Aideed ostentatiously welcomed the humanitarian mission and assured it of his full cooperation. By February, the famine, which had in fact begun to ease even as U.S. troops were landing, was over. But as civil conflict had precipitated it, conditions for its renewal were still in place. The expeditionary force had insisted on disarmament only in instances where locals evinced hostile intent. Militias remained mobilized and armed, the economy inert, the infrastructure devastated. There were neither courts nor any civil administration in most of the country other than that provided by the subclan leaders in areas they respectively dominated. In a number of populous areas, preeminently Mogadishu itself, no group dominated and a tenuous equilibrium of forces prevailed. The eye of the famine area remained contested territory, its indigenous population the historically weakest among the country's ethnic subgroups. Nevertheless, the new Clinton Administration and particularly the Joint Chiefs were eager to pull out and leave rehabilitation and peace building to the United Nations, the successor Bush had named when asked at the outset of the intervention who would take over once the U.S. had fed and left. Bush had diplomatically failed to mention that the U.S. was not only the U.N.'s most important member, notionally obligated to pay a quarter of its expenditures, it was also the only one able to provide the air and sea lift capability, the air power, the tactical intelligence, the long-term logistical support and the sophisticated communications systems that a successful humanitarian intervention or peace enforcement operation would urgently require.

Boutros-Ghali, an intelligent and sophisticated diplomat of long experience, not surprisingly acted like a man being asked to accept the leash of a famished and pathologically belligerent pit bull. He was faced, in essence, with assuming responsibility not only or simply for rehabilitation, but for helping reestablish the Somali state, a project generally assumed to require, among other things, demobilization and disarmament of the subclan militias. And he was to do that with a mixed force composed of units of varying size, training and equipment primarily from Third World middle powers like India and Pakistan, plus smaller contingents from Italy, Belgium, France, and a host of other states. Air cover would be thin to diaphanous. Units would arrive according to an uncertain timetable and with varying instructions from their capitals. Even when fully deployed, the force would be incomparably weaker than the one it would be replacing, the one that had determinedly resisted the much more ambitious tasks facing its successor. Boutros-Ghali delayed, the U.S. insisted, and finally in May 1993, the handover took place, although many of the promised units had yet to arrive. Instead of 38,000 crack troops armed to the teeth under an umbrella of air power, the U.N. deployed hardly 16,000. Its only advantage was a political accord negotiated the prior March in Addis Ababa by the 16 subclan factions organized into pro- and anti-Aideed coalitions. The accord committed them to disarmament, but contained no details about how that phenomenon would occur. And it envisioned reestablishment of the judiciary and the national police together with a rolling electoral process beginning with district council elections. Negotiated in a moment of tranquility under intense diplomatic pressure from the U.S. and U.N. officials, by the time of the handover it was already beginning to unravel.

Even before assuming responsibility, Boutros-Ghali and his colleagues appeared to have decided that Aideed could not be part of a political solution to the country's enduring agony, that he was too arrogant, too ambitious, determined in their judgment to lead the country virtually as a reward for playing, at least in his mind, the central role in overthrowing Siad Barre. Ambassador Oakley's successor as the chief U.S. diplomat in the area, Bob Gossendi, appeared to agree. That explains, I think, why both Gossendi and Jonathan Howe, the retired U.S. Admiral selected by Boutros-Ghali to head the mission in the role of Special Representative of the Secretary-General, shunned Oakley's practice of going to see Aideed frequently. They doubtless thought that such visits to the General enhanced his prestige.

The handover had hardly occurred when the U.N. mission, with U.S. support, set about appointing judges to serve in Mogadishu. They dismissed Aideed's complaint that the effort, unless carried out with his support, constituted an illegal intervention in the country's internal affairs, an imperialist intrusion into its politics that he would not tolerate. The former national radio station, which he now controlled, began a barrage of vituperative attacks on the U.N. Spurred on by the anti-Aideed coalition, U.N. officials began to wonder whether prudence dictated the station's seizure. Aideed sent word to Howe and Gossendi that communication was breaking down between him and them. They responded by saying they thought communication was not a problem, but in any event, their doors were always open to Aideed should he express the desire to visit.

It was in this incendiary climate that the U.N. decided to initiate disarmament of the militias by a sudden "baseline audit" of the weapons sites where Aideed (in parallel with other militia leaders) had ostensibly stored his heavy weapons at Oakley's request near the beginning of the year. One of these so-called authorized weapons sites was the compound of the National Radio Station. Suddenly informed on the 4th of June that the audits would occur the following morning and that managers of the sites should have the doors open to receive U.N. inspectors, Aideed's chief of security said he would have to consult with his superiors. The U.N. colonels who had brought the message replied that there was nothing to consult about, since the U.N. was authorized under its Security Council mandate, as well as the March accord, to act. If you do this, the chief of security said, "it will mean war." Whatever it means, the colonels replied, we will be there.

The following morning, as Pakistani troops accompanying one of the inspection teams were headed back to base, they were caught in a murderous cross fire and when another unit dispatched to help approached the scene of the initial attack, hitherto concealed automatic weapons opened fire from another site creating a deadly killing zone. At roughly the same time, Pakistani units in other parts of south Mogadishu came under attack. In a statement issued the next day, Aideed declared that all this amounted to a spontaneous response to the killing of a civilian in front of the radio station earlier in the morning. He called for negotiations and a new start. The United Nations and the United States decided instead to hunt down Aided and remove him from the political game. Thus began the battle of Mogadishu and the beginning of the end of the U.N. peace operation in Somalia.

It has often been said that the mission failed because neither the United States nor the United Nations understood Somalia and the Somalis. In fact, Gossendi had spent three years in the country a decade earlier and senior U.N. advisors had a fairly sophisticated grasp of the clan structure and history. If we think of understanding in terms of information, literally of knowledge, it was not the source of failure. There was knowledge; however, knowledge is not a synonym for judgment. Judgments were made in good faith in pursuit of noble goals in an unforgiving environment; but neither the faith nor the goals were enough.

Strategies for Peace Operation with Military Bite

Somalia offers a number of lessons.[12] One is that if the motives of states supporting a peace operation are truly humanitarian, as they were for the most part in Somalia, then the participating governments will rarely have a stomach for casualties and that is particularly true of the Western Democracies. Whereas, one commander of national forces put it to Jonathan Howe, troops are not sent to engage in heroic actions, then the United Nations cannot assign them even moderately dangerous jobs.

We may be one world in economic terms, but in terms of compassion, we still reserve the greater part of it for members of our separate imagined communities, the nation-states. In other words, compassion still tends to thin out when it crosses frontiers. One conclusion we may draw from that is the following: where serious force is required in order to restore or help the people of a war-torn state to build for the first time a participatory political order likely to protect human rights, you can count most on those states motivated by interests as well as ideals. And where you cannot find interested states with the requisite muscle and will, then interventions must seek more modest ends. In the first quarter of the 21st century, the liberal democracies of the West—particularly the U.S., Germany, the U.K., and France—will generally be the only states with the ideological inclination backed by potentially effective means for humanitarian interventions on behalf of human rights and representative government. U.S. willingness to lead remains the critical variable. Economic sanctions will rarely be the answer. Thus, the U.S. will not lead very far as long as its military doctrine shuns the twilight world of peace operations in conflicted societies.[13]

What is actually needed is doctrine that identifies options integrating military operations with all of the other instruments for reestablishing or establishing for the first time[14] a consensual political order. With the withdrawal of Serbian forces from Kosovo, NATO has demonstrated that air power alone can sometimes compel a regime to suspend a campaign marked by crimes against humanity and to acquiesce in the occupation of its territory by humanitarian intervenors and peace enforcers. But it also demonstrates the difficulty of preventing a well-armed, organized, and determined adversary from devastating a target population it controls before succumbing to military pressure. And it highlights the material costs to the target territory the intervenors may have to impose in order to repress the will of the repressor, costs the intervenors may themselves have to bear in order to reconstruct a viable social order.

Air power may be most effective where the humanitarian crisis is linked to an armed conflict between organized military groups. In that setting, outside actors can leverage air power to restrain attacks on the civilian population and to press the parties toward peace by threatening to deploy it on behalf of the first belligerent that demonstrates the willingness to respect the civilian population and to explore a peaceful settlement. This strategy clearly requires considerable subtlety of judgment for its effective application, since if, with the aid of foreign air power, one faction achieves decisive local supremacy, leverage will, of course, be lost. Therefore, other than in cases where one faction has irreproachably liberal credentials, the strategy must intend the creation and maintenance of a military balance between the belligerents, although in the short term its imperative must be to create disincentives to ethnic cleansing and massacre. This strategy should work best where there are only two important indigenous forces and they are relatively organized and coherent in their political aims.

Ideally, as I suggested above, intervenors will be able and willing to deploy economic incentives and disincentives in ways that reinforce the military ones.

But where conflict and humanitarian crises coincide, this can be particularly difficult. Somalia suggests why. In December 1992, at the time U.S.–led coalition troops landed in the country, and thereafter when the baton was passed to the U.N. force directed by the Secretary-General, simmering or actual conflict reigned only in parts of Somalia. Elsewhere local groups had worked out understandings that permitted daily life to occur without constant fear of attack and enabled international relief and rehabilitation organizations to operate more or less normally. Thus they were a pole apart from Mogadishu following the outbreak of hostilities between the U.N. and General Aideed's clan. Once conflict erupted, by which time the famine was largely over, relief flagged and rehabilitation efforts practically collapsed. Yet Mogadishu remained the epicenter of the U.N. civil-military operation and the intergovernmental and NGO relief operations associated with it, however grudgingly.

This international presence, centered in south Mogadishu, virtually constituted the city's economy, such as it was, and the principal beneficiaries of that economy were members of General Aideed's subclan. By day, Habr Gedir workers toiled inside the U.N.'s so-called fort helping to build and maintain its facilities. By night, Habr Gedir militia episodically lobbed shells inside. The U.N. rented cars and houses from Habr Gedir landlords and employed subclan members as guards for the latter. While it also rented facilities in the anti-Aideed northern part of the city, the center of its operations was in the south where it had first established itself in the former U.S. Embassy compound and the adjoining ruins of the National University. Since subclan members undoubtedly financed the subclan militia, in essence the U.N. was subsidizing its opponent.

A U.N. pull out from Mogadishu would have dealt a stunning blow to the subclan economy and to the financial interests of particular Aideed associates. That was true before the conflict began, as well as after. To underscore the advantages both of intergroup conciliation and cooperation with the international community, the U.N. could, in theory, have poured aid into precisely those areas where inter-group accommodation prevailed. Unfortunately, the bulk of the Somali population, including great numbers of displaced persons, were concentrated in precisely those areas where accommodation did not prevail. Moreover, because it possessed the only major port facilities in the populous part of the country and the only airport equipped to handle large planes and because the few all-weather roads radiated from the city, in pure logistical terms, it was by far the most efficient place to mount relief, rehabilitation, and development efforts.

As far as I know, a strategy of encouraging accommodation by limiting international assistance operations to those areas that achieved it was never seriously discussed, at least during the period before the October 1993 fire fight in downtown Mogadishu that killed eighteen Americans and effectively ended U.S. support for the entire mission. If it had surfaced as a strategic option, it would probably have stirred opposition among NGO leaders. Humanitarian relief organizations, like their human rights counterparts, often see themselves as operating outside the discourse of politics and strategy. Their task is to feed the hungry, heal the sick, vaccinate the children. What they ask of the humanitarian intervenors is to secure an environment where they can perform their aid-giving mission. Any move to abandon large areas of the country, for as long as it might take, in the hope of influencing local political leaders would rub across the grain of humanitarian institutional identity. In the workaday world of international relief operations, humanitarian appeals and horrific images tend to impact more strongly on popular sentiment in Western countries than the cool discourse of strategic calculation.

Civil-military tension is native to humanitarian operations where troops trained primarily if not exclusively for high-intensity warfare are deployed. On top of the difference in institutional culture and mission is the difference in the median personality the respective missions attract. Recognizing this fact of life, countries like Canada that have a strong commitment to peace operations train military units for operations in the complex environment of humanitarian relief. Training includes discussion and operational simulations conducted with civilian relief agencies. But where relief and protection efforts confront a hostile environment and particularly where speed is of the essence, the natural if not necessary spearhead of an intervention force will be precisely those units exquisitely refined to the remorseless tasks of battle.

The heroine of a novel by F. Scott Fitzgerald remarks, "The only thing you can learn from life is that there is nothing to learn from life." Contrary to her despondent view, which unconsciously anticipates chic postmodern despair over matters epistemological, the study of humanitarian intervention and peace operations generally since the end of the Cold War offers various lessons to those willing to learn. Among them, I would underscore two. One is the need in the U.N. and in national security establishments for strategic planning units that begin at the first sign of crisis within a country to elaborate disaster scenarios and strategies of response. Officials of relief and development organizations, public and private, should be incorporated into this humanitarian war gaming. The number of countries on any latent-crisis list, each miserable and explosive in its own distinctive way, is large enough to overwhelm the human resources either the U.N. or national governments are likely to deploy for this purpose. At little cost, however, planning cadres could be reinforced by experts from universities and research centers who are generally eager to incorporate their scholarship into the public policy process. They could be identified, vetted, and prepared to join planning teams at short notice. Contemporary communications technology vastly facilitates the use of outside experts.

The other lesson is captured in the response of the protagonist in A.J. Cronin's pre–World War II novel about the English medical profession, *The Citadel*. A young and innocent doctor, when asked at the end of a crucial oral examination what is the most important lesson he has learned in his first years of practice, responds: to doubt. In other words, the only iron rule of strategy and tactics is that there is no iron rule. For instance, the air power that could not prevent the devastation of Kosovo might have at least slowed the momentum of massacre in Rwanda and given time for the Tutsi insurgents to save many of their kin. Economic sanctions proved ineffective to halt Serbian atrocities in Bosnia or restore democracy in Haiti, but helped in the overthrow of Idi Amin and, if they had been threatened (rather than support at least implicitly promised), might have curbed the torture and executions that followed Augusto Pinochet's seizure of power in Chile. That success, in any case, requires a well-judged and sustained strategy adopted in light of available resources and will is self-evident. But which strategy and which associated tactical choices promise success in any given case? In the end, we are left with the irreducible need for wise judgment and the conviction, resting on experience, that it is one of our scarcer commodities.

Notes

1   Jonathan Moore, *The UN and Complex Emergencies* (Geneva: United Nations Research Institute for Social Development, 1996), pp. 49-50.

2   Ibid., p. 50.

3   *Consolidating Peace Through Practical Disarmament Measures and Control of Small Arms*, a Report by Winrich Kuhne from an international workshop sponsored by Stiftung Wissenschaft

und Politik, Ebenhausen, Germany, 1998, see esp. p. 3.

4   Ibid., p. 14.

5   Jonathan Moore, supra note 2, p. 15.

6   Ibid.

7   See comment of senior U.N. official Leonard Kapungu in the Stiftung Wissenschaft report, supra note 3, p. 86.

8   On the recent experience of the international community with respect to elections and internal peacemaking, see Krishna Kumar, ed., *Postconflict Elections, Democratization & International Assistance* (Boulder: Lynne Rienner, 1998).

9   For a detailed treatment, see Tom Farer, *War Clouds on the Horn of Africa* (Washington: The Carnegie Endowment, 2nd. ed., 1979).

10 See Antonia Handler Chayes and George Raach, ed., *Peace Operations: Developing an American Strategy* (Washington: National Defense University Press, 1995), pp. 71-72.

11 Ibid., p. 72.

12 Two useful monographic studies with a policy orientation are Jaret Chopra et al., *Fighting for Hope in Somalia*, No. 6 in the Norwegian Institute of International Affairs studies of Peacekeeping and Multinational Operations (Oslo 1996) and Terrence Lyons and Ahmed I. Samatar, *Somalia: State Collapse, Multilateral Intervention, and Strategies for Political Reconstruction* (Washington, D.C.: The Brookings Institution, 1995).

13 Prominent among general works on the subject of peace operations not cited in the text are the following: William J. Durch, ed., *U.N. Peacekeeping, American Policy, and the Uncivil Wars of the 1990s* (New York: St. Martin's Press, 1996); I. William Zartman, ed., *Elusive Peace: Negotiating an End to Civil Wars* (Washington, D.C.: The Brookings Institution, 1995). Valuable monographic studies (other than those already cited) include Cameron Hume's *Ending Mozambique's War* (Washington, D.C.: United States Institute of Peace Press, 1994), and Ian Johnstone, *Rights and Reconciliation: U.N. Strategies in El Salvador* (Boulder, CO: Lynne Rienner, 1995).

14 The collapse of order and ensuing humanitarian crisis prompting intervention will sometimes stem, as in the Somali case, from a decline in the repressive power of an authoritarian regime. Being inspired by liberal values, humanitarian intervention by its nature precludes recourse to a strategy of restoring order by restoring the ancient regime or establishing a new one, which, like its predecessor, can only hope to maintain order by recourse to means that violate human rights norms.

CHAPTER FIVE

On the Prevention of Genocide: Humanitarian Intervention and the Role of the United Nations

George J. Andreopoulos*

The international community's recent responses to the crises in Kosovo and East Timor have rekindled the debate over the doctrine of humanitarian intervention.[1] The debate has focused on its moral assumptions, its legality, and its use as the ultimate intrusive tool exercised by the international community to deal with gross and systematic human rights violations, often amounting to "acts of genocide/genocide."[2] Both the NATO-led action against the Federal Republic of Yugoslavia, and the Australian-led peacekeeping force in East Timor have raised the legal and political stakes in the discussion surrounding the evolution of sovereignty, and the legitimacy and universality of the principles on which intervention is to be based.[3]

In his comments on the Kosovo conflict in September 1999, the U.N. Secretary-General noted that "it has cast in stark relief the dilemma of so-called 'humanitarian intervention.' On the one hand, is it legitimate for a regional organization to use force without a U.N. mandate? On the other, is it permissible to let gross and systematic violations of human rights, with grave humanitarian consequences, continue unchecked?"[4] Addressing the issue in last year's Millennium Report, and acknowledging the dilemma posed by the contrasting exigencies of sovereignty and humanity, he emphasized the moral legitimacy of U.N.–authorized armed intervention against the perpetrators of crimes against humanity: "Where such crimes occur and peaceful attempts to halt them have been exhausted, the Security Council has a moral duty to act on behalf of the international community."[5]

The Secretary-General's remarks on the need to take the forcible option seriously in cases of gross and systematic violations of human rights, in conjunction with his comments on sovereignty,[6] generated a lot of controversy in the debate that followed his opening remarks at the 1999 annual session of the General Assembly. The responses ranged from concerns about the misuse of the humanitarian option with its adverse impact on the sovereign prerogatives of member states,[7] and the sanctioning of the U.N.'s involvement in endless "humanitarian wars,"[8] to the inconsistencies and inequities of interventionist policies[9] and their potential encouragement of secessionist movements.

Kofi Annan's observations on sovereignty and his related comments on intervention did not really break any new ground conceptually. The controversy generated had less to do with the originality of his utterances, and more to do with their timing and the prominence with which his concern for the "humanitarian challenge" was displayed in his Report to the General Assembly.[10] His views are reflective of a perspective, which can be traced back to the early post–Cold War period, and the reactivation of the collective security machinery of the organization during the Persian Gulf crisis. Shortly after Iraq's defeat, and in the midst of exuberant remarks about a "New World Order" relating to the enhanced normative status of the rule of law and of collective security, then Secretary-General Javier Perez de Cuellar claimed that:

> We are clearly witnessing what is probably an irresistible shift in public attitudes towards the belief that the defense of the oppressed in the name of morality should prevail over frontiers and legal documents.[11]

Although de Cuellar was careful to avoid grand pronouncements on novel legal doctrines (after all, the ambiguous reference to "public attitudes" is telling), the early post–Cold War euphoria, reinforced with U.N. Security Council Resolution 688[12] concerning the Iraqi civilian population, led several analysts to references of a "new humanitarian order."[13]

One of the key characteristics of this "new humanitarian order" was the emphasis on prevention. This was clearly indicated during the first meeting held by the Security Council at the level of Heads of State and Government in January 1992. In its concluding statement, the leaders asked the Secretary-General to prepare an analysis and recommendations on ways of strengthening and making more efficient within the framework and provisions of the Charter the capacity of the United Nations for preventive diplomacy, for peacemaking and for peacekeeping.[14] The resulting document, An Agenda for Peace, devoted substantial attention both to preventive diplomacy, and to a new concept, postconflict peace building with clearly preventive features. The Agenda defined preventive diplomacy as an "action to prevent disputes from arising between parties, to prevent existing disputes from escalating into conflicts and to limit the spread of the latter when they occur."[15] Postconflict peace building was defined as an "action to identify and support structures which will tend to strengthen and solidify peace in order to avoid a relapse into conflict."[16] Thus, the international community's responsive capacities to challenges to peace and security were to be perceived as part of continuum, ranging from preventive measures, to postconflict peace building. The former was geared toward the resolution of disputes before crossing the threshold into violence, while the latter was the ultimate form of successful prevention. In between, lay peacemaking and peacekeeping, whose task was to ensure that the measures adopted under peace building would lead to nonrecurrence rather than constitute a temporary interlude to a renewed cycle of violence.

As with sovereignty, a concern with prevention has been manifested throughout the nineties, with its fortunes fluctuating in accordance with the fate of different U.N.–authorized and (in certain instances) led multidimensional, or multifunctional peacekeeping operations.[17] However, the recent attention devoted to prevention at both the international and regional levels,[18] and the proliferation of think-tank studies and nongovernmental organizations (NGO)–related activities, may signal the international community's willingness to accord prevention more than the "flavor of the month" status. What is the reason for the renewed interest in the "culture of prevention?"[19] Part of the reason has to do with the aforementioned operations which, ranging from partially successful to outright disastrous, have—among other things—highlighted the inherent limitations in the range of responsive action which traditional agents of humanitarian intervention are prepared to undertake, even in the face of severe abuses of human rights amounting to genocide. An important facet of this problem is the uneasy cohabitation of humanitarian work and enforcement action. Another critical issue relates to the questionable assumptions underlying the relief-rehabilitation-development continuum deemed essential to the success of peace building. The latter issue is addressed in another chapter of this volume.[20]

If these observations are tolerably accurate, they point to another explanation. Given the complexities of humanitarian action in the context of massive humanitarian emergencies, and the prolonged and costly engagement that peace building necessitates, preventive action can save lives, energy, and money. Yet, the more one talks about prevention, the more the intangibility of its benefits become apparent. In his 1999 Annual Report, Kofi Annan refers to the fact that prevention's benefits "lie in the distant future," while its costs "have to be paid in the present"; and to the fact that the benefits relate to "wars and disasters that do not happen."[21] Thus, the prevention paradox severely curtails any serious consideration of preventive strategies. Does this mean that this renewed interest is there simply because we have otherwise reached a dead end, that it is "more rhetorical than substantive?"

The simple and not very satisfactory answer here is that nobody knows. Definitely, if the past is to be of guidance, the signs are not very encouraging. However, the controversies surrounding the modalities of the international community's response to humanitarian emergencies,[22] offer a useful entry point for a reassessment of the most intrusive tool of interventionary diplomacy, and its potential role in the prevention of the most heinous of international crimes, the crime of genocide.

Political vs. Humanitarian Considerations

One of the key characteristics of the post–Cold War era has been the U.N. Security Council's increasing willingness to link humanitarian crises to threats to international peace and security. During the Cold War era, such linkages were very rare and affected near-universally considered pariah regimes, i.e., Southern Rhodesia (Zimbabwe) and South Africa.[23] On the one hand, the Security Council's foray into the arena of humanitarian crises has contributed to a more human rights-sensitive agenda; on the other hand, it has brought into sharper focus the challenging task of the conceptualization and operationalization of the intersections between the humanitarian and the peace maintenance goals of the U.N. system.

Several views have been put forward to explain the nature of the relationship between humanitarian action and peace maintenance.[24] One view holds that humanitarian action cannot be separated from peace operations, since it constitutes part and parcel of the "political rubric" of the United Nations. This view is based on the critical role of humanitarian work in any peace operation; thus, any attempt to separate the two would be tantamount to an artificial compartmentalization of operations that are part of the same continuum. Many supporters of the relief-to-development continuum share this integration approach.[25]

The second view holds that, although humanitarian activities cannot be separated from peace maintenance operations, they should be insulated so as not to be subjected to partisan agendas, which would undermine their credibility, and eventually their effectiveness.[25] Proponents of this view point to the importance of the key principles of "humanity, neutrality and impartiality" in the delivery of humanitarian assistance, as reaffirmed in the relevant U.N. General Assembly Resolution, and in the *Agenda for Peace*.[26] Political measures, especially when they result in coercive action (whether forcible or nonforcible),[27] compromise the integrity of the humanitarian space, and the security of the humanitarian relief providers. Supporters of the insulation approach point to the schizophrenic behavior of the United Nations in situations like the crisis in the Former Yugoslavia to justify their quest for a self-contained humanitarian track of U.N. action.

The final view holds that humanitarian activities must be kept separate and distinct from peace operations, which whether undertaken multilaterally, or (even worse) unilaterally, tend to subject humanitarian concerns to the primacy of political and military considerations. Several NGOs adhere to this view, with the International Committee of the Red Cross (ICRC) constituting probably the best example of an organization whose strict adherence to the "holy trinity" of humanitarian assistance principles, renders it incapable of tolerating any type of association even with consensual (Chapter VI of the U.N. Charter) operations.[28] Proponents of this view stress the traditional emphasis of humanitarian work on *service,* as opposed to *advocacy,* which is the hallmark of human rights work.[29]

The tensions between political and humanitarian objectives are not new. After all, Medecins Sans Frontieres (MSF), the organization that has challenged more consistently and effectively the sanctity of the "holy trinity," was created in 1971 by a group of doctors clearly disillusioned with the political conditions attached to traditional aid operations. To the ICRC's belief that humanitarian intervention is a contradiction in terms, MSF, which also opposes the use of the term, counterposes the lack of clear political objectives in U.N.–led interventions; lack that exacerbates the difficulties inherent in these operations.[30] Yet, the recent prominence of these tensions is attributable to certain key features of the types of intrastate conflicts the international community has been grappling with since the end of the Cold War.

For the purposes of this essay, two of these features need to be stressed.[31] The first relates to the increasing perception among combatants that the delivery of humanitarian assistance constitutes a nonneutral act. This perception is sustained by the nature of these conflicts where often civilian targeting constitutes one of the expressed aims of the belligerents rather than "collateral damage." As the Secretary-General has noted, "...combatants perceive the provision of humanitarian assistance and protection to vulnerable populations as being not a neutral but rather a politically motivated act. In intrastate conflicts...even the accommodation of the most basic needs of the populations may be perceived as direct interference with the war effort."[33]

Moreover, it is rendered more acute as a result of the decentralized conduct of war, where decisions pertaining to access have to be continuously screened through successive layers of—at times—loose command structures, and as a consequence of the dispersion of "enemy" enclaves throughout the contested territory. If, for example, a local commander of forces belonging to ethnic group A is laying siege to an enclave populated by ethnic group B, his sole war objective is the fall of the enclave. The delivery of even minimal amounts of nonlethal aid to the besieged civilians would be perceived by that commander as an attempt to enhance his opponent's ability to sustain their war effort. Thus, it is highly unlikely that the commander in question will be persuaded by arguments relating to the international community's "balanced" delivery of humanitarian assistance to all enclaves and communities throughout the contested territory. For him, the local picture is the only one that matters by virtue of constituting the sole area of his operational responsibility.

The second flows from the first. In the eyes of the parties to the conflict, the increasing politicization of humanitarian relief operations necessitates their disruption, or attempts to divert them from their original mission to contribute to the combatants' own war aims. This sooner or later generates the need for the forcible protection of humanitarian missions. Thus, it is no accident that in two major cases, in the Former Yugoslavia and Somalia, the Security Council was prepared to authorize the use of force to secure the delivery of humanitarian assistance. In the Yugoslav case, the Security Council, acting under Chapter VII, called upon states in resolution 770 to take "all measures necessary to facilitate...the delivery...of humanitarian assistance" and demanded that all parties concerned "take the necessary measures to ensure the safety of United Nations and other personnel engaged in the delivery of humanitarian assistance."[34]

Likewise, in the Somalia case, it was the very "extortion, blackmail and robbery to which the international relief effort was subjected and the repeated attacks on the personnel and equipment of the United Nations" that led to the adoption of Security Council Resolution 794 authorizing the use of "all necessary means to establish as soon as possible a secure environment for humanitarian relief operations in Somalia."[35] In this case, the overall picture became more complicated as a result of the U.N.'s (UNOSOM I)[36] earlier "collaborative relationships on an ad hoc basis with some Somali partners," to ensure "the effective delivery and distribution of humanitarian assistance."[37] This arrangement had created two major security problems for UNOSOM I: first, threats by the very same armed guards ("the technicals") regarding conditions of work and their fees; and second, threats by other Somali factions excluded from these collaborative arrangements, over the increasingly "partisan posture" of UNOSOM I.

In a nutshell, one of the key contentious issues in the political/humanitarian interface relates to the nature of humanitarian assistance. In the humanitarian realm, the strategic value of aid is supposed to be minimal to nonexistent; otherwise, there can be no guarantee as to its secure delivery. On the political realm, the situation on the ground necessitates policies that will take into consideration the rising strategic value of aid. The only way that this tension can be resolved is through a commitment to a comprehensive disarmament program covering all parties to the conflict; a program prepared to use "all necessary means" to that effect.

No case is more instructive than Somalia. In fact, one of the reasons why Somalia has cast such a long shadow on U.N. peace maintenance operations and has generated a cottage industry on the "lessons" of the "new interventionism" is precisely because this dilemma was brought into sharp focus at the time that Operation Restore Hope was launched.[38]

One of the common misperceptions about the Somali case is the difficulty of explaining how the U.N. operation turned into a partisan operation (especially the UNOSOM II attempt to capture Aideed), when it had been launched with the best of humanitarian intentions. There is no doubt that many mistakes characterized specific policies adopted during the UNITAF, as well as during the UNOSOM II phase, which contributed to the unfortunate turn of events in the summer and early fall of 1993; developments which destroyed whatever prospects were left for the successful completion of the mission. However, one of the major problems that had haunted the operation from its inception was the *deliberate ambiguity on issues relating to the agency and extent of the disarmament program.*

The disarmament of combatants is critical to the long-term prospects of any peace maintenance operation. It is the first phase of a process that should include the disarmament, demobilization and (eventual) reintegration (DDR) of ex-combatants into a society committed to postconflict recovery and the prevention of a renewed cycle of violence. This process, as one analyst has aptly noted, "is not just a technical military issue: it has political, security, humanitarian and development dimensions as well."[39] Any peace maintenance activities that avoid/downplay the importance of disarmament, and unfold in a context insensitive to its indispensability as a key component of a holistic process (with its aforementioned interconnected dimensions), are doomed to failure. Operation Restore Hope is a telling example of a short-term and piecemeal responsive action.

Policymakers were keenly aware of the fact that they were not sending troops to Somalia to set up soup kitchens, but to carry out an operation that could cost lives. By the end of the summer of 1992, it was a well-established fact that security was a major issue for the orderly functioning of UNOSOM I, and a major impediment to the implementation of its mandate. The Pakistani soldiers who were part of the UNOSOM I deployment had to hire "technicals" as security guards for the Mogadishu airport. Mohamed Sahnoun, the experienced Algerian diplomat who headed UNOSOM I, notably remarked, while addressing a donors' conference in Geneva in October 1992, that "One important area where many respectable elders have repeatedly asked for assistance is the disarmament of the population and the demobilization of irregular forces. *The Somali Nation has become hostage to gunmen.*"[40] Likewise, the Secretary-General, in his letter to the Security Council arguing for a Chapter VII operation to deal with the situation in Somalia, urged that the disarmament of all irregular forces should constitute one of the main purposes of the mission.[41] Finally, President Bush, in announcing his decision to send the troops to Somalia, said the following: "Our mission is humanitarian, *but we will not tolerate armed gangs ripping off their own people, condemning them to death by starvation...the outlaw elements in Somalia must understand this is serious business.*"[42]

These observations were indicative of the realization that access to food and other nonlethal aid was used as an instrument of war in both inter and intraclan conflict; and that any long-term solution would have to curtail the combatants' ability to engage in the type of abusive conduct that sustained their war effort. The first step in that direction would have been a comprehensive disarmament program. But who would carry out such a disarmament program? A closer look at Security Council Rresolution 794 demonstrates that the United States, contrary to the repeated calls of the Secretary-General for disarmament to achieve national reconciliation, was reluctant to commit its troops to this task. In fact, while paragraph 7 of the enabling resolution acknowledged the Secretary-General's recommendation, key paragraph 10, which authorized under Chapter VII the use of "all necessary means to establish a secure environment for humanitarian relief operations," expressly referred to paragraph 8 and the U.S. offer.[42] Thus, as one analyst has observed, "the relevant issue was whether the U.S. offer included disarming of the Somali factions to bring about national reconciliation."[43]

As the record has shown, the U.S. Administration was not prepared to undertake such a commitment, although fully cognizant of the fact that no long-term solutions to the Somali crisis could materialize in an environment that tolerated fully armed hostile factions. Once deployed, UNITAF did engage in sporadic disarmament actions, but such efforts did not affect the power of the warlords, who could count on minimal challenges by the interventionary force. In their obsessive preoccupation with an "exit strategy" (with the focus on exit rather than on strategy), U.S. policymakers simply postponed the need to address problems that logically followed from the decision to intervene.[44] The postponement would put UNOSOM II— UNITAF's successor—at a distinct disadvantage. UNOSOM II's mandate included the task of assisting in "the re-establishment of national and regional institutions and civil administration in the entire country"[45]; a task which UNOSOM II had to undertake with less fire-power, a more uncertain command and control structure,[46] and in the midst of fully armed factions with a critical stake in the outcome. To the argument that part of the problem was "mission creep,"[47] a closer look at Resolution 794 undermines the view of a qualitative leap from Resolution 794 to 814.[48] On the contrary, what really distinguished the two resolutions was that many of the unfinished tasks under 794 would have to be addressed under 814 by a new force with a more specific mandate and much less clout. Operation Restore Hope never really had a chance given the clear reluctance of key actors to implement a policy consistent with their initial acknowledgment of the political dimensions of the humanitarian crisis.[49]

This institutional reluctance coupled with a mission creep–focused interpretation of the Somali debacle has shaped the subsequent debate at the highest echelons of the United Nations. To be sure, there have been several verbal acknowledgments to the contrary. For example, in its presidential statement of July 8, 1999, the Security Council recognized that

> *disarmament, demobilization and reintegration cannot be seen in isolation but rather, as a continuous process which is rooted in and feeds into a broader search for peace, stability and development...Taking into account that the process is closely linked to economic and social issues, the question must be addressed comprehensively so as to facilitate a smooth transition from peacekeeping to peace-building.*[50]

This realization in conjunction with the holistic approach advocated in the Agenda for Peace document would support the argument that peace-building activities, the ultimate form of preventive action, should constitute a key component of the Security Council's competencies in the area of peace maintenance. In fact, there is a verbal acknowledgment to that effect in the Secretary-General's first Report on the Protection of Civilians in Armed Conflict[51]:

> *It is now generally recognized that the maintenance of international peace and security requires action by the Security Council at all stages of a conflict or potential conflict. Whenever possible, action must be taken to address the root causes of the conflict and to prevent disputes from escalating into violence...In the aftermath of war, all efforts must be directed at peace keeping and peace-building, including reconciliation amongst groups pulled apart by the conflict....*[52]

When, however, the report turns to critical issues affecting post-conflict civilian welfare, and in particular to the issue of disarmament and demobilization, the discussion of any long-term perspective is conspicuously absent. The report states "The disarming and demobilizing of combatants must be a top priority in any United Nations peacekeeping/peace-building operation"[53]. Yet, except for a reference to the importance of the demobilization and reintegration of child soldiers, the report says nothing on how this would be achieved, let alone on what the Security Council's role should be in the process. The low key language used in the Protection of Civilians Report is striking, especially when contrasted to the bolder language used on issues of humanitarian access and intervention.[54] A similar approach is evident in the Secretary-General's follow-up report on the same subject.[55] While the second report focuses on the humanitarian aspects of protection, there is a verbal acknowledgment of the importance of "ending a conflict and building sustainable peace" as the most effective means of achieving civilian protection.[57] Once again, except for a reference to a general statement issued by the President of the Security Council,[58] the report is noticeably silent on the specific measures in need of adoption, as well as on the modalities of their implementation.

Preventing Genocide: What Are the Options?

Given some of the problems associated with peace maintenance operations, especially those deployed under circumstance of massive civil strife, and state actors' reluctance for long-term commitments, are there any grounds for expecting better responses in genocidal, let alone genocide-prone situations?

On the normative level, it is not difficult to answer this question in the affirmative. After all, the Genocide Convention's importance lies well beyond the fact that it constitutes the very first U.N.–sponsored human rights treaty. Coming on the immediate aftermath of World War II, the Genocide Convention was the first legal instrument to officially disentangle the most heinous of crimes against humanity from the war nexus requirement.[59] To the Nuremberg Charter's subordination of crimes against humanity to crimes against the peace, or to the primacy it conferred upon sovereignty concerns over human rights concerns, the Genocide Convention counterposed in its very first article genocide's international crime status "whether committed in time of peace or in time of war." Moreover, it was the first U.N. legal instrument to indicate that individuals can attract international criminal responsibility irrespective of whether they act on behalf of a state or not.[60] Yet when it came to the implementation provisions, especially those relating to punishment, the Convention reflected the continuing grounding of human rights norms by the exigencies of sovereignty. State parties to the Convention were expected to enact the "necessary legislation to give effect" to its provisions, "and, in particular, to provide effective penalties for persons guilty of genocide."[61] Barring the creation of an international penal tribunal, the Convention would be unenforceable, since the only adjudicative option would be the courts of the perpetrator state (except, of course, in cases in which the genocidal regime was overthrown, and the successor regime embarked on judicial proceedings against key members of the predecessor regime).[62]

There was, however, another option with potentially far-reaching implications. Article VIII provided state parties with the opportunity to "call upon the competent organs of the United Nations to take such action under the Charter of the United Nations as they consider appropriate for the prevention and suppression of acts of genocide." Since one of the competent organs is the Security Council, which can authorize the use of force, Article VIII could be used as the legal basis for enforcement measures under Chapter VII. In addition, it could be used, as the legal basis for the Security Council's creation of subsidiary organs (Article 29 of the U.N. Charter) deemed necessary "for the performance of its functions." Thus, ever since January 12, 1951,[63] the international community had at its disposal several tools to deal with genocide—tools that transcended the limited measures provided for in Article VI. These tools ranged from the creation of subsidiary organs (including the creation of ad hoc international criminal tribunals as eventually happened with the International Criminal Tribunal for the former Yugoslavia (ICTY) in 1993, and with the International Criminal Tribunal for Rwanda (ICTR) in 1994) to the ultimate tool (U.N.-authorized use of force) for the prevention and suppression of genocide. To be sure, the provision in question was of a nonmandatory nature; thus states could refrain from invoking it without breaching their obligations under the Genocide Convention. Nevertheless, the Genocide Convention, at a time when the human rights discourse was still inchoate, did authorize the ultimate U.N. sanction against perpetrators of genocide.

Why when the international community had so much potentially at its disposal, did it end up doing so little, so late? The question has been revisited with a vengeance ever since the Rwanda tragedy. Despite the fact that it is now commonplace to speak of the Rwanda tragedy as a case of "failure" on the part of the international community, the ease with which the term failure is applied must give us some pause. After all, failure means inability to achieve an outcome consistent with the professed policy objectives. Before this conclusion is confidently reached, some uncomfortable questions need to be asked; in particular, what were the international community's objectives in Rwanda? Were the policies pursued consistent with the said objectives? If not, what accounts for the discrepancy?

It is beyond the scope of this essay to address all these critical questions. In addition, a more authoritative assessment of the information available to policymakers prior to the genocide will have to await the release of official records.[64] However, for the purposes of genocide prevention, several issues can be highlighted. First, it was clear from the time of the Arusha Peace Agreement between the Government of Rwanda and the Rwandan Patriotic Front (RPF), that the parties were clearly expecting a more robust U.N. presence on the ground than the one eventually approved by Security Council Resolution 872. While in a joint request to the Security Council the two parties had asked for a force which "would assist in searches for weapons caches, neutralization of armed bands...disarmament of civilians and the cessation of hostilities,"[65] Resolution 872 made no reference to these provisions.[66] Instead, the peacekeeping force was empowered "to *investigate*, at the request of the parties, or on its own initiative, instances of alleged non-compliance with the provisions of the Arusha Peace Agreement."[67] Moreover, the parties' request for the provision of security to the civilian population was drastically changed to a commitment "to *investigate* and *report* on incidents regarding the activities of the gendarmerie and police."[68] Such a conscious effort to moderate mission goals and downplay expectations can only be understood by reference to the "shadow" of Somalia.[69] In its quest for a policy on disarmament and demobilization, the United Nations had to deal with the ghosts of the past (an eerie reminder of the earlier dispute on the nature and extent of the disarmament program) and the debacle of the present (Resolution 872 was adopted two days after the battle in Mogadishu).[70]

Second, although much has been made of the famous "genocide fax"[71] sent by the United Nations Assistance Mission in Rwanda (UNAMIR) Commander Major General Dallaire to Kofi Annan's military advisor concerning the Interahamwe's plans for possible extermination of Tutsi in Kigali, this was not an isolated early warning.[72] Between November 1993 and April 1994, there were several instances in which both UNAMIR and foreign intelligence sources came across information indicating that something more than a renewed cycle of ethnic strife was at stake. In particular,

1. On November 23, 1993, General Dallaire requested, in a draft set of Rules of Engagement (ROE) for UNAMIR, permission to use force in response to the commission of crimes against humanity and related offenses, "There may also be ethnically or politically motivated criminal acts...which will morally and legally require UNAMIR to use all available means to halt them." Dallaire never received a formal response to his request from the U.N. headquarters.[73]

2. In a December 3, 1993, letter by senior officers of the Rwandan Armed Forces to General Dallaire, they informed him that the recent killings of civilians were part of a series of massacres which "are being prepared and are supposed to spread throughout the country, beginning with the regions that have a great concentration of Tutsi....This strategy aims to convince public opinion that these are ethnic troubles...."[74]
3. In a February 25, 1994, letter to the Belgian Ambassador at the U.N., the Belgian Ministry of Foreign Affairs urged the strengthening of UNAMIR's mandate. In the letter, the Ministry warned that in case of a deteriorating situation *"public opinion would never tolerate having Belgian peacekeepers remain passive witnesses to genocide and having the U.N. do nothing."*[75]
4. Last, but not least, at a meeting held during the third week of March, the officer in charge of the Rwandese Army's intelligence is quoted as saying to a group that included Belgian military advisers that "if Arusha were implemented, they were ready to liquidate the Tutsi."[76]

Finally, Dallaire repeatedly requested permission from the U.N. headquarters to raid the weapons caches in Kigali. It is important to note that in his fax to Baril, Dallaire indicated that the deterrent arms recovery operation was well within UNAMIR's mandate.[77] It was only after the response from the headquarters notifying him that it was not within the force's mandate that Dallaire repeatedly sought permission to engage in such action.[78]

Could genocide have been prevented in Rwanda? Such a question addresses two separate issues. First, could the timely projection of *a credible deterrent posture* via the proposed arms recovery operation have acted as a catalyst against the extermination plans? Second, once the genocidal killing began, could the timely deployment of an intervening force under Chapter VII have stopped the genocide?[79]

Taking into consideration the inherent limitations of counterfactual argumentation, there were indeed some missed opportunities. Concerning the first question, one has to take seriously Dallaire's repeated requests for the confiscation of weapons. Given his knowledge of the situation on the ground and the intelligence on the activities of both military and paramilitary groups, a determined response on the part of the peacekeeping force would have signaled UNAMIR's determination not to simply stand by.

Having said that, however, what if the Rwandan Government Forces (RGF) were to respond by the use of force, thus opting for escalation? Would they have called UNAMIR's bluff? We will never know. In the context of the "shadow" of Somalia, a forcible response on the part of the RGF may have led to another debacle. Nevertheless, a credible argument can be made that it was UNAMIR's responsibility to exhaust all means at its disposal consistent with its limited mandate. Could UNAMIR have engaged in such an operation without violating the letter of Resolution 872? UNAMIR's responsibility to "contribute to the security of the city of Kigali...within a weapons-secure area established by the parties in and around the city," a responsibility not conditioned by any request to that effect by the parties concerned, did enable it to undertake such an operation. If UNAMIR's operation had led to any violations, these would have been violations relating to the *spirit*, rather than to the *letter* of Resolution 872; namely, it would have gone against the wishes of the contributing countries concerning potentially "controversial" actions on the ground.

The U.N. report on the genocide in Rwanda is rather equivocal on this point. The report notes the divergence of views between Dallaire and the Secretariat, and concludes that the key is the interpretation of the mandate's reference to "weapons secure area established by the parties." Given the divergence, the report is not critical of the Secretariat on this issue. While the report lays the blame on the follow-up to the cable, and in particular on the fact that the issue was not raised with the Security Council "*as a fundamental weakness in the mandate of the mission*," it is instructive that it acknowledges the deterrent potential of the arms recovery operation.[80] This acknowledgment, in conjunction with the aforementioned observations, render the report's conclusion less than satisfactory. The way to make the Security Council face up to its responsibilities relating to the "weaknesses" inherent in UNAMIR's mandate would have been for the Secretariat to authorize the arms recovery operation, and then let the Security Council deal with its potential consequences. Such a course of action would have delivered a potentially deterrent message, and would have put pressure on the Council to clarify the nature and extent of UNAMIR's role in Rwanda. While this course of action might not have prevented what followed, it would have at least confronted Council members with the limitations inherent in the calculated ambiguity that appeared to mark their actions. The infamous "acts of genocide" provision in Resolution 925 should be viewed as the most "surreal" manifestation of this trend, *since it raised the question of the number of acts of genocide necessary for the determination of genocide;*[80] the sarcastic overtones of such a question are—if anything—a fitting commentary on the international community's inaction during the crisis.

The issue of the restrictive vs. expansive interpretation of UNAMIR's mandate has another morally questionable dimension. While, as noted previously, the Secretariat was obsessed with the need to contain Dallaire's "discretionary interpretations" of the mandate, no such concern was expressed in the case of the national operations to evacuate expatriates mounted—during the early days of the crisis—by the United States, Belgium, France, and Italy. In fact, in a cable to Dallaire, Kofi Annan requested his cooperation with Belgian and French commanders in these operations and added: "You should make every effort not to compromise your impartiality or to act beyond your mandate *but may exercise your discretion to do should this be essential for the evacuation of foreign nationals.*"[81] Thus, the Secretariat could exhibit considerable interpretive elasticity when it came to saving foreign nationals, but not when it came to an arms recovery operation with potentially considerable deterrent implications within the Rwandan context. There is little doubt that contextual factors, rather than strict textual analysis, provide the key to the Secretariat's sudden flexibility.[82]

The other question, which is directly related to the issue of humanitarian intervention, is more difficult to answer. The debate focuses less on the size of the intervening force and on the timing of its deployment, and more on the phased nature of combat operations.[83] At a January 1997 conference, General Dallaire outlined the operational plan he would have undertaken had the appropriate level of military support been provided during the critical weeks of April 1994.[84] He argued that the deployment under Chapter VII of a 5,000-strong force with the mandate to: (1) stop the genocide; (2) conduct a peace enforcement mission; (3) assist in the return of refugees and displaced persons; (4) ensure the successful delivery of humanitarian aid; and (5) assist in a cessation of hostilities, could have brought the situation under control. Such an operation could have been conducted by a multinational force in six phases, taking into consideration the capabilities of the combatants, and the most likely scenarios of opposition activity.[85] Most of the criticism leveled at Dallaire's plan centered on its sequential nature. The concern related first to the inability of the intervening force to distinguish—in such a situation—between civil war violence and genocidal violence[86]; second, to the uncertainty concerning the RPF's response, especially if they were winning the war; and third, to the perception of partisanship on behalf of the RPF that such a phased deployment would create among RGF supporters. Given these concerns, critics counterposed a plan that, although a Chapter VII operation with a force of the same size would have led to the simultaneous not sequential deployment of the said force. The force's mandate would have included: (1) its interposition between the combatants, and (2) the imposition of the same standards of behavior on all involved in the conflict, in particular, the determined suppression of all acts of violence irrespective of the source and context.[87]

Two comments are of relevance here. The critics' plan is clearly more sensitive to the challenges that have confronted intervening forces in situations of massive civil strife manifesting the widespread and systematic commission of inhumane acts. Most importantly, it acknowledges the perennial challenge of neutrality. As some critics pointed out, if the force was directed to stop only the genocide "could run into the unenviable position of having its efforts viewed by the government forces as assisting the rebels, and by the rebel forces as enabling the government to devote more troops to the civil war."[88] To be sure, there is no interventionist posture that can render those undertaking it immune from accusations of partisanship. However, *a posture of "zero tolerance" towards violent acts irrespective of provenance, coupled with robust rules of engagement offer the best chance of minimal challenges.*

Second, it is very difficult for an intervening force thrust in the middle of an ongoing conflict to be able to distinguish different categories of crimes so as to selectively suppress them. Suppose that members of this force were to enter a village and witness several individuals who appear to be civilians killing other civilians. What crimes are being committed here? War crimes (if the perpetrator civilians are actually members of a paramilitary group), crimes against humanity, or genocide? What if some of them are engaged in self-defense? Given the absurdity of selective suppression, *only a policy of general and indiscriminate suppression can create the appropriate environment for the subsequent punishment of all those responsible for the commission of genocidal acts.*

This debate, irrespective of the particularities of mandates and rules of engagement, points to one of the options for the prevention of genocide. Having acknowledged the need for a force, how does the international community go about creating it? The issue has been on the international agenda ever since the adoption of the Charter and the ill-fated article 43, whose provisions have never materialized. It was reactivated on the aftermath of the Gulf War, when the Secretary-General urged member states to bring into being the special agreements foreseen in article 43, a measure "essential to the credibility of the United Nations as a guarantor of international security."[90] This suggestion, as well as his proposal on peace enforcement units,[91] have to this day never seriously been considered.

The problem is compounded by the fact that the U.N. Standby Arrangements System (UNSAS) will be of limited use, even when fully functional (which is not yet the case). The system grew out of the need to meet the demands for rapid deployment, and in 1994 the Standby Arrangement Management Unit was created with the task of completing its implementation.[92] The system is "based upon conditional commitments by Member States to contribute specified resources with agreed response times for United Nations peacekeeping operations."[93] Although this is an attempt to create a system of dependable and timely contributions to U.N. peacekeeping, with expectations of its evolution into a semipermanent mechanism for force recruitment, so far the system has failed to meet the expectations that its launching had generated. To be sure, there have been some encouraging recent developments, in particular the creation of the High Readiness Brigade (HRB). While the HRB is not a U.N. formation, it was established by small and medium-sized states participating in the system, in response to the Secretary-General's call for a rapid deployment force. The main purpose of the HRB is to train units to the same standards (including the compatibility of command and control procedures) for rapid deployment in Chapter VI operations.[94]

Despite this and related improvements, there are certain structural problems that will render, even a properly functioning UNSAS, of little or no impact on the prevention of genocide: (1) the system is geared toward Chapter VI rather than Chapter VII operations; and (2) despite the growing number of member states willing to sign the Memorandum of Understanding (MOU) on Standby Arrangements with the United Nations,[95] Section III of the Memorandum entitled *Condition of Provision* clearly states that "The final decision whether to actually deploy the resources...remains ...a(n)...national decision."[96] Let us not forget that, at the time of the Rwanda genocide, none of the 19 standby arrangements already in existence could be activated in response to the unfolding tragedy.[97] The Rwanda debacle stands as a disturbing reminder of the limits of reforms that, although well intentioned, are unresponsive to organizational capabilities.

Attempts to break this deadlock have led to suggestions for the creation of a special force under U.N. auspices. In this vein, proposals have included the creation of a modest rapid reaction capability, and the formation of a U.N. volunteer military force. From the various proposals on rapid reaction, one of the most comprehensive is the one prepared by the Canadian Government on the fiftieth anniversary of the organization.[98] Despite its wealth of recommendations and its overall grounding by the realities of the United Nations system, the proposed measures are primarily intended to refine and strengthen the UNSAS. There is no doubt that some suggestions, like the Vanguard group, have—if implemented—the potential of providing the United Nations with a more coherent, multi-functional presence in a preventive or conflict management role during the early stages of a crisis. However, the critical question is what happens next. The report acknowledges that once this token physical presence on the ground has fulfilled its mandate, it may be necessary to replace it with "a subsequent 'follow-on' force along more traditionally-organized lines."[99]

The U.N. Volunteer Force proposal is a variation of Boutros-Ghali's idea on peace-enforcement units articulated in the *Agenda for Peace* document.[100] The Volunteer Force is envisaged as a measure to fill an important gap in the Security Council's arsenal, by enabling it "to back up preventive diplomacy with a measure of immediate peace enforcement."[101] Such a force (minimum strength: 5,000) would receive training in both peacekeeping and peace enforcement tasks. Acting under the exclusive authority of the Security Council, it would be deployed quickly at an early stage of a crisis to bring the situation under control before another operation could take over.

These proposals share the need to create a mechanism for a timely and decisive projection of international concern in a potentially critical situation. The underlying assumptions here are: first, that such a projection would act as a credible deterrent to further escalation, and second that, if challenged, the initial operation would buy valuable time for the preparation and launching of a commensurate to the challenge response. These are questionable assumptions. Any credible deterrent posture must answer the inevitable question of what follows in case of deterrence failure: have those forces challenging the deployment managed to call the international community's bluff, or have they done it at the risk of unleashing an overwhelming response? If the former, the whole plan would amount to an exercise in futility. If the latter, then we would go back to square one: Are states prepared to take seriously their obligations under the Genocide Convention? This, however, is only part of the problem. Let us suppose that a 10,000-

strong force is created. From all the recent humanitarian crises, such a force could have been instrumental in Rwanda, but it would have been clearly inadequate for both Somalia and Bosnia. Moreover, given that these crises came in rapid succession and overlapped considerably, how could such a force intervene in Somalia if it were already tied down in Bosnia? How useful would it be in Rwanda if it were already engaged in Somalia? Under these circumstances, only the timely deployment of a follow-on force could enable the volunteer force to extricate itself from one crisis and move onto the next. Once again, we are back to square one.

Volunteer force proponents would argue that it is better to try to do something rather than nothing, and that the dismal response record necessitates some type of action, which, in certain circumstances, could be effective. Although there is some merit to this view, there is an element of naïve incrementalism that undergirds it. If some modest operations centered on a U.N. force were to prove successful, such a structure might constitute the first step toward more supranational initiatives in the future. Thus, slowly but steadily, the international community would build upon this initiative, eventually leading to a comprehensive framework for the U.N., as opposed to U.N.–authorized actions. Yet, there is another side to this coin. States might welcome these initiatives, not because they would favor this transition, but for precisely the opposite reason—to derail it. To put it bluntly, the tarnished reputation of the United Nations offers the perfect vehicle for half-hearted measures in situations that would otherwise necessitate a more serious commitment on the part of member states. In this context, one of the crucial lessons of the U.S. and European responses to the Bosnia crisis, of the U.S. reaction to the Somalia crisis, and of the much-publicized Security Council "failure" in the Rwanda crisis is the consistent quest for the politics of virtual reality.[101]

The second option is the subcontracting of humanitarian responsibilities to multilateral organizations (NATO, OAS, ECOWAS), or individual states: UNITAF-United States in Somalia, and Operation Turquoise-France in Rwanda. This subcontracting, by conferring operational responsibilities upon states or groups of states, even when under nominal U.N. supervision, is in the end hostage to geopolitical considerations, and to the problems that have bedeviled peace maintenance operations, including the reluctance for long-term commitments and recurring perceptions on the often thinly-veiled partisanship of the intervening forces.[102]

The NATO-led action against Yugoslavia in defense of the Kosovo Albanians has generated a great deal of controversy. Debates have centered on the lawfulness of the NATO action, its precedential effect, and its impact on the uncertain doctrine of humanitarian intervention.[104] Troubling questions have been raised concerning the bypassing of the Security Council, the nature of the air campaign against the Federal Republic of Yugoslavia, and the postconflict prospects for a democratic and multiethnic Kosovo. These issues have to be analyzed and assessed within the context of an ongoing humanitarian crisis that had characterized the situation in Kosovo, and of the limited availability of responsive options.

Among the defining characteristics of the Kosovo crisis, the following are of particular relevance here.

1. The bypassing of the Security Council. Although in the past the Security Council has remained silent on the use of force by multilateral organizations, most prominently in the case of ECOWAS in Liberia and has ended up with a retroactive, implicit or explicit, endorsement of their conduct,[105] the Kosovo case was different. Contrary to the Liberia case, the Security Council was already actively seized of the matter before the NATO bombing began. In fact, the Security Council had already adopted a series of resolutions on the crisis that invoked Chapter VII of the Charter.[106] Thus, this was a situation in which the Security Council was already engaged, then bypassed (primarily because of veto concerns), and eventually brought back into the picture to legitimize the outcome with Resolution 1244. What are the implications (legal, moral, political) of this roller-coaster ride? One of the key issues relevant to subcontracting is the following: Does Resolution 1244 point to the direction of an emerging norm whereby prior authorization is not necessary and should be considered as implicitly conferred, if the outcome is explicitly endorsed in a subsequent resolution? Does it make any difference whether the Security Council was already seized of the matter in question (Kosovo) or not (Liberia)? In a nutshell, could an argument be made that Resolution 1244 retroactively conferred subcontracting status to NATO action? If not, what exactly is the retroactive status of Resolution 1244?[107]

2. The way in which Operation Allied Force was conducted. This may well turn out to be one of the most important issues in the

overall assessment of the operation, with critical long-term implications for the future of forcible humanitarian action. The air campaign has been criticized as being more sensitive to allied casualties rather than to the welfare of victimized civilians that it was supposed to protect. In fact, NATO complaints at the start of the operation that weather conditions prevented it from engaging into an effective bombing campaign cannot be accepted at face value. As one analyst has pointed out "what the cloud ceiling prohibited was not all bombing...but rather perfectly safe bombing."[108] To be sure, the laws and customs of war do not provide for a separate set of rules for forcible humanitarian operations as opposed to regular military operations. In fact, it is within the very context of universally accepted customary rules of international humanitarian law (discrimination between combatants and non-combatants, protection of civilian objects, adherence to the principle of proportionality), that the conduct of operations has been criticized. From a strictly humanitarian perspective, an argument on the disproportionate nature of NATO's bombing can be made on two grounds: for its adverse impact on the Serb civilian population, and for its failure to protect (absence of ground forces) the victims of ethnic cleansing.[109] It is in a similar vein, I would argue, that the "controversial" comments by the United Nations High Commissioner for Human Rights (UNHCHR) must be read: "Mrs. Robinson said that since the conflict had regrettably victimized innocent people on all sides,...it was all the more crucial and pressing that diplomacy and peacemaking be stepped up to bring about a peaceful solution. Unless diplomacy succeeded, Kosovo would be thoroughly cleansed of Albanians while Serbs would be bombed without end."[110]

The Kosovo case is a reminder that precisely because of their humanitarian component, humanitarian interventions—often accompanied by heavy "just war" pronouncements—generate higher *moral* expectations of lawful conduct.[111]

The third and last option involves arming the victims. Although this is not usually couched in the language of humanitarian intervention, the primary concern is clearly humanitarian: namely, the empowerment of the victims so as to enable them to suppress or prevent the abusive conduct orchestrated by the perpetrators. This option was raised in connection with the wars in Bosnia and Kosovo.[111] In the former case, it even constituted one of the provisional measures requested by the Government of Bosnia and Herzegovina in its petition against the Federal Republic of Yugoslavia before the International Court of Justice (ICJ). The ICJ, in both of its orders on provisional measures, declined the Bosnian request.[112] The issue of arming the victims resurfaced during the NATO campaign at a time when the alliance was exhibiting growing centrifugal tendencies, and policymakers began to look seriously at other options. Discussion centered on the merits of bringing the Kosovar Liberation Army (KLA) into the picture, as the most credible vehicle for the campaign against Milosevic. The elevation of KLA's profile even received presidential endorsement,[113] and certain analysts characterized it as the best of all available alternatives.[114]

From a humanitarian perspective, this is a problematic option for two basic reasons. First, there is no guarantee that victims will refrain from directing their anger against their opponents' civilian population. On the contrary, if they are going under, and desperation sets in, civilian targets may become quite an attractive option (in both of the aforementioned cases, Bosnian Muslims and Kosovar Albanians have been accused of atrocities and terrorist actions).[115] Second, arming the victims says nothing about the outcome. If, for example, Operation Allied Force was indeed a "just war" (as President Clinton claimed), any policy geared toward the KLA must have ensured an outcome consistent with a just cause. And here lies the problem. Supporters of this "humanitarian" option do not commit themselves to a specific outcome. Instead what they are saying is that Bosnian/Kosovar freedom fighters should be given a chance. *If they are given a chance and they fail, what next? Has an outcome consistent with the humanitarian objectives of the original campaign been achieved?* Once again, we are back to square one and to an eerie reminder of the politics of virtual reality.

Concluding Remarks

What is the future role of humanitarian intervention in the prevention of genocide? Any answer to this question must deal with the lessons of the recent crises. While a comprehensive assessment of recent interventions will have to await the availability of key records, certain preliminary observations are in order. Peace enforcement operations with a humanitarian component will still be plagued by the inherent tensions between political and humanitarian considerations. One of the lessons of both Somalia and Bosnia is the sober reminder of the low tolerance for casualties when the strategic value of humanitarian aid (for the belligerents) is high, and the political value of the issues at stake (for the intervening forces) is low. This would seem to favor low-key operations with more modest ends. As one commander of a national contingent said to the Secretary-General's Special Representative for Somalia, when "troops are not sent to engage in heroic actions, then the United Nations cannot assign them even moderately dangerous jobs."[117] Genocide, however, poses two particular problems to such an unheroic prescription. First, given its exterminatory nature, modesty in pursuit of its prevention, let alone suppression will clearly be inadequate. Second, stopping the killings will simply not be enough, since the international community must ensure that the conditions that led to their unleashing do not recur. This, of course, leads to the other major problem associated with interventions, namely their lack of long-term perspective. In a nutshell, if one international crime necessitates a heroic mission par excellence, this is genocide.

The realization that, almost fifty years since the "lessons" of the war, our responsive actions still leave a lot to be desired, is tantamount to overstating the obvious. Have the "lessons" of Rwanda and now of Kosovo made any difference? What is so maddening about the former is that a less than heroic mission may have prevented it. What is so frustrating about the latter is that while the outcome is consistent with certain humanitarian objectives, the modalities of the operation raised serious legal and humanitarian concerns. Feeling his way between the Scylla of inaction and the Charybdis of unilateral/multilateral unauthorized action, the Secretary-General noted:

> The choice must not be between council unity and inaction in the face of genocide—as in the case of Rwanda—and council division, but regional action, as in the case of Kosovo. In both cases, the U.N. should have been able to find common ground in upholding the principles of the charter, and acting in defense of our common humanity.[118]

Oratorical exhortations aside, what would the quest for a "common ground" entail? Here is where the need for a new definition of national interest meets the concern for a "culture of prevention." What the Secretary-General seems to be saying is that the growing intersections between the pursuit of national well-being and that of transnational goals and values would sensitize member states to prompt interventionary responses below the forcible option. It is in this context that his proposals linking humanitarian access to peace and security must be viewed: prompt Security Council response to such challenges would hopefully minimize the need for subsequent massive intervention.[119] In a similar vein, in his recent report on the prevention of armed conflict, Kofi Annan emphasized the importance of "providing periodic regional or subregional reports to the Security Council on threats to international peace and security."[120] The focus of these reports "would be on cross-border issues" that may adversely impact on international peace (illicit arms, mercenaries, refugees, irregular forces), and, in particular, "on the security implications of their interaction."[121] Thus, the emphasis on cross-border issues and on their interactive effect provides a useful entry point for the reaffirmation of the indivisibility of peace, a key attribute of collective security. In extreme cases, however, and if all else fails, the "common ground" would necessitate intervention under Chapter VII to deal with "systematic and widespread breaches of international humanitarian and human rights law, causing threats of genocide, crimes against humanity and war crimes...."[122]

While all this sounds promising have we really moved forward, or is it an ad hoc response to the latest controversy? An argument can be made that some of the aforementioned utterances are simply refinements of earlier proposals found in the Agenda for Peace (with a Kosovar twist).[123] To be sure, recent reports and discussions on the future of peacekeeping operations seem to indicate a concerted effort to upgrade the system's rapid deployment capabilities.[124] But even in this context, some of the most far-reaching proposals, like the formation of "coherent brigade-sized forces" as a means of enhancing the UNSAS, will have to await "further dialogue and consultations" with member states.[125]

This brings us back to square one: member states and their political objectives. In the midst of the most recent crisis, calls for the empowerment of the United Nations have a clearly deja vu flavor. Cynicism aside, some of these appeals may indeed be issued in earnest (especially when emanating from countries that have traditionally taken their U.N. responsibilities seriously). However, if the past is of any guidance here, beware of appeals whose "glossy" surface masks another attempt to simply take us once again down the path of great expectations with minimal means of fulfilling them; namely, appeals which at critical junctures can exploit the weaknesses and mistakes of the organization in order to scapegoat it. When a crisis necessitates the use of the ultimate interventionary tool, as is the case with genocide, any credible responsive action rests and will continue to do so with member states. Have we learned at least this lesson yet? The answer will have to await the next crisis, when we will reconvene to dissect the reasons for our "failure" to take the appropriate course of action.

Notes

* An earlier version of this chapter was presented at the Genocide Studies Program Seminar Series, Yale University. I would like to thank Richard Falk of Princeton University, and Peter Juviler of Columbia University, for their very helpful and constructive comments on earlier drafts of this essay.

1 There is no consensus on a definition of humanitarian intervention. For the purposes of my work, I define humanitarian intervention as the nonconsensual projection of military force to prevent or stop large-scale killings, contemplated or committed by forces led or controlled by the government of the target state against its own citizens, or by forces accountable to no discernible authority in situations of total or near-total anarchy. For a discussion of the concept of humanitarian intervention, see Richard Lillich, ed., *Humanitarian Intervention and the United Nations* (Charlottesville: University Press of Virginia, 1973); Sean D. Murphy, *Humanitarian Intervention. The United Nations in an Evolving World Order* (Philadelphia: University of Pennsylvania Press, 1996); and George Andreopoulos, "Humanitarian Intervention and Relief," in Council on Foreign Relations, *Encyclopedia of U.S. Foreign Relations* vol. 2 (New York: Oxford University Press, 1997), pp. 322-326.

2 On jurisprudential grounds, there are no distinctions between "genocide" and "acts of genocide." Yet, many governments have engaged in definitional hair-splitting for obvious reasons. The best example of this tendency is Security Council Resolution 925 concerning Rwanda which, adopted two months after the killings began, referred in one of its preambular provisions to "reports indicating that acts of genocide have occurred in Rwanda"; United Nations Department of Public Information, *The United Nations and the Situation in Rwanda*, New York, DPI/1484/AFR/PKO (August 1994 edition), October 1994, p. 38. According to the United Nations report on the genocide in Rwanda, the resolution's original draft did use the term genocide. It was eventually changed to "acts of genocide" "as a compromise after China objected to use of the term genocide on its own"; *Report of the Independent Inquiry into the Actions of the United Nations During the 1994 Genocide in Rwanda, 15 December 1999*. http://www.un.org/News/ossg/rwanda report.htm (hereinafter, *The Rwanda Report*). This, however, is part of a bigger and more serious problem: the systematic avoidance of the "G" word during critical phases of ongoing crises (Bosnia, Rwanda). The most notorious precur-

sor of "G" avoidance is the Cambodia case, where only in 1991 was the occurrence of genocide officially recognized in an international document; Ben Kiernan, "The Inclusion of the Khmer Rouge in the Cambodian Peace Process: Causes and Consequences," in Ben Kiernan ed., *Genocide and Democracy in Cambodia. The Khmer Rouge, the United Nations and the International Community* (New Haven: Monograph 41/Yale University Southeast Asia Studies, 1993), p. 230. On the other hand, in the Kosovo crisis, the U.S. administration acknowledged the existence of "indicators that genocide is unfolding" shortly after the beginning of the NATO-led bombing campaign against the FRY; Francis X. Clines, "Flood of Refugees," *The New York Times*, March 30, 1999.

3   Although forcible action was taken against the Federal Republic of Yugoslavia (FRY) in order to protect the Kosovar Albanians, as opposed to the nonforcible measures taken in support of the East Timorese, the presence of an international peacekeeping force in East Timor was not exactly consensual. It is true that the Indonesian Government did finally consent to its presence, but only after tremendous pressure was exerted by foreign governments, culminating with President Clinton's stern warning that "If Indonesia does not end the violence, it must invite, it must invite the international community to assist in restoring security." Philip Shenon, "Clinton Demands End of Violence in East Timor," *The New York Times*, September 10, 1999.

4   Kofi Annan, "Two concepts of sovereignty," *The Economist*, 18 September 1999.

5   Millennium Report of the Secretary-General of the United Nations, *We the Peoples. The Role of the United Nations in the 21st Century*, http://www.un.org/millennium/sg/report/full.htm; in a similar vein, a year earlier, Kofi Annan had noted that "Nothing in the Charter precludes a recognition that there are rights beyond borders"; UN Press Release SG/SM/7136GA/9596, 20 September 1999, *Secretary-General Presents His Annual Report To General Assembly*, http://www.un.org/News/Press/docs/1999/1999 0920.sgsm7136.html

6   "State sovereignty...is being redefined...by the forces of globalization and international co-operation. States are now widely understood to be instruments at the service of their peoples, and not vice versa. At the same time individual sovereignty—by which I mean the fundamental freedom of each individual...has been enhanced by a renewed and spreading consciousness of individual rights"; "Two concepts of sovereignty," supra note 4.

7   The Chinese Foreign Minister, Tang Jiaxuan, noted that any deviation from respect for national sovereignty and noninterference would lead to gunboat diplomacy; likewise, Jaswant Singh, the Indian Foreign Minister, noted that it would be erroneous "to assume that the days of the State are over. The state continues to have a crucial role and relevance...The UN was not conceived as a super State...there is no viable substitute to the sovereign State"; Barbara Crossette, "China and Others Reject Pleas That U.N. Intervene in Civil Wars," *The New York Times*, September 23, 1999; and Agenda item 9:

General Debate, *Statement by Mr. Jaswant Singh, Minister for External Affairs on September 22, 1999,* http://www.un.int/india/ind39.htm.

8   David Rieff, "Wars Without End?" *The New York Times,* September 23, 1999.

9   The Indonesian Foreign Minister speaking about the "recklessness" which has characterized member states' attitudes and its spillover effect on the United Nations, observed that "...we have the spectacle of a U.N. Security Council...venturing out to take over the work of other U.N. organs in such fields as human rights, democracy and humanitarian aid. The unhappy truth is that the inequities and imbalances and discrimination in international relations that the United Nations is supposed to cure have infected its own vital organs and processes"; *Statement by H. E. Mr. Ali Alatas, Minister for Foreign Affairs, Republic of Indonesia, at the 54th Session of the U.N. General Assembly,* New York, September 23, 1999, http://www.un.int/indonesia/speeches/ga/plenary/ga-092399.html

10 United Nations General Assembly Official Records, Fifty-fourth Session, Supplement No. 1 (A/54/1), *Report of the Secretary-General on the Work of the Organization,* United Nations, New York, 1999 (hereinafter, Annual Report).

11 U.N. Press Release SG/SM/4560, *Secretary-General's Address at University of Bordeaux,* 1991.

12 S.C. Res. 688, U.N. SCOR, 46th Sess., 2082 mtg, U.N. Doc. S/RES/688 (1991).

13 See, for example, the following statement by Francis M. Deng and Larry Minear: "By overriding Iraqi sovereignty to provide humanitarian assistance and protection to the Kurds, the U.N. Security Council has paved the way for the current discussion of a new humanitarian order in which governments are held—by force, if necessary—to higher standards of respect of human life"; *The Challenges of Famine Relief. Emergency Operations in the Sudan* (Washington, D.C.: The Brookings Institution, 1992), p. 8.

14 United Nations General Assembly, Report of the Secretary-General on the Work of the Organization, *An Agenda for Peace. Preventive Diplomacy, peacemaking and peace-keeping,* U.N. Doc. A/47/277/S/24111, 17 June 1992, p. 1 (hereinafter, *Agenda for Peace*).

15 Ibid., p. 5.

16 Ibid., p. 6.

17 Multifunctional is the term used in the *Supplement to an Agenda for Peace.* It refers to the type of peacekeeping operations that have usually come into being upon the conclusion of negotiations and, in the words of then Secretary-General Boutros Boutros-Ghali, "with the mandate of helping the parties implement the comprehensive settlement they had negotiated." These settlements covered not only military issues, but also

an extensive list of civilian matters, including the return of refugees and displaced persons; the verification of respect for human rights; the design and supervision of constitutional, judicial, and electoral reforms; and the coordination of support for economic rehabilitation and reconstruction. United Nations General Assembly, Report of the Secretary-General on the Work of the Organization, *Supplement to an Agenda for Peace: Position Paper of the Secretary-General on the Occasion of the Fiftieth Anniversary of the United Nations*, A/50/60/S/1995/1, 3 January 1995, p. 6 (hereinafter, *Supplement*).

18 For preventive initiatives on light weaponry, see Edward Laurance, *Light Weapons and Intrastate Conflict. Early Warning Factors and Preventive Action* (Washington, D.C.: Carnegie Commission on Preventing Deadly Conflict, 1998), pp. 42-50.

19 Expression used in Carnegie Commission on Preventing Deadly Conflict, *Preventing Deadly Conflict: Final Report* (Washington, D.C.: Carnegie Commission on Preventing Deadly Conflict, 1997), p. xiv. Most recently, the notion of culture of protection was emphasized in the Secretary-General's second report on the protection of civilians in armed conflict; United Nations Security Council, *Report of the Secretary-General to the Security Council on the protection of civilians in armed conflict*, S/2001/331, 30 March 2001.

20 See Tom Farer, *Rescuing Human Rights: The Prospect for Humanitarian Interventions*.

21 Annual Report, supra note 10, p. 3.

22 In defining humanitarian emergencies, I follow the definition provided in the U.S. Mission to the U.N. Study on Global Humanitarian Emergencies, namely "a situation in which large numbers of people are dependent on humanitarian assistance—especially, food, water, medical care, and shelter—from sources external to their own society in order to avoid serious malnutrition or death; and/or large numbers of people are in need of physical protection in order to have access to subsistence or external assistance"; *Global Humanitarian Emergencies, 1996*, p. 1. Humanitarian Emergencies are usually distinguished between man-made and nature-made (natural disasters). It is beyond the scope of this essay to deal with the merits of such distinction. Suffice to say at this point that Kofi Annan makes a good point when in his 1999 Report he observes that natural disaster "has to become an increasingly anachronistic misnomer. In reality, human behaviour transforms natural hazards into what should really be called unnatural disasters"; Annual Report, supra note 10, p. 2.

23 I am referring to U.N. Security Council Resolutions 232, December 16, 1966, and 253, May 29, 1968, both pertaining to Southern Rhodesia; and U.N. Security Council Resolution 418, 4 November 1977, pertaining to South Africa.

24 I use the term peace maintenance generically to include both traditional peacekeeping and peace enforcement action under Chapter VII. Both relate to the maintenance of international peace and security, one of the main purposes of the United Nations as expressed in article 1, section 1 of the U.N. Charter.

25 For a discussion of the integration as well as of the other approaches, see Larry Minear, "The Evolving Humanitarian Enterprise," in Thomas G. Weiss, ed., *The United Nations and Civil Wars* (Boulder, CO: Lynne Rienner, 1993), pp. 89-106; and Larry Minear, "Humanitarian Action and Peacekeeping Operations," *Journal of Humanitarian Assistance*, http://www-jha.sps.cam.ac.uk/a/a024.htm posted on July 4, 1997.

26 Ibid.

27 United Nations General Assembly, *Strengthening of the coordination of humanitarian emergency assistance of the United Nations*, A/RES/46/182, 14 April 1992; *Agenda for Peace*, supra note 14, p. 9.

28 For example, Security Council resolutions invoking Chapter VII of the U.N. Charter. This, however, need not be the case. One of the most controversial resolutions, the aforementioned 688 on the aftermath of the Gulf War, makes no reference to Chapter VII. An argument can be made that, given the language used in some of its provisions (*Demands that Iraq....Insists that Iraq*), the legal basis for the intervention can be inferred from the Security Council's general powers to maintain and restore international peace and security. For a thorough discussion of Resolution 688, see Sean D. Murphy, supra note 1, pp. 182-198.

29 Larry Minear, supra note 25; for a discussion on the problematic nature of these principles, in particular the principle of neutrality, see George Andreopoulos, *Neutrality and Humanitarian Operations*, paper presented at the Workshop on Humanitarian Operations and Civil Conflicts, John Jay College of Criminal Justice, CUNY, December 1-2, 2000.

30 For a discussion of the growing convergence between human rights and humanitarian norms, see George Andreopoulos, *Non-State Armed Groups and the Limits of International Law*, paper presented at the CISS/ISA Conference, Heidelberg, June 25-26, 2001.

31 For a more detailed discussion through the prism of a series of case studies, see Francois Jean, ed., *Life, Death and Aid. The Medecins Sans Frontieres Report on World Crisis Intervention* (London: Routledge, 1993). MSF was among the first major humanitarian organizations to adopt a clearly human rights (advocacy-related) approach in its work.

32 I have discussed this issue in greater detail in George Andreopoulos, "Enforcing Humanitarian Action: Lessons from UNPROFOR and UNOSOM," Stefano Bianchini and Robert Craig Nation, eds., *The Yugoslav Conflict and Its Implications for International Relations* (Ravenna: Longo Editore, 1998), pp. 71-82; see also *Supplement*, supra note 17.

33 *Report of the Secretary-General to the Security Council on the protection of civilians in armed conflict*, supra note 19.

34 United Nations Security Council Resolution 770, 13 August 1992; United Nations Department of Public Information, *The United Nations and the Situation in the Former Yugoslavia,* New York, DPI/1312/Rev. 4, July 1995, p. 129.

35 United Nations Security Council Resolution 794, 3 December 1992, United Nations Department of Public Information, *The United Nations and the Situation in Somalia,* New York, DPI/1321/Rev. 3, June 1994, p. 41.

36 UNOSOM I was established as a result of Security Council Resolution 751 of April 24, 1992 as a traditional peacekeeping operation to "facilitate an immediate and effective cessation of hostilities and the maintenance of a cease-fire throughout the country in order to promote the process of reconciliation and political settlement in Somalia and to provide urgent humanitarian assistance"; ibid., p. 34.

37 Mohamed Sahnoun, *Somalia. The Missed Opportunities* (Washington, D.C.: United States Institute of Peace Press, 1994), p. 34. For a critical look at U.N. policies prior to the passage of Resolution 794, see pp. 25-41. See also John L. Hirsch and Robert B. Oakley, *Somalia and Operation Restore Hope* (Washington, D.C.: United States Institute of Peace Press, 1995), pp. 17-47.

38 Elsewhere, I have characterized Somalia as the Vietnam of the post–Cold War era. By this, I mean two things: first, the aforementioned cottage industry on the merits of the new interventionism, as Vietnam generated one on containment; second, as an example of how policymakers misuse historical analogies for political purposes. For an excellent study of the latter, see Ernest May, *'Lessons' of the Past: The Use and Misuse of History in American Foreign Policy* (New York: Oxford University Press, 1973). The Somalia (but also the Yugoslavia) case would be most appropriate for inclusion in such a study.

39 Dirk Salomons, *The Moment of Truth: Disarmament, Demobilization and Reintegration of Former Combatants as Indicators of a Successful Peace Process,* paper presented at the Workshop on Humanitarian Operations and Civil Conflicts, John Jay College of Criminal Justice, CUNY, December 1-2, 2000.

40 My emphasis; Mohamed Sahnoun, supra note 37, p. 34.

41 Letter dated 29 November 1992 from the Secretary-General to the President of the Security Council, U.N. Doc. S/24868 (1992).

42 My emphasis; George Bush, Humanitarian Mission to Somalia: Address to the Nation, Washington, D.C., December 4, 1992, *U.S. Department of State Dispatch,* vol. 3, no. 49, December 7, 1992; quoted in Walter Clarke and Jeffrey Herbst, "Somalia and the Future of Humanitarian Intervention," *Foreign Affairs,* vol. 75(2), March/April 1996, pp. 74-75.

43 Paragraph 10 refers to paragraph 8 which states that the Security Council "Welcomes the offer by a Member State described in the Secretary-General's letter to the Council of November 29, 1992 (S/24868) concerning the establishment of an operation to create such secure environment"; United Nations Security Resolution 794, supra note 35.

44 Sean D. Murphy, supra note 1, pp. 226-227.

45 Walter Clarke and Jeffrey Herbst, supra note 42, p. 75.

46 United Nations Security Council Resolution 814, March 26, 1993; United Nations Department of Public Information, *The United Nations and the Situation in Somalia*, supra note 35, pp. 43-44.

47 Walter Clarke and Jeffrey Herbst, supra note 42, p. 76.

48 See, for example, The Associated Press Story on IFOR entitled *U.S. Trying to Apply Somalia Lessons to Bosnia Mission*, November 25, 1995, http://www.nando.net/newsroom/nt/1125somalia.html. After quoting then Defense Secretary William Perry saying that "We're not going in there to fight a war, we're not planning to fight our way in," the report states "That is one lesson from Somalia being applied to Bosnia: No "mission creep."

49 Let us not forget that one of the key preambular provisions of Resolution 794 stressed the Security Council's determination "to restore *peace, stability and law and order with a view to facilitating the process of a political settlement under the auspices of the United Nations, aimed at national reconciliation*" and its encouragement of the Secretary-General's efforts and those of his Special Representative "to continue and intensify their work *at the national and regional levels to promote these objectives*" (my emphasis); *The United Nations and the Situation in Somalia*, supra note 35, p. 40.

50 An acknowledgment which apparently was not communicated to the troops. In an interesting study of U.S. Army soldiers' evolving attitudes toward Operation Restore Hope, Miller and Moskos found that at the initial stage, participating soldiers felt that the task would be purely humanitarian: "A key factor in soldiers' expectations for the mission in Somalia was the model of army relief work in Florida following Hurricane Andrew in the summer of 1992"; Laura L. Miller and Charles Moskos, "Humanitarians or Warriors?: Race, Gender, and Combat Status in Operation Restore Hope," *Armed Forces and Society*, vol. 21(4), Summer 1995, p. 619.

51 My emphasis: United Nations, *Statement by the President of the Security Council*, S/PRST/1999/21, 8 July 1999, http://www.un.org/Docs/sc/statements/1999/prst9921.htm

52 *Report of the Secretary-General to the Security Council on the protection of civilians in armed conflict,* S/1999/957, 8 September 1999, http://www.reliefweb.int/library/documents/civilian html.

53 My emphasis; *Report of the Secretary-General,* ibid.

54 Ibid. The importance of the DDR process was reaffirmed in the Secretary-General's recent report on the prevention of armed conflict, where he urged the Security Council "to include, as appropriate, a disarmament, demobilization and reintegration component" in U.N. peacekeeping/peace-building mandates; United Nations General Assembly/Security Council, Report of the Secretary-General, *Prevention of armed conflict,* A/55/985-S/2001/574, 7 June 2001, p. 23.

55 As we shall see below.

56 *Report of the Secretary-General to the Security Council on the protection of civilians in armed conflict,* supra note 19.

57 Ibid.

58 United Nations Security Council, *Statement by the President of the Security Council,* S/PRST/2001/5, 20 February 2001.

59 For a discussion of this issue, see George Andreopoulos, "Offenses Against the Laws of Humanity: International Action," in Neil J. Smelser and Paul B. Baltes, *International Encyclopedia of the Social and Behavioral Sciences* (New York: Pergamon Press, 2001); and Beth Van Schaack, "The Definition of Crimes Against Humanity: Resolving the Incoherence," *Columbia Journal of Transnational Law,* vol. 37(3), 1999, pp. 787-850.

60 Article IV of the Genocide Convention.

61 Article V of the Genocide Convention.

62 There have been several studies of the debilitating political compromises that shaped the drafting of the Genocide Convention. One of the best is Leo Kuper, *Genocide: Its Political Use in the Twentieth Century* (New Haven, CT: Yale University Press, 1982).

63 Date in which the Genocide Convention entered into force.

64 While this is generally the case, it is also true that some legislatures have been more willing to scrutinize their executive branch on its knowledge and objectives concerning the situation on Rwanda during the critical months before and after the genocide. An example is the Belgian Senate Committee of Inquiry which, initiated by Senator Alain Destexhe, unearthed important information concerning the Belgian Government's access to information: "Concerning the period before the genocide, our Committee con-

cluded that, at the latest, in mid-January 1994, the Belgian authorities *had a series of relevant information regarding if not the preparation of a genocide, at least the preparation of large-scale massacres*" (my emphasis); *Rwanda: Genocide and the Continuing Cycle of Violence.* Testimony of Alain Destexhe before the Subcommittee on International Operations and Human Rights of the Committee on International Relations. One Hundred Fifth Congress. Second Session. May 5, 1998, http://commdocs.house.gov/committees/intlrel/hfa49306.000/hfa49306_0.htm.

65 *The United Nations and the Situation in Rwanda*, supra note 2, p. 2.

66 In fact, the United Nations Report on the Rwanda Genocide identified the absence of a role in the recovery of arms as a critical omission in UNAMIR's mandate; *The Rwanda Report*, supra note 2.

67 United Nations Security Council Resolution 872, 5 October 1993, ibid., p. 27.

68 Human Rights Watch, *Leave None to Tell the Story. Genocide in Rwanda*, March 1999, wysiwyg://10/http://www.hrw.org/reports/1999/Rwanda/.

69 On May 3, 1994, President Clinton signed Presidential Decision Directive (PDD) 25 which placed—half a year after the Mogadishu debacle—severe restrictions on United States support for United Nations peace operations; *United States: Administration Policy on Reforming Multilateral Peace Operations, May 1994*, 33 I.L.M. 795.

70 Although, as it is argued below, even this scaled-down mandate did empower UNAMIR to raid the weapons caches in Kigali. For a discussion of the October 3, 1993, battle and its impact on U.S. policy, see John L. Hirsch and Robert B. Oakley, *Somalia and Operation Restore Hope. Reflections on Peacemaking and Peacekeeping* (Washington, D.C.: United States Institute of Peace Press, 1995), pp. 124-135.

71 Philip Gourevitch, "The Genocide Fax," *The New Yorker*, May 11, 1998, pp. 43-46.

72 DALAIRE/UNAMIR/KIGALI to BARIL/DPKO/UNATIONS, 11 January 1994, http://www.pbs.org/wgbh/pages/frontline/shows/evil/warning/cable.html.

73 *The Rwanda Report*, supra note 2. The quoted passage is from the same report.

74 *Leave None to Tell the Story*, supra note 68. This information is included in the chapter entitled *Warnings*, which also includes a comprehensive chronology of events during the critical months preceding the genocide; http://www.hrw.org/reports/1999/rwanda/Geno4-7-01.htm. For a useful overview of events leading up to the genocide, see Gerard Prunier, *The Rwanda Crisis. History of a Genocide* (New York: Columbia University Press, 1995), pp. 192-212.

75 Emphasis added; *Leave None to Tell the Story*, ibid.

76 Ibid.

77 In his fax, Dallaire stated that "It is our intention to take action within the next 36 hours." This is to be contrasted to the language used for the protection of his informant "It is recommended that informant be granted protection and evacuated out of Rwanda." In the latter case, Dallaire clearly sought authorization, while in the former case, he was simply informing the headquarters of his proposed course of action; supra note 71; see also the section entitled *The 11 January Cable* in *The Rwanda Report*, supra note 2.

78 In one of his subsequent cables (February 3, 1994), Dallaire wrote: "We can expect more frequent and more violent demonstrations, more grenade and armed attacks on ethnic and political groups, more assassinations....Each day of delay in authorizing deterrent arms recovery operation will result in an ever deteriorating security situation and may if the arms continue to be distributed result in the inability of UNAMIR to carry out its mandate in all aspects"; General Dallaire to U.N., New York, Code Cable MIR 267, February 3, 1994; quoted in *Leave None to Tell the Story*, supra note 74. Despite Dallaire's repeated requests and warnings, the Secretariat's response stuck to a very restrictive interpretation of UNAMIR's mandate. In his reply to another Dallaire cable which pointed to the inability of the Rwandan gendarmerie and army to conduct cordon and search operations, Kofi Annan (then Under Secretary-General for Peacekeeping Operations) insisted that Resolution 792 "only authorized UNAMIR 'to contribute to the security of the city of Kigali, i.a., within a weapons secure area *established by repeat by the parties'* " (emphasis added), *The Rwanda Report*, supra note 2. The Secretariat's insistence on a restrictive interpretation of UNAMIR's mandate is also stressed in the OAU Report on the Rwanda Genocide: Organization of African Unity, International Panel of Eminent Personalities to Investigate the 1994 Genocide in Rwanda and the Surrounding Events, *Rwanda: The Preventable Genocide*, 7 July 2000 (hereinafter, *The Preventable Genocide*). The discussion of the U.N.'s role can be found primarily in chapter 13 of the report (*Before the Genocide: The Role of the United Nations*); http://www.oau-oua.org/document/ipep/report/rwanda-e/EN-13-CH.htm.

79 In this context, timely deployment would have meant deployment before the last week of April. After that date, any interventionary plans would have necessitated a major military commitment because the killings had spread to the countryside; Scott R. Feil, "Preventing Genocide. How the Early Use of Force Might Have Succeeded in Rwanda," *A Report to the Carnegie Commission on Preventing Deadly Conflict* (New York: Carnegie Corporation of New York, 1998), p. 22.

80 *The Rwanda Report*, supra note 2.

81 The United Nations report characterizes the delay in identifying the events as genocide as "*a failure by the Security Council*" the *Rwanda Report*, supra note 2. This, however, once again begs the question: What were the Security Council's policy objectives that the chosen course of action failed to achieve?

82   Emphasis added; *the Rwanda Report,* supra note 2.

83   The OAU report is extremely critical of this cable which is viewed as "emblematic of a larger pernicious reality: the lives of Africans were considered less valuable to the world community than the lives of citizens of western nations." The report notes that this conclusion is inevitable, given Dallaire's instructions to assign his troops to the evacuation of expatriates in the midst of an ongoing genocide; *The Preventable Genocide,* supra note 78, para 5.

84   In a recent article on the Rwandan Genocide, Alan J. Kuperman has questioned the "claim that 5,000 troops deployed at the outset of the killing in April 1994 could have prevented the genocide"; "Rwanda in Retrospect," *Foreign Affairs,* vol. 79(1), January/February 2000, p. 94. Within the limits of counterfactual argumentation, Kuperman makes some good points on the limits of alternative interventionary scenarios, and claims that maximum credible intervention (division-size force) would not have prevented the genocide, but it would have saved about 125,000 Tutsi (25% of the ultimate toll), p. 108. There are, however, some problems with Kuperman's assertions that go beyond word games (I do not think that any credible analyst argues that preventing genocide after April 6 would have meant zero casualties; rather prevention in this context would have meant slowing down the rate of killings and eventually stopping them altogether). One major problem relates to his assumption that "President Clinton could not have known that a nationwide genocide was under way in Rwanda until about April 20"; p. 101. This is a statement based on very questionable assumptions. First, Kuperman acknowledges that U.S. intelligence reports remain classified. From this observation, he proceeds to conclude that they "probably mirrored those of the international news media, human rights organizations, and the U.N.—because U.S. intelligence agencies committed virtually no in-country resources" to Rwanda (p. 101). This is a very unsatisfactory conclusion since it ignores the U.S.'s impressive intelligence gathering capacity via satellites; capacity that relates to the ability to intercept communications among key actors (in this case, between the Hutu government and the Presidential Guard, the regular army, the interahamwe, and the national police). To be sure, there is only one way to ascertain this: the U.S. government should declassify (with congressional oversight) all relevant intelligence reports from that period. In the absence of detailed knowledge of what the U.S. government knew and when, it is rather far-fetched to equate its knowledge with that of news media and human rights NGOs. But even if that were to be the case, NGOs did notify the U.S. Administration early on (April 7) that Hutu soldiers had been killing Tutsi; see Alison Des Forges' reply to Kuperman, "Alas, We Knew," *Foreign Affairs,* vol. 79(3), May/June 2000, p. 141. Second, Kuperman does not address at all the revelations of James Woods, former Deputy Assistant Secretary of State for African Affairs, who has stated that the Administration was aware "within 10 to 14 days" of the plane crash that the killings were "premeditated, carefully planned,...executed according to plan with the full connivance of the then-Rwandan government"; quoted in the *Preventable Genocide,* Chapter 15 (*The World During the Genocide: The United Nations, Belgium, France and the OAU*) para 15, http://www.oau-oua.org/document/ipep/report/rwanda-e/EN-15-CH.htm   Finally,

it is clear that Kuperman did not have any access to the U.N. confidential files on the genocide. However, both the U.N. inquiry (the *Rwanda Report*) and the OAU Panel (*the Preventable Genocide*) did. According to the latter, on April 17, Dallaire in a cable to General Baril (Headquarters) stated that "UNAMIR's troops were increasingly demoralized and were not merely refusing to protect civilians, but actually surrendering them to the killers without a fight"; quoted in the *Preventable Genocide*, chapter 15, para. 14. The picture may have been more muddled at the time, as Kuperman has argued in his response to Des Forges (p. 143), but not to the point of not recognizing intentional killing, if Dallaire could send such a cable to Headquarters.

85   A detailed outline of Dallaire's operational plan and the alternative plan offered by those critical to it can be found in Scott R. Feil, supra note 79, pp. 7-23.

86   Scott R. Feil, ibid., pp. 7-14; in outlining his plan, Dallaire also took into consideration the action of the evacuation forces in Kigali to extract expatriates, and the largely uncontested French intervention under Operation Turquoise. For an official French assessment of Operation Amaryllis (to extract French and foreign citizens from Kigali), including responses to criticisms leveled at the selective nature of the operation, see Chapter V of the report of the French Parliamentary Commission on Rwanda; Assemblee Nationale, *Mission d'information sur le Rwanda*, http://www.assemblee-nationale.fr/2/dossiers/rwanda/r1271.htm.

87   While testifying before the House Subcommittee on International Operations and Human Rights, Shaharyar M. Khan, former Special Representative of the U.N. Secretary-General in Rwanda, cited the civil war scenario as one of the reasons for the Security Council's slow response to the genocide: "But the only information coming to the Security Council, the representative of the Rwandan Government itself, who happened to be the representative of the FRG, and he is saying to his colleagues...that the situation is that one side is killing the other, it is a horrible civil war, don't interfere..."; *Rwanda: Genocide and the Continuing Cycle of Violence*, supra note 64.

88   Scott R. Feil, supra note 79, pp. 15-16.

89   Ibid., p. 16.

90   *Agenda for Peace*, supra note 14, p. 12.

91   Peace-enforcement units were envisaged as part of the reference to provisional measures in article 40 of the Charter. Their main task would have been to restore and maintain a cease-fire; ibid., p. 13.

92   Cdr(SG) R.T. Mentzen, *Annual Update Briefing to Member States on Standby Arrangements*, November 4, 1998, http://www.un.org/Depts/dpko/rapid/anb.htm.

93   *Enhanced UN Standby Arrangements System for Military and Civilian Police Capabilities,* http://www.un.org/Depts/dpko/rapid/sys.htm, updated 26 July, 2001.

94   *Progress Report of the Secretary-General on Standby Arrangements for Peacekeeping,* http://www.un.org/Depts/dpko/rapid/anr.htm, updated 1 May 2000. The HRB currently comprises units from Argentina, Canada, Denmark, the Netherlands, Norway, Poland, and Sweden; *Report of the Secretary-General to the Security Council on the protection of civilians in armed conflict,* supra note 19.

95   According to the latest report from the UNDPKO, 90 countries have expressed their willingness to participate in UNSAS, 69 have provided a list of capabilities that they will make available, 49 have completed the Planning Data Sheet with detailed information on these capabilities, and 35 have signed MOUs with the United Nations; United Nations Department of Peacekeeping Operations, *Annual Update on the United Nations Standby Arrangements System. (Presented to Member States on 22 November 2000),* http://www.un.org/Depts/dpko/rapid/anb.html, updated 26 July, 2001.

96   United Nations Department of Peacekeeping Operations, *Model of Memorandum of Understanding (MOU),* http://www.un.org/Depts/dpko/rapid/mou.htm.

97   *Supplement,* supra note 17, p. 11.

98   Department of Foreign Affairs and International Trade, *Towards a Rapid Reaction Capability for the United Nations,* September 1995, http://www.dfait-maeci.gc.ca/english/news/newsletr/unrap1.htm.

99   Ibid.; the proposal envisages the Vanguard group as a multifunctional group of up to 5,000 military and civilian personnel.

100 Supra note 91. According to its proponent, the idea originated with the first U.N. Secretary-General. In the midst of the 1948 Arab-Israeli War, Trygve Lie proposed the creation of a small U.N. guard force "to put an end to factional fighting in Jerusalem and to shore up the truce decreed by the Security Council." The proposed force, recruited by the Secretary-General, would be under the command and control of the Security Council; Brian Urquhart, "For a U.N. Volunteer Military Force," *The New York Review of Books,* June 10, 1993, p. 3.

101 Brian Urquhart, ibid.

102 Otherwise known as the "politics of being seen to do something;" see relevant comments by John Hillen, "Peace(keeping) in Our Time: The U.N. as a Professional Military Manager," *Parameters. U.S. Army War College Quarterly,* Autumn 1996, http://carlisle-www.army.mil/usawc/Parameters/96autumn/hillen.htm; see also the comments on the importance of having gratis officers for peacekeeping operations at the U.N. in Robert L. McClure and Morton Orlov II, "Is the UN Peacekeeping Role in

Eclipse?," *Parameters. U.S. Army War College Quarterly*, Autumn 1999, http://carlise-www.army.mil/usawc/Parameters/99autumn/mcclure.htm; "Properly employed and supported, U.N. peacekeeping operations are a force multiplier for the United States in the sense that an effective U.N. peacekeeping operation means one less potential demand on our already limited military resources."

103 As discussed at great length above. On the question of partisanship, Operation Turquoise has raised troubling questions concerning the relationship between the French forces and the FAR. The OAU Panel Report, while acknowledging that the Operation did save thousands of Tutsi, argued that its other task "was to give support to the interim government," thus providing a safe haven for many genocidists; *The Preventable Genocide*, supra note 84, para. 68. On the other hand, the report issued by the French Parliamentary Commission on Rwanda has a very different assessment of French action, claiming that the principal goal of the Operation "was to save human lives by protecting without distinction the threatened populations, whether they be hutu or tutsi (our translation); *Mission d'information sur le Rwanda*, supra note 86.

104 See the debate in the Editorial Comments: "NATO's Kosovo Intervention," *American Journal of International Law*, vol. 93(4), October 1999, http://www.asil.org/ajil/kosovo.htm I have discussed some of the relevant issues at greater length in *Operation Allied Force. Challenges and Opportunities for World Order* (forthcoming). Some of the ensuing arguments and passages follow closely this forthcoming piece.

105 Although ECOMOG (ECOWAS's Military Observer Group) was characterized as a peacekeeping force, it did respond aggressively to military challenges. ECOMOG forces landed in Monrovia on August 24, 1990; it was not until November 19, 1992 that the Security Council commended in Resolution 788 ECOWAS "for its efforts to restore peace, security and stability in Liberia"; United Nations Department of Public Information, *The United Nations and the Situation in Liberia*, New York DPI/1697/Rev. 1, March 1997, p. 37. There was also an earlier statement by the President of the Security Council to the effect that members of the Council commended ECOWAS's efforts "to promote peace and normalcy in Liberia"; *Statement by the President*, 22 January 1991 (S/22133), ibid., p. 36.

106 United Nations Security Council Resolution 1160, S/RES/1160, 31 March 1998, http://www.un.org/peace/kosovo/98sc1160htm; United Nations Security Council Resolution 1199, S/RES/1199, 23 September 1998, http://www.un.org/peace/kosovo/98sc1199.htm; and United Nations Security Council Resolution 1203, 24 October 1998, http://www.un.org/peace/kosovo/98sc1203.htm.

107 There is also an argument that denies any retroactive dimension to Resolution 1244. This seems to be Jonathan Charney's underlying assumption, when he argues that Resolution 1244 "only prospectively authorized foreign states to intervene in the FRY to maintain the peace"; "Anticipatory Humanitarian Intervention in Kosovo," supra note 104. I do not agree with this assessment. The issue here is the exact nature of the

resolution's retroactive status, not whether it has any. The Security Council would have further undermined its already weakened status if it appeared to endorse the outcome of an action that it thought was clearly unlawful. Such an adherence to a strict textual level of analysis fails to capture the complexity of the "decisional contexts;" for an argument on the limitations of legalistic analysis, see Richard Falk, "Kosovo, World Order, and the Future of International Law," supra note 104.

108 Edward N. Luttwak, "Give War a Chance," *Foreign Affairs*, July-August 1999, p. 40.

109 See relevant comment by Christine Chinkin, "Kosovo: A "Good" Or "Bad" War?," supra note 104.

110 United Nations Press Release, *High Commissioner for Human Rights Urges Peaceful Resolution of Conflict in Kosovo*, HR/CN/99/65, 30 April 1999, http://www.unhchr.ch/huricanen...28b3961891e80256766003280c0?OpenDocument.

111 This is also one of the reasons why allegations of misconduct by personnel involved in humanitarian missions create great embarrassment for the government concerned. In this context, see the Canadian Government's report on the Somalia mission, Report of the Commission of Inquiry into the Deployment of Canadian Forces to Somalia (Executive Summary), *Dishonoured Legacy. The Lessons of the Somalia Affair* (Ottawa: Canadian Government Publishing, 1997).

112 In both instances, a Security Council resolution imposing an arms embargo was in effect. In the case of Bosnia, it was Resolution 713, 25 September 1991, covering the whole territory of the Former Yugoslavia; in the case of Kosovo, it was resolution 1160, 31 March 1998, covering the Federal Republic of Yugoslavia, including Kosovo.

113 International Court of Justice, *Order on Request for the Indication of Provisional Measures in Case Concerning Application of the Convention on the Prevention and Punishment of the Crime of Genocide* (Bosnia and Herzegovina v. Yugoslavia (Serbia and Montenegro)), April 8, 1993, 32 I.L.M. 888 (1993); and the subsequent ruling on provisional measures issued on September 13, 1993, which basically reaffirmed the measures it ordered on April 8, 1993.

114 In an op-ed piece entitled "A Just and Necessary War," *The New York Times*, May 23, 1999.

115 See, for example, the op-ed piece by Michael Doyle and Stephen Holmes, "Arm the K.L.A.," *The New York Times*, May 25, 1999.

116 In the Kosovo case, Resolution 1160 called upon the "Kosovar Albanian leadership to condemn all terrorist action."

117 Tom Farer, supra note 20.

118 "Two concepts of sovereignty," supra note 4.

119 *Report of the Secretary-General to the Security Council on the protection of civilians in armed conflict*, supra note 52.

120 *Prevention of armed conflict*, supra note 54, p. 12.

121 Ibid.

122 *Report of the Secretary-General to the Security Council on the protection of civilians in armed conflict*, supra note 52.

123 According to the Secretary-General, one of the factors which the Security Council must consider before acting under Chapter VII is "the limited and proportionate use of force, with attention to repercussions upon civilian populations and the environment"; ibid.

124 United Nations General Assembly, *Report of the Special Committee on Peacekeeping Operations*, A/54/839, 20 March 2000; United Nations General Assembly/Security Council, *Report of the Panel on United Nations Peace Operations*, A/55/305-S/2000/809, 21 August 2000; United Nations General Assembly, *Report of the Secretary-General on the Implementation of the Report of the Panel on United Nations Peace Operations*, A/55/502, 20 October 2000.

125 United Nations General Assembly, *Report of the Secretary-General. Implementation of the recommendations of the Special Committee on Peacekeeping Operations and the Panel on United Nations Peace Operations*, A/55/977, 1 June 2001.

CHAPTER SIX

A Glass Half Full: The NAFTA Labor Agreement and Cross-Border Labor Action

Lance Compa

The North American Agreement on Labor Cooperation (NAALC) creates a new arena for creative transnational action by labor rights advocates. With its unusual "cross-border" complaint mechanism—described in more detail below—the NAALC provides an opportunity for workers, trade unions, and their allies in the United States, Mexico, and Canada to work together concretely to defend workers' rights against abuses by corporations and governments.

Critics have often called this "labor side agreement" to the North American Free Trade Agreement (NAFTA) weak and ineffective— "toothless" is the most common invective. The NAALC is certainly flawed and far from what labor rights advocates would craft if they had the power to do so alone. But they did not. NAFTA's labor side agreement was negotiated by three governments with contending interests. The governments also had to take into account the balance of power (or rather, more accurately, imbalance of power) between workers and employers in each country. The result was a compromise leaving no one happy, including trade unionists and allied workers' rights advocates. But a "glass half-full" analysis of the NAALC reveals stages and spaces for more developed forms of international labor solidarity.

The NAALC sets forth eleven "Labor Principles" on which the three signatory countries commit themselves to take effective action:

1. Freedom of association and protection of the right to organize
2. The right to bargain collectively
3. The right to strike
4. Forced labor

5. Child labor
6. Minimum wage, hours of work, and other labor standards
7. Nondiscrimination
8. Equal pay for equal work
9. Occupational safety and health
10. Workers' compensation
11. Migrant worker protection

In the six years since it took effect, NAFTA's labor side agreement has given rise to a varied, rich experience of international labor rights advocacy. More than twenty complaints and cases have arisen under the NAALC, embracing worker organizing, occupational safety and health, migrant worker protection, minimum employment standards, and other issues.

Before analyzing the cases as vehicles for international action, an understanding of NAALC institutions and mechanisms is needed. The following is a brief description.

NAALC Background

The NAALC resulted from tensions in the U.S. political arena during the 1992 presidential election. Candidate Bill Clinton was faced with a dilemma. His opponent, President George Bush, had signed the NAFTA in August 1992 with Prime Minister Brian Mulroney of Canada and President Carlos Salinas of Mexico.[1] Bush was touting the NAFTA as a major achievement of his administration that promised expanded trade and job creation throughout the continent.

Labor, environmental, and human rights organizations pressured candidate Clinton to renounce NAFTA. They argued that the trade pact was a giveaway to multinational corporations and investors that would destroy jobs, drive down wages, harm the environment, and undermine human rights. However, Clinton was heavily dependent for campaign support on business interests, especially in high-tech industries and among Wall Street investment specialists who supported NAFTA.

The result was a compromise. Clinton promised to support NAFTA, but only if "side agreements" addressing labor and environmental issues were added to the trade arrangement. After winning the election, the new Clinton administration insisted on side agreement negotiations, to which

Canada and Mexico acceded. In August 1993 the three countries signed the NAALC and the North American Agreement on Environmental Cooperation (NAAEC). The NAFTA, the NAALC, and the NAAEC took effect January 1, 1994.

NAALC Institutions

Commission for Labor Cooperation (Ministerial Council and Secretariat)

The NAALC creates a Commission for Labor Cooperation composed of the labor ministers of the three countries and a Secretariat now based in Washington, D.C. (it was originally located in Dallas, Texas, but moved to Washington in 2000). The ministers meet once a year to review the work of the Commission and the implementation of the Agreement. Deputy ministers from the three countries meet 3–4 times a year to guide the work of the Commission and to review the work of the Secretariat. Between meetings, the deputy ministers maintain steady contact with the Executive Director of the Secretariat.

The Secretariat is charged with conducting regular and special research reports on comparative labor law and labor market issues as well as serving as the administrative arm of the Commission. The 12-person professional staff of the Secretariat is drawn equally from the three countries, with an executive director from one country (currently Mexico) and a director from each of the other two countries, one for labor law and economic research and one for administration. Secretariat employees have the status of international civil servants who cannot take instruction from any government.

National Administrative Offices (NAOs)

The NAALC also creates within each country's department of labor a National Administrative Office (NAO). Besides undertaking cooperative activities under the NAALC, NAOs receive, review, and report on "public communications" under Article 16(3) of the NAALC involving labor law matters that arise in the territory of one of the other countries. "Public communication" is the technical phrase for what the NAOs generally refer to as a "submission" and what unions, NGOs, and the media usually call a "complaint."

The cross-border feature of the NAALC is the key to understanding how it promotes international labor solidarity work. An NAO does not review submissions on matters that arise in its own country but in one of the other countries party to the agreement.

Evaluation Committee of Experts (ECE)
Following an NAO review and report and a stage of ministerial consultations, the NAALC provides for establishment of an independent, nongovernmental 3-person Evaluation Committee of Experts (ECE) under Article 24 of the NAALC. The request of one party is sufficient to form an ECE. The Committee performs a comparative study "in a nonadversarial manner" of one or more "technical labor standards" (Labor Principles 4–11) subject to prior ministerial consultation. The ECE may issue recommendations with its report. These recommendations are not binding, but their public declaration would likely create pressure for action on a government's part.

Arbitral Panel
For three Labor Principles, those covering minimum wage, child labor, and occupational safety and health, two countries can agree to require the establishment of an Arbitral Panel under Article 29 of the NAALC to consider an alleged "persistent pattern of failure to effectively enforce" domestic labor law by the third country. The nongovernmental 5-person Arbitral Panel (2 from the country that originally moved the case forward, two from the country complained against, and a neutral chair) is empowered to fine an offending government or, upon failure to pay such a fine, to impose trade sanctions on the firm, industry, or sector giving rise to the submission.

NAALC Complaint Procedures
Any "labor law matter" related to one or more of the 11 Labor Principles can be the subject of a NAALC complaint. Any person or organization may file a complaint. In practice, a wide range of trade unions, human rights organizations, labor lawyers associations, student groups, and other NGOs have presented complaints to all three NAOs. There are no citizenship requirements for filing a submission; any citizen of any country or organization based in any country may submit a complaint to any of the NAOs.

The NAOs of Canada and the United States provide for public hearings on submissions brought before them. Each has held such public hearings, often with dramatic testimony from affected workers and with widespread media coverage. In contrast, the NAO of Mexico provides for "informative sessions" conducted privately and less formally. The first such session in connection with a submission was held December 2, 1998, in Mexico City. A delegation of migrant Mexican workers from the Washington State apple industry presented testimony on workers' rights violations there. Although the session itself was closed to the media, the NAO of Mexico and the workers' delegation both issued press releases and held press conferences describing the event.[2]

The following is a representative sample of cases and related cross-border action by trade unionists and labor rights advocates.

Cases Involving Alleged Workers' Rights Violations in Mexico

Honeywell and General Electric (U.S. NAO Case Nos. 940001 and 940002). In February 1994, two U.S. unions, the International Brotherhood of Teamsters and the United Electrical Workers, filed the first NAALC complaints with the U.S. NAO. Citing violations of Labor Principle 1 and the failure of Mexican labor law authorities to adequately protect the right to organize, the unions charged that several workers at a Honeywell electronic controls plant and at a General Electric motor plant in the state of Chihuahua were dismissed for union activity. The two unions were allied with an independent Mexican labor organization, the Frente Auténtico del Trabajo (FAT), which was seeking to gain bargaining rights at the factories.

The U.S. NAO accepted the submissions for review in April 1994, and held a public hearing in Washington, D.C., in September 1994. Workers from the Honeywell and GE factories in Mexico testified at the hearing, along with Mexican labor lawyers and U.S. union representatives. Neither of the companies appeared at the hearing. They defended their actions in written statements to the U.S. NAO, arguing that the dismissals were for lawful causes unrelated to union activity.

The U.S. NAO noted that its review "reveals disagreements about the events at each of the plants" as to whether or not workers were fired because of union activity. The NAO made no finding on the reasons for the workers' discharge, but it noted that "the timing of the dismissals appears to coincide with organizing drives by independent unions at both plants." The U.S. NAO cited "other relevant issues" including "difficulties in establishing unions in Mexico, the hurdles faced by independent unions in attaining legal recognition, company blacklisting of union activists...and government preference for and support of official unions."[3]

Despite this background, the U.S. NAO declared itself "not in a position to make a finding that the Government of Mexico failed to enforce the relevant labor laws." The NAO noted that the dismissed workers' acceptance of severance pay as indemnization for relinquishing their legal claims were in keeping with Mexican labor law.[4]

The case did not advance further, but in the course of these proceedings the firms reinstated several of the fired workers and paid additional severance pay to others who chose not to return to work. One General Electric official at corporate headquarters stated, on condition of anonymity, that top GE management instructed managers in Mexico not to dismiss union supporters again "because we didn't want any other 'GE case' to embarrass us" under NAFTA's labor agreement.[5]

Sony (U.S. NAO Case No. 940003). In August 1994, a coalition of four NGOs in the U.S. and Mexico filed a complaint alleging discharge of workers and discrimination against dissident unionists at a Sony Corp. factory that manufactures magnetic tapes for video cassettes. The plant is located in a Mexican *maquiladora* industrial park in Nuevo Laredo, Tamaulipas, along the border with Texas. In their complaint the International Labor Rights Fund, the Coalition for Justice in the Maquiladoras, the American Friends Service Committee, and the *Asociación Nacional de Abogados Democráticos* (ANAD) of Mexico cited collusion by management, incumbent union leaders and local political officials to crush an attempt by union members to elect new leadership. Dissident union leaders were fired, and police attacked a peaceful march of independent union members.

The U.S. NAO accepted the submission in October 1994, and held a public hearing in San Antonio, Texas, in February 1995. Mexican workers, their attorneys, and U.S. supporters addressed the hearing. Sony management refused to appear at the hearing. Much of the testimony dealt with Mexico's Conciliation and Arbitration Boards (CABs), tripartite agencies with government, and labor and management representatives that adjudicate all labor disputes.

Citing "serious questions" on union registration issues, the U.S. NAO recommended the first Ministerial Consultations under the NAALC.[6] Ensuing consultations resulted in a program of activities including (1) trinational workshops and public conferences in Mexico and in the U.S. on union registration and certification, (2) a special study by independent Mexican experts on labor law dealing with union registration and its implementation, and (3) a series of meetings by officials of the Mexican Department of Labor and Social Welfare with Sony workers, local labor authorities, and company representatives.

In December 1996, the U.S. NAO delivered a follow-up report on the Sony case. The report discussed the current status of Sony workers, initiatives in Mexico to change the labor law, and decisions of the Mexican Supreme Court that appeared to provide greater rights for independent union organizers. It concluded that "potentially significant developments" continue to take place in Mexico in a wide range of labor matters, including labor legislation, labor-management relations, labor-government relations, and within labor organizations themselves. Though the situation on the ground did not change, independent union advocates in Mexico maintain that the international attention sustained the independent Sony workers' movement, which is still active.[7]

Pesca Union (U.S. NAO Case No. 9601). In June 1996, the International Labor Rights Fund, Human Rights Watch/Americas, and the Mexican lawyers group ANAD filed a complaint with the U.S. NAO on behalf of an independent union that had long represented employees of the Mexican fisheries ministry. The union lost its representation rights when the fisheries ministry merged with a larger ministry of environment and natural resources where a progovernment union held bargaining rights.

The submission alleged that the new ministry and the labor authorities improperly revoked the Pesca union's registration and granted recognition and favorable treatment to the larger, progovernment union at the environment and natural resources ministry. Complainants also charged that the participation in the tripartite *Junta de Conciliación y Arbitraje* of union representatives who might have a conflict of interest in ruling on disputes with another union violated the NAALC's requirement for impartial labor tribunals.

The U.S. NAO accepted the petition for review in August 1996. It held a public hearing in Washington, D.C., in December 1996, with testimony from representatives of the submitting U.S. and Mexican organizations, union representatives and counsel from the contending unions, interested public citizens, and from a representative of the Mexican labor department.

As part of its review, the U.S. NAO also commissioned special studies on labor law enforcement in the federal sector.

In January 1997, the U.S. NAO issued a report[8] that recommended Ministerial Consultations on relevant legal doctrines in Mexico, including the effects on Mexican labor law of constitutional provisions assuring freedom of association, "for the purpose of examining the relationship between and the effect of international treaties, such as the International Labour Organization (ILO) Convention 87, and constitutional provisions on freedom of association on the national labor laws of Mexico." Mexico agreed to engage in consultations in March 1997.

No specific follow-up program was devised in the *Pesca* union case, because it became unnecessary. A series of court decisions found in favor of the independent union. In related cases, the trade union monopoly in the public employee sector was found unconstitutional by the Supreme Court of Mexico.[9] In the end, registration was restored to the *Pesca* union. It has continued to try to organize the merged ministry in competition with the bigger union. It has not been successful in this, but the union and its leaders still play a role in the independent labor movement in Mexico.

Maxi-Switch (U.S. NAO Case No. 9602). The Communications Workers of America (CWA) filed a complaint with the U.S. NAO in October 1996 on behalf of the Mexican telephone workers' union, the Sindicato de Telefonistas de la República Mexicana (STRM). The submission alleged that workers' attempt to organize a union affiliated with the STRM at the Maxi-Switch facility in Cananea, Sonora, was thwarted by a collusive "protection contract" between the company and another union affiliated with the dominant union federation. The submission argued that the contract was made without employees' knowledge or consent, and that the local *Junta de Conciliación y Arbitraje* improperly denied registration to the STRM group.

In December 1996, the U.S. NAO scheduled a public hearing on the matter in Tucson, Arizona, on April 18, 1997. Testimony was to be received from Maxi-Switch workers and from representatives of the CWA and the STRM. However, on April 15, 1997, the CWA withdrew the submission at the request of the STRM because the labor authorities in Mexico took steps to resolve the matter to the satisfaction of the STRM. The public hearing was canceled.

Pregnancy Testing in the Maquiladora (U.S. Case No. 9701). Two U.S.–based human rights groups, Human Rights Watch and the International Labor Rights Fund, along with the ANAD of Mexico, filed a complaint with the NAO of the United States in May 1997 alleging "a pattern of widespread, state-tolerated sex discrimination against prospective and actual female workers in the *maquiladora* sector along the Mexico-U.S. border."[10] The submission alleged a common practice of requiring pregnancy testing of all female job applicants and denying employment to those whose test results are positive. The submission also said that employers pressure employees who become pregnant to leave their jobs.

The submitters argued that the practice by employers and the failure of the labor authorities to combat it—sometimes by omission, sometimes by overt support for the employers' discriminatory policy—violates Mexico's obligations under the NAALC. The complaint sought a U.S. NAO review, public hearings in cities along the Mexico-U.S. border, and the formation of an Evaluation Committee of Experts to report on employment practices related to pregnancy in Canada, Mexico, and the United States.[11]

In January 1998, the U.S. NAO issued a report confirming widespread pregnancy testing that discriminates against women workers. Concluding ministerial consultations in October 1998, the labor secretaries of Canada, Mexico, and the United States approved a program of workshops for government enforcement officials, outreach to women workers, and an international conference on gender discrimination issues. These programs have been under way, most recently with an international conference on women workers held in Mexico in March 1999, and with "outreach sessions" for women workers held along the U.S.-Mexico border in Texas. In the meantime, some U.S. companies in the *maquiladora* zones announced they would halt pregnancy testing, and the federal government has prohibited pregnancy testing of women applying for employment in federal ministries. The pregnancy testing case may still give rise to the first ECE under the NAALC.

Echlin/ITAPSA (U.S. NAO Case No. 9703; Canada NAO Case No. 98-1). A broad coalition of more than thirty U.S., Canadian, and Mexican unions and human rights groups filed two separate NAALC complaints, one with the U.S. NAO in late 1997 and one with the Canadian NAO (the first case filed in Canada) in mid-1998. The submission involves efforts by an independent FAT-affiliated union in Mexico to supplant a progovernment

CTM union at a Mexico City auto parts factory called ITAPSA owned by U.S.–based Echlin Corporation. The complaints also cite health and safety violations involving exposure to asbestos and other toxic substances without adequate personal protective equipment.

Concerned in part about health and safety hazards, a majority of ITAPSA workers sought to enlist the independent union STIMAHCS to represent them. The CTM launched a campaign of threats and violence against STIMAHCS supporters. Company management sided with the incumbent union, firing several independent unionists and hiring new employees sent by the CTM to break up the independent organizing drive. Events culminated on the day of an election between the two unions, which was held not by secret ballot but by an open declaration in front of company and CTM officials. On the day of the election dozens of men armed with sticks, chains, bars, and metal rods from the CTM were given free run of plant premises, where they threatened to kill any workers who voted for STIMAHCS.

The election, like reinstatement appeals from fired workers, were all conducted by a tripartite Conciliation and Arbitration Board (CAB) made up of government, employer, and labor representatives. The labor officials on the CAB handling the Echlin case were all from the CTM, creating an inherent conflict of interest.

Both the U.S. and Canadian NAOs held public hearings in the two Echlin cases where workers recounted these events and supporters voiced outrage. U.S. unionists organized protests at Echlin stockholders' meetings. Unions were also instrumental in convincing the state legislature of Connecticut, Echlin's corporate home, not to pass legislation sought by Echlin management protecting Echlin against a hostile takeover. Such a takeover was accomplished by Dana Corp., the largest U.S. auto parts manufacturer, and the union coalition entered negotiations with Dana to resolve the Echlin dispute. In the meantime, the U.S. and Canadian NAOs issued hard-hitting reports in 1998 and 1999 on the apparent violations of workers' rights, and recommended ministerial consultations on the matter. Following these developments, the labor ministers of the 3 NAALC countries were reportedly close to completing a ministerial agreement with an extensive follow-up program.[12]

TAESA (U.S. NAO Case No. 9901). On November 10, 1999, the AFA and ASSA filed a new complaint on violations of freedom of association, minimum employment standards, and health and safety rules affecting flight attendants at TAESA, a low-cost airline that flies to a number of U.S. cities including Oakland and Chicago. Some 100 flight attendants who supported ASSA were fired by the airline when they voted in favor of ASSA and against an incumbent, government-affiliated union. The vote was taken at company headquarters in a procedure where each worker had to declare support for ASSA or for the official government and employer-sponsored union in the presence of company and union officials, who openly took notes on how workers voted. Reprisals were taken almost immediately against ASSA supporters. The complaint also cited the company's violations of overtime, pension and wage requirements, and health and safety violations affecting both flight attendants and the flying public.

In January 2000, the U.S. NAO accepted the case for review and scheduled a public hearing in Washington, D.C. At the March 2000, hearing, the presidents of the two unions, joined by dismissed flight attendants, labor lawyers, and the AFL-CIO's Mexico representative, testified on the election, minimum labor standards violations, and health and safety hazards. Witnesses presented compelling and disturbing testimony about threats and intimidation during the election, excessive overtime and lack of emergency training, unsafe passenger cabin conditions, and company failure to make timely and complete payments for workers' health insurance, pension, and housing funds.

The U.S. NAO issued its report in the case in May 2000, crediting workers' accounts of serious violations of freedom of association, minimum labor standards, and occupational health and safety. Ministerial consultations were recommended, and labor ministers moved to design a program of public forums in the United States and in Mexico that would include participation by national and international trade union leaders.

Autotrim/Breed Technologies (U.S. NAO Case No. 2001-01). In July 2000, a coalition of more than twenty trade unions, NGOs, and student organizations filed a complaint with the U.S. NAO over events at the U.S.-based corporation Breed Technologies' Autotrim plant in the Mexican state of Tamaulipas. Autotrim supplies wheel covers and gearshift covers for General Motors, Ford, and Daimler-Chrysler. Petitioners included current and former workers at the plant, the Coalition for Justice in the Maquiladoras, Mexican labor, human rights and religious organizations, the AFL-CIO and several affiliated unions, a number of worker health and safety support groups, and students from human rights clinics at St. Mary's Law School in San Antonio, Texas and Columbia University Law School in New York.

The complaint focused on health and safety matters in the Autotrim plant, citing widespread illnesses and injuries from exposure to toxic materials and muscular-skeletal disorders caused by poor ergonomics. Illnesses and injuries are underreported and undercompensated, said the submitters. The complaint charges that the Mexican government fails to monitor compliance and investigate suspected violations, fails to require record-keeping and reporting, fails to seek appropriate sanctions or remedies, fails to guarantee access to tribunals for enforcement, and fails to ensure that all proceedings for the enforcement of labor law are fair, equitable, transparent, and are not unnecessarily complicated or involve unwarranted delays regarding the fulfillment of obligations stemming from the NAALC.

A written report by the U.S. NAO was scheduled for issuance in 2001.

Cases Involving Alleged Workers' Rights Violations in the United States

Sprint (Mexico NAO Case No. 9501). The *Sindicato de Telefonistas de la República Mexicana* (STRM) filed a complaint with the NAO of Mexico in February 1995, on the sudden closing of a Spanish-language telemarketing facility of the Sprint Corp. in San Francisco, California. The complaint alleged that the shutdown was motivated by antiunion bias. The STRM collaborated with its U.S. counterpart, the Communications Workers of America (CWA), which was the union seeking to organize the Sprint facility.

The NAO of Mexico accepted the submission for review and issued a report on May 31, 1995, concluding that it was "concerned about the effectiveness of certain measures intended to guarantee [freedom of association and the right of workers to organize]" and "possible problems in the effective application of U.S. law," and recommended ministerial consultations in the matter. Ensuing consultations resulted in an agreement among the labor secretaries of Mexico and the United States and the labor minister of Canada in February 1996, calling for a three-part program:

1. A public forum to be held in San Francisco, California.

2. A special report by the Secretariat on the effects of sudden plant closings on the principle of freedom of association and protection of the right to organize in Canada, Mexico, and the United States.

3. Updating by the Secretary of Labor of the United States to the Secretary of Labor of Mexico on developments in proceedings under U.S. domestic labor law of the case that prompted the submission and the ministerial consultations.

In February 1996, the public forum called for by the ministers was held in San Francisco with presentations by workers affected by the plant closing, by union representatives from the STRM, the CWA, and unionists from Germany and Great Britain. Testimony was also offered by a law professor speaking on behalf of Sprint and by academic analysts.

In December 1996, the U.S. National Labor Relations Board (NLRB) ruled that the plant closing by Sprint was motivated by antiunion animus, and ordered the employer to rehire affected workers into openings in other divisions of the company and to provide back pay for lost wages. Sprint appealed the NLRB decision to a U.S. federal court of appeals.

In April 1997, the Secretariat issued a 140-page special report titled *Plant Closings and Labor Rights*. The report explained legal frameworks and union organizing systems in the U.S., Canada, and Mexico, and reviewed administrative tribunal and court decisions in each of the three countries dealing with plant closings and threats of plant closings to resist union organizing efforts by workers. The Secretariat found that such antiunion tactics are widespread in the United States but less prevalent in the other countries. In Canada, this is due to stronger enforcement. In Mexico, it is due to differences in the union organizing system, which rarely involves an election "campaign" where threats of closing or decisions to close are made.[13]

In November 1997, the court of appeals reversed the NLRB's decision that had found Sprint liable for an unlawful plant closing motivated by antiunion bias. The court ruled in favor of the company, finding that the closing was motivated by legitimate business considerations, not by antiunionism.[14] This decision effectively foreclosed any further action under the NAALC, since the agreement does not provide a means of overturning or reversing a ruling by domestic labor authorities.

Washington State Apple Industry (Mexico NAO Case No. 9802). A coalition of Mexican trade unions and farm worker organizations filed a wide-ranging NAALC complaint in May 1998, alleging failure of U.S. labor law to protect workers' rights in the Washington State apple industry. The submission cited the lack of legal protection for farm worker union organizing, widespread health and safety violations, discrimination against migrant workers, and employers' use of threats and intimidation in recent union representation elections in apple packing and shipping facilities.

The *Unión Nacional de Trabajadores* (UNT), a new independent labor federation, the *Frente Auténtico del Trabajo* (FAT), another independent labor group, and the *Frente Democrático Campesino* (FDC) of Mexico filed the complaint with the Mexican NAO. In preparing the submission, they collaborated with the U.S. Teamsters Union and the United Farm Workers Union, which are conducting organizing campaigns in the apple sector. The complaint called on the Mexican government to pursue multiple stages of review, consultation, evaluation, and arbitration under the NAALC.

The NAALC apple workers' submission is the broadest case yet filed under the NAALC, citing labor law violations and inadequate enforcement in areas encompassed in 7 of the NAALC's 11 labor principles. Most earlier cases addressed union organizing issues. The Washington State apple industry complaint covers the right to organize, collective bargaining, minimum labor standards, nondiscrimination in employment, job safety and health, workers' compensation, and migrant worker protection. The filing generated a burst of publicity calling attention to conditions of migrant workers and the opportunity for advocacy presented by the NAALC.[15]

The NAO of Mexico accepted the Washington State apple case for review in August 1998. In December 1998, the NAO of Mexico held its first-ever hearing on a NAALC complaint. It was not a public hearing in the quasilegal style of the U.S. and Canadian NAOs, but rather an "informative session" under the Mexican NAO procedural guidelines conducted in private in a roundtable setting. A delegation of workers from packing sheds and orchards in Washington State attended the hearing and presented direct testimony about pesticide poisoning, discharge for union activity, minimum wage violations, discrimination in the workers' compensation system, discrimination against migrant workers, and other violations of workers' rights.

The hearing garnered widespread publicity in the news media of both the United States and Mexico.[16] The NAO of Mexico was to issue its report in February 1999, but the report was delayed by personnel changes in the department of labor and the NAO. The report was finally issued in August 1999, and on August 20 Mexico's secretary of labor formally requested ministerial consultations with the U.S. secretary of labor. This development sparked a new round of publicity and related attention to the conditions of migrant workers in the industry.[17]

In April 2000, the governments announced a program of events resulting from the consultations, including a public forum in the apple-growing region for workers, unions, employers, and government officials and an "outreach" effort by labor law enforcement personnel.

Cases Involving Alleged Workers' Rights Violations in Canada

McDonald's (U.S. NAO Case No. 9803). Joined by the Quebec Federation of Labor and the International Labor Rights Fund, the Teamsters Union and its Quebec affiliates filed a NAALC complaint in October 1998, on the closure of a McDonald's restaurant in St-Hubert, Quebec shortly before the union was certified to bargain for workers there. This was the first NAALC case implicating labor law in a Canadian jurisdiction.

Submitters argued that McDonald's used loopholes and delaying tactics to string out union representation proceedings before the Quebec labor board for one year. The company prolonged proceedings by arguing falsely that the restaurant was part of a larger chain where workers transferred among different facilities. McDonald's routinely appealed decisions in the union's favor. Finally it shut the restaurant when the union certification was about to be issued.

Although Quebec labor law is generally favorable to workers and unions, it is impotent dealing with antiunion workplace closures. The Quebec courts evolved a doctrine allowing employers to close facilities to avoid unionization with impunity—the only jurisdiction in North America that does so.[18]

In December 1998, the U.S. NAO announced that it accepted the McDonald's case for review.[19] In April 1999, the petitioners withdrew their complaint following an agreement by the Quebec government to undertake a special study of the question of antiunion plant workplace closures in the context of an overall review of the Quebec Labor Code.[20]

Overview

Some trade union and NGO critics have called the NAALC weak and toothless and have disparaged the results. They argue that there has not been discernible progress in domestic labor law enforcement to protect workers' rights. They point to the absence of common minimum standards and specific remedies for workers whose rights are violated, such as reinstatement of workers dismissed for union activity or recognition of independent unions.[21]

At the other extreme, some employer critics see the NAALC providing a powerful new weapon for trade unionists and anticorporate campaigners, citing the submission procedure and the attendant publicity and public scrutiny of employer conduct.[22] Commenting on the Washington State apple industry complaint, an industry spokesman said "unions on both sides of the border are abusing the NAFTA process in an effort to expand their power....NAFTA's labor side agreement is an open invitation for specific labor disputes to be raised into an international question" and "could open the door to a host of costly and frivolous complaints against U.S. employers." He said, "the labor section of NAFTA should be revised or industry support for future trade agreements will be severely eroded."[23]

The U.S. Council for International Business (CIB) argued that the NAALC "has unduly emphasized [submissions] over positive cooperative activities...it sets the wrong tone and focus." The U.S. CIB said that NAO acceptance of a submission should be an "exceptional act" after all domestic legal procedures have been exhausted and that the sole results of submissions should be "joint studies and technical cooperation and assistance." Furthermore, citing the practice of the ILO and the Organization for Economic Cooperation and Development (OECD), the U.S. employer council argued that the name of a specific company should not be part of the record in any submission and that NAOs should not hold public hearings because they are "too confrontational."[24]

Mexican employer groups criticized the "publicity" surrounding NAALC cases in connection with "premature" acceptance of cases. They called public hearings by the U.S. NAO "contrary to Mexican sovereignty" and argued that no submission or related report should contain the name of a specific company.[25]

Between the contrasting critical perspectives of labor and business, many academic analysts see substantive, positive results in the NAALC's addressing of workers' rights in the region. The NAFTA Committee of the

Industrial Relations Research Association, for example, said "the NAALC has had several positive effects that make it worth exploring further as a mechanism to shed light on labor rights violations in the three countries." The Committee cited improved ability of policymakers to understand labor relations practices and laws, valuable research reports from the Secretariat, the broad subject matter of the 11 Labor Principles, opportunities for unions to collaborate across borders with each other and with advocacy groups outside of the labor movement, and the positive effects of "sunshine" generated by the publicity surrounding NAALC cases.[26]

Other analysts have noted that "Despite the skepticism of critics, the NAALC and the institutions it has spawned have had some modest successes in labour's favor. Although the agreement contains procedures that are far from ideal, they do have the capacity to advance the struggle for labour rights."[27] Another commented, "It is clear that the NAALC's primary contribution to the transnational labor rights regime to date has been to create a forum for regional public awareness of labor rights issues....Despite its limitations, the NAALC stands as a groundbreaking step toward regional collaboration in the development of labor rights."[28]

The NAALC has many positive features for labor rights advocates. First, it establishes for the first time in any international trade agreement the principle of a labor rights-trade linkage, backed up by potential economic sanctions even if under limited circumstances. This fundamental step should not be deprecated, especially in light of scant progress on a "social clause" in other trade and investment regimes.[29]

The NAALC's Labor Principles set forth a broad range of labor rights and labor standards that fall under the Agreement's obligations. It does not limit consideration to "core" labor standards such as those adopted by the ILO in its June 1998 Declaration (freedom of association, forced labor, child labor, and nondiscrimination) but goes further to take up such matters as occupational safety and health, minimum wages, and conditions for migrant workers.

There are no "standing" requirements for filing NAALC claims. Trade unions or employers can raise complaints, obviously, but so can human rights organizations, community coalitions, student groups, and even private individuals with no "interest" other than concern for workers' rights. There are no citizenship requirements, either. Any person from any country can file a NAALC complaint with the NAO of any country. This makes for a flexible, accessible instrument that labor rights advocates can creatively exploit as they build a movement to support workers in the three NAFTA countries.

Sometimes the mere threat of a NAALC complaint gets action. In 1996, for example, the conservative provincial government in Alberta announced plans to privatize health and safety standards enforcement. Public employee unions and their allies responded with a promise to file a submission under the NAALC. The government then dropped its proposal.[30]

In other cases, the pressure of international scrutiny got results on the ground—recognition of the independent union in the Maxi-Switch case, the recognition and survival of the independent union in the *Pesca* case, the halting in some *maquiladora* factories of pregnancy testing of female employees, and others.

Even where no immediate concrete results are apparent, the claims procedure and its public hearings, public reports, and attendant publicity have dramatically increased public awareness and concern over labor standards in North America. The Secretariat's 1997 special report *Plant Closings and Labor Rights*, a product of ministerial consultations in the *Sprint* case, is a valuable analysis comparing labor law in the three countries on an issue critical for trade relations. On the political front, the activity connected to the NAALC claims procedure created a powerful record that helped persuade Congress to refuse new fast-track negotiating authority for President Clinton because the fast-track legislation proposed by the Republican leadership failed to address issues of workers' rights and labor standards.

The NAALC and International Labor Solidarity

Another key outgrowth of the NAFTA labor side accord and its complaint mechanism is an unprecedented increase in exchange, communication, and collaboration among labor rights advocates and labor researchers at the trinational level. Since a submission about workers' rights violations in one country must be submitted with the NAO of another country, submitters are encouraged to seek partners in the other country to help pursue the case in the other country's NAO review process. Nearly every submission has been signed by a coalition of organizations based in at least two countries, and sometimes all three.

Even before the NAFTA, the United Electrical (UE) Workers Union and the Mexican FAT fashioned a 1992 strategic organizing alliance. Much like the FAT, the UE is a small, independent union outside the main national labor federation but with strong local unions in workplaces around the country and a national contract with General Electric. The Teamsters Union—historically distinct from the UE's traditions but brought closer by the reform leadership of then-president Ron Carey—also worked with the FAT without the formality of a written agreement. The two U.S. unions helped FAT organizing attempts in *maquiladora* factories of General Electric and Honeywell. The assistance flows both ways, though. In 1995, FAT organizers helped the UE win an organizing victory at a large manufacturing plant in Milwaukee, Wisconsin, with a high complement of immigrant Mexican workers.

The CWA has developed close ties with the STRM, the national telephone workers union of Mexico. The two unions have held a series of joint educational seminars and coordinated strategy in dealing with moves by AT&T, Sprint, and other U.S. telecommunications companies into the Mexican market.

The U.S. ladies' garment and men's clothing workers' unions, now joined in UNITE, have carried out joint programs with unions in Mexico and Canada. In one "twin plant" setting with unionized shops in Eagle Pass, Texas, and Piedras Negras, Coahuila, for example, the UNITE local collaborated with its Mexican counterpart to achieve key contract gains in both factories.

Mexican unionists who filed the Washington State apple workers' complaint in Mexico came to Washington's apple valleys to help the Teamsters union in National Labor Relations Board (NLRB) election campaigns in January 1998. In December 1998, the Mexican supporters hosted a delegation of Washington State apple workers who presented their case in the first "informative session" held by the NAO of Mexico. While in Mexico, the U.S. workers met with many trade union, farm worker, and human rights organizations, with widespread press coverage.

The coalition of unions in the Echlin case before both the U.S. and Canadian NAOs has created a lasting forum for labor rights advocacy as the case continues to advance. Autoworkers, steelworkers, machinists, and electrical workers from the three countries are all involved in the case and pressing the NAOs for what may be the first case susceptible to arbitration, on the basis of a health and safety claim.

Mexican workers, union organizers, and labor lawyers testified in all the public hearings held by the U.S. and Canadian NAOs. Migrant Mexican workers joined Mexican-American and Anglo-American workers and union organizers in the first hearing of the Mexican NAO. Labor rights advocates from Canada, Mexico, and the United States spoke out at public forums held by the three governments as part of their ministerial consultations.

In the recent TAESA case, leaders of flight attendants' unions from the United States and Mexico agreed that collaborating on the NAALC complaint and the public hearing "brought us closer together than we've ever been." A dismissed flight attendant who testified at the hearing declared, "It's tremendous that we have an international forum where we can shine a spotlight on the abuses we have suffered." Another stated, "It means a lot that I can go back and tell my colleagues that the U.S. government took us seriously and is studying our complaints."[31]

The TAESA experience is a capsule version of a bigger phenomenon. Working on NAALC complaints has required careful coordination to shape common positions. As those involved get to know each other better, contacts proliferate. Trade unionists and union economists, lawyers, and other staffers from the three NAALC countries now regularly send delegates to each other's conventions, conferences, and other activities. They are trading bargaining information, translating papers and studies, and finding new ways to link their movements. While it is not *only* the labor side agreement driving these actions, the NAALC creates a framework for concrete work—developing strategies, drafting submissions, planning testimony, writing press releases, setting up demonstrations, meeting with government officials, and participating in the Agreement's cooperative activities program and events that flow from Ministerial Consultations. All the time, social actors are learning about each other's countries and labor movements.

What we are witnessing is a deepening of labor rights advocacy in North America. Before NAFTA and the NAALC, cross-border solidarity took place at a thin, high level of bureaucratic meetings among top union officials and occasional letters of support to workers in struggle. Now trade union leaders and activists up and down the line are working together in concrete projects dealing with the effects of economic integration in their continent.

A review of experience under the NAALC is just the first chapter in what will surely be a lengthy saga recounting the promotion of workers' rights in connection with expanded trade. The story will not be one of straight-line advances, either. The forces arrayed against workers' interests are powerful and do not easily yield to trade union demands for greater voice in trade and investment matters.

Looming negotiations on a Free Trade Agreement of the Americas (FTAA) raise the stakes for a labor rights-trade linkage. In the FTAA context, the experience and the views of labor movements in Mercosur countries (Brazil, most significantly) and other hemispheric bodies will be important. The NAALC by itself will not be the only example of workers and their allies grappling with the effects of global trade and investment on their unions and their wages and working conditions. However, it is an example that provides valuable experience and insights into fashioning a strong social charter to advance workers' rights in the 21st century.[32]

Notes

1 *North American Free Trade Agreement*, Dec. 17, 1992, U.S.-Can.-Mex., 32 I.L.M. 605.

2 See, for example, Molly Moore, "Mexican Farmhands Accuse U.S. Firms: Panel Hears Washington Apple Pickers," *Washington Post*, December 3, 1998, p. A36.

3 *See* U.S. NAO, *Public Report of Review*, October 12, 1994, pp. 28-30.

4 *Ibid.*, pp. 30-31.

5 Author interview with GE manager, Fairfield, Connecticut, October 8, 1997.

6 *See* U.S. National Administrative Office, *Public Report of Review*, April 11, 1995.

7 *See* U.S. NAO, Submission No. 940003 *Follow-Up Report*, December 4, 1996, p. 10.

8 See U.S. NAO, *Public Report of Review*, NAALC Submission No. 9601, January 27, 1997.

9 *See* Sam Dillon, "Mexico: Gain for Independent Unions," *The New York Times*, May 13, 1999, p. A16.

10 *See* U.S. NAO Case No. 9701, *Submission Concerning Pregnancy-Based Sex Discrimination in Mexico's Maquiladora Sector*, p. 4.

11 *Ibid.*, pp. 37-39.

12 Author interview with NAALC officials, January 20, 2001.

13 It should be noted that the Secretariat's study focused on plant closures and threats in the context of efforts to unionize a nonunion workplace. The terms of reference under which the Secretariat carried out its study did not instruct it to address the broader issue of plant closures and threats in the collective bargaining context, where closures or threats might be used to extract concessions from workers already represented by a trade union. The terms of reference can be found on page 15 of the Secretariat's report.

14 See *Sprint Corporation v. NLRB*, 129 F.3d. 1276 (D.C. Circuit 1997).

15 See, for example, Steven Greenhouse, "Mexicans Were Denied U.S. Rights, Suit Says," *New York Times*, May 28, 1998, p. A18; Ken Guggenheim, "U.S. Unions Find New Tool," *Seattle Post-Intelligencer*, May 29, 1998, p. C1; Raul Trejo Delarbre, "Casablanca Laboral," *La Crónica*, June 1, 1998.

16 *See* Molly Moore, "Mexican Farmhands Accuse U.S. Firms: Panel Hears Washington Apple Pickers," *Washington Post*, December 3, 1998, p. A36; Elizabeth Velasco, "Trabajadores agrícolas denuncian explotación en EU," *La Jornada*, December 3, 1998, p. 41; Arturo Gomez Salgado, "Denuncian migrantes violaciones laborales," *El Financiero*, December 3, 1998, p. 19.

17 *See*, for example, Arthur C. Gorlick, "State's Apple Hands Abused, Mexico Says: Complaint Could Lead to Special Investigation and Even Sanctions," *Seattle Post-Intelligencer*, September 9, 1999, p. A1; "Farm Workers *Are* the Subsidy" lead editorial, *Seattle Post-Intelligencer*, September 19, 1999 (beginning: "Mexico's accusation that Washington tolerates abuse of farm workers will be debated...but there's no debating that some agricultural sectors owe their success to systematic exploitation of migrant workers").

18 *See* reference to Quebec law and jurisprudence in Secretariat of the Commission for Labor Cooperation, *Plant Closings and Labor Rights* (1997), p. 34.

19 *See* Toronto Star, *U.S. labour body probes anti-union move in Quebec*, December 21, 1998, p. D3 (Associated Press wire story).

20 *See* letter from Claude Melançon, Teamsters Canada attorney, to Irasema Garza, U.S. NAO Secretary, April 14, 1999.

21 See, for example, Jerome I. Levinson, *NAFTA's Labor Agreement: Lessons from the First Three Years*, Institute for Policy Studies and International Labor Rights Fund, November 12, 1996 (calling the NAALC "fatally flawed").

A Glass Half Full

22   See letters from employers in NAALC cases on file with the U.S. NAO, Washington, D.C.

23   *See* Evelyn Iritani, "Mexico Charges Upset Apple Cart in U.S.," *Los Angeles Times*, August 20, 1998, p. D1.

24   See *ibid.*, *Public Comment* of Abraham Katz, President, U.S. Council for International Business.

25   See *ibid.*, *Public Comment* of Juan Gallardo on behalf of these organizations.

26   See *Making Free Trade More Fair: Developments in Protecting Labor Rights*, Final Report of the IRRA-NAFTA Committee for 1996-1997. Anil Verma of the University of Toronto served as Committee Convenor; also serving on the Committee were Maria Lorena Cook of Cornell University, Enrique de la Garza of the Universidad Autonoma de Mexico, Morley Gunderson of the University of Toronto, Russell Smith of Washburn University, and Mark Thompson of the University of British Columbia.

27   *See* Roy J. Adams and Parbudyal Singh, "Early Experience with NAFTA's Labor Side Agreement," *Comparative Labor Law Journal*, vol. 18 (Winter 1997), pp. 161-181.

28   *See* Sarah H. Cleveland, "Global Labor Rights and the Alien Torts Claims Act," *Texas Law Review*, vol. 76 (May 1998), pp. 1533-1579.

29   See, for example, the decision of the World Trade Organization (WTO) at its December 1996 Ministerial Conference renouncing any linkage between labor rights and WTO trade disciplines, referring all labor matters to the International Labour Organization (ILO).

30   See Allan Chambers, "Privatization of Labor Rules Raises Fears: Law May Face NAFTA Challenge," *Edmonton Journal*, September 6, 1996, p. 1; "Province's Halt of Privatization Plan Ends Looming NAFTA Complaint," *Inside NAFTA*, December 25, 1996, p. 14.

31   Author interview, March 23, 2000 (the author served as counsel to the two unions in the case).

CHAPTER SEVEN

The Right to Education and Human Rights Education

Richard Pierre Claude*

In this chapter I will undertake three tasks. First, I will review the origins of Article 26 of the Universal Declaration of Human Rights which, in its core provision, says that "Everyone has the right to education." Second, I will discuss education *about* human rights in the light of Article 26, and finally, I will profile some of the creative programs which today seek to implement such education in projects under way in the context of the "United Nations Decade for Human Rights Education, 1995-2004," as designated by the General Assembly a few years ago.

The Right to Education in the UDHR

World War II led to the greatest effort in history to promote human rights. The reaction against totalitarian aggression and genocide produced support for the founding of the United Nations, and the U.N. Charter of 1945 in Article 55 says that by virtue of joining the U.N., member states solemnly promise (among other things) to *"promote...universal respect for, and observance of human rights and fundamental freedoms...."* Article 56, correspondingly pledges members to the same objectives. These articles constitute the cornerstone of later U.N. efforts to project human rights on a global basis.[1] Nevertheless, while at the same time binding member states to respect and promote human rights, the U.N. Charter does not actually define them.

Because of the general language of the U.N. Charter on human rights, a widespread debate in the mid-1940s ensued regarding whether the Charter's wording on the subject needed further clarification, or whether, as some argued, no time should be wasted on wishful thinking about rights for everyone and visions of civilizing a brutal world. Despite such skepticism, the first member states at the U.N.'s inception in 1945 quickly turned to efforts to specify the meaning of the Charter's references to human rights and called for the drafting of an International Bill of Rights.[2] The initial result was the Universal Declaration of Human Rights (UDHR), adopted by the U.N. General Assembly on December 10, 1948, without any negative votes.[3] This declaration of 30 articles affirms such traditional civil liberties as privacy and the right to seek and disseminate information, freedom of speech, press, assembly and religious liberty, as well as rights exercised in the economic, social and cultural areas, such as the right to education, to work, to join trade unions, to health care, and to participate freely in the cultural life of the community.

Discussion about the importance of education as a requisite for post-War "reconstruction" emerged in the earliest work of the United Nations Human Rights Commission. That body was first set up in 1946 by the Economic Social and Cultural Council of the U.N., to make recommendations for promoting respect and observance of human rights. The 18 members began their work on January 27, 1947, and Mrs. Eleanor Roosevelt was elected to chair the Commission.[4] The Commission's Rapporteur, Dr. Charles Malik (Lebanon) said that from the beginning all the Commission members knew that their task of composing a declaration of human rights was itself an educational undertaking. He said: We "must elaborate a general Declaration of Human Rights defining in succinct terms the fundamental rights and freedoms of [everyone] which, according to Article 55 of the Charter, the United Nations *must* promote. This responsible setting forth of fundamental rights will exert a potent doctrinal and moral and educational influence on the minds and ways..." of people everywhere.[5] The same view is embodied in the language of the Preamble to the Universal Declaration saying the instrument was designed as a common standard of achievement for all peoples and all nations and therefore "every individual and every organ of society," keeping this Declaration in mind, "shall strive by teaching and education to promote respect for these rights and freedoms...."

Between June 1947, when the Secretariat's draft outline[6] of a Bill of Human Rights was first considered by the Drafting Committee[7] of the Commission on Human Rights,[8] and December 1948, when the General Assembly adopted and proclaimed the Declaration as the first part of the Bill of Human Rights, an immense amount of work was done. For example, the text prepared by the Drafting Committee and revised by the Commission was sent to every member government for its comments and suggestions.

The draft Declaration, as completed by the Commission on Human Rights, was sent to the General Assembly convening in Paris in September 1948. There, despite the exhaustive examination already given every article during the preceding two years, the Assembly's Social, Humanitarian and Cultural Committee ("The Third Committee") composed of most U.N. representatives, tore it apart once more and revised it line by line and even word by word.[9]

Regarding the dynamics of the process producing the Universal Declaration of Human Rights, U.N. records and memoirs of participants show that Mrs. Roosevelt, as Chairman of the Human Rights Commission, placed substantial responsibility on the agency's Secretariat and its Director, the Canadian Professor John P. Humphrey. At the beginning of the Commission's work he prepared a 408-page compilation of rights and liberties provisions of national laws worldwide and a draft outline for a bill of rights with 48 suggested articles, referred to as the "Secretariat Draft."[10] According to Director Humphrey, the text of the UDHR had no one dominant progenitor or inspired authors, as he said, "in the sense that Jefferson was the father of the American Declaration of Independence." Nevertheless, in his autobiography, Humphrey claimed that the first early Secretariat draft was largely his responsibility. His role in specifying a proposed right to education is important because it is clustered with other socioeconomic rights, seen as problematic by some delegates leery of expanding the menu of safeguards beyond civil and political rights. A social democrat, Humphrey said he guessed it unlikely "that economic, and social rights would have been included in the final text if I had not included them in mine." One not given to idle boasting, Humphrey said this was true because "once the Secretariat had included something in its draft, it was very difficult for a government to object to its being there."[11] This account is confirmed by Professor Johannes Morsink of Drew University in his book, *The Universal Declaration of Human Rights, Origins, Drafting and Intent*. Morsink rejects most people's assumption that the presence of social, economic and cultural rights in the Declaration was the result of the Marxist voice of the communist delegations. Rather, from the start the Declaration included these rights because Humphrey (who wrote the first draft) was intimately acquainted with the socialist tradition of Latin America. And what Humphrey had put in, the delegations from Latin America made sure stayed in the Declaration.[12]

In Professor Humphrey's draft, the right to education specified that primary schooling should be compulsory and free. Following the introduction and consideration of this proposal, the French delegate, Professor René Cassin, in his typically analytical fashion, summarized Commission points of consensus and debating items relating to education. He said that in most of the proceedings, in fact, the right to education had been hardly contested at all. However, he noted that: "Three points...had attracted contention: that education should be free, that it should be compulsory, and the question of the influence of parents."[13]

On all of these points, Latin American votes were invariably positive and usually decisive. Going far to explain this consensus is the fact that only the previous year Hemispheric countries meeting in Mexico City had participated in formulating United Nations Educational, Scientific and Cultural Organization (UNESCO) standards on education. With enthusiasm, the delegate from Venezuela, Miss Zuloaga said the definition of education adopted by UNESCO at its conference in Mexico in 1947 should be retained, emphasizing free and compulsory education because it was seen to be the sole means of ending the illiteracy which was still widespread in the world.[14] The upshot of this debate is found in Section 1 of Article 26 which says, "Everyone has the right to education. Education shall be free, at least in the elementary and fundamental stages. Elementary education shall be compulsory." Again reflecting UNESCO standards, the Section goes on to say "Technical and professional education shall be made generally available and higher education shall be equally accessible to all on the basis of merit."

Before the Third Committee of the General Assembly, recollections of Nazi oppression came to life in debates over the final provisions of the Education Article; that is, Section 3 specifies that "Parents have a prior right to choose the kind of education that shall be given to their children." On this measure, the Lebanese, Belgians, and Dutch led the battle for parental rights bearing on education. Thus the Dutch delegate reminded others of a fundamental principle, namely, "The family could not be replaced by any public or private institution which contributed to education." He said, "This idea might seem a truism had it not been for recent experience...with Nazi Germany, where the Hitler Youth deprived parents of control over their children. This provided an experience which should never be permitted to recur."[15] The specter of fascism was also invoked when the Commission opened an opportunity to NGOs to comment. Ms. Schaefer for the International Union of Catholic Women's Leagues observed that if the right to education is said to require free and compulsory elementary education, these standards by themselves could lead to "a recurrence of situations such as that which prevailed in Germany under Hitler." She meant that state responsibilities must be balanced by recognition of parental duties to educate their children as they saw fit."[16] In a similar vein, but addressing a broader topic, Mr. Bienenfeld for the World Jewish Congress noted that fascist countries had historically acted as if they recognized a right to education, but importantly, "the doctrines on which that education had been founded had led to two world wars. Thus any formulation of a right to education should define the spirit in which future generations were to be educated."[17]

The Universal Declaration shows that its framers realized that education is not value neutral. The Soviets, being most ideologically sensitive, were the first to speak on this point. Mr. Pavlov for the U.S.S.R. told Commission members in one of their preliminary meetings that the U.N. must formulate a right to education, viewing it as a preventive measure against human rights violations "based on the principles of the Charter, the experience gained during the war," and foreclosing "any attempt at a revival of fascism." Pavlov argued that one of the fundamental factors in the development of fascism and Nazism was "the education of young people in a spirit of hatred and intolerance."[18] As it finally turned out, Article 26 took up Pavlov's point that education inescapably has political objectives but ignored his ideologically rigid ideas on exactly what goals education should pursue. Thus Article 26, in its second and most contentiously debated section, says that the right to education should be linked to specific educational goals. The final wording adopted on this point states, "Education shall be directed to the full development of the human personality and to the strengthening of respect for human rights and fundamental freedoms. It shall promote understanding, tolerance and friendship among all nations, racial or religious groups, and shall further the activities of the United Nations for the maintenance of peace."

This arresting notion of a human being's full personality, while abstract, is important as a thematic thread running through the UDHR. Its significance in framing a holistic concept of human nature as essentially free, social, potentially educated, and entitled to participation in critical decision-making is bolstered by repetition at several points:

1. Article 22 says everyone's rights to social, economic, and cultural rights are "indispensable" for the "free development of his personality."
2. Article 26 posits a right to education, and says, "Education shall be directed to the full development of the human personality...."
3. Article 27 links sharing the benefits of science in the larger context of the right to "participate in the cultural life of the community, to enjoy

the arts and to share in scientific advancement and its benefits."
4. Article 29 repeats the holistic vision of human rights, saying: "Everyone has duties to the community in which alone the free and full development of his personality is possible."

The language linking these provisions in terms of "the full development of the human personality" illustrates the organic nature of the Declaration whereby diverse rights flowed from a belief in the equality of all human beings and the fundamental unity of all human rights. The often reiterated right to "the full development of the human personality" was seen by most delegates as a right reinforced by community and social interaction. It linked and summarized all the social, economic, and cultural rights in the Declaration. Given the goal of the full development of the human personality in the context of society—the only context in which this can occur, it follows that the right to education is a social right, a social good, and a responsibility of society as a whole.

The educational directives described above point to three distinguishable goals. In each instance, some of the justificatory language advanced in the drafting process is worthy to recall. After this exercise is complete, I will use the three-pronged framework to profile some present-day examples of human rights education directed to each of the three goals.

The first goal is education for the *"full development of the human personality and strengthening respect of human rights."* Having specified a right to education, the Human Rights Commission adopted the view that they should prescribe a normative link between the right to education and a cluster of appropriate goals. As you may guess, this is the type of issue debated frequently among faculty in schools of education. To my knowledge, only one education scholar or professor of education was called upon to address the novel idea of identifying the goals of education in the context of a right to education. In a memorandum invited by UNESCO, Isaac L. Kandel, Professor Emeritus of Education, Columbia Teachers College, observed that "historically...education...was directed to indoctrinating the young in religious beliefs and...to develop[ing] a sense of loyalty to the political group or nation." But now to move toward education for what Kandel called "freedom as a human being" will require pedagogical innovation because "education for freedom demands a type of discipline in learning, among other things, to appreciate the moral consequences of one's actions."[19] In his view, education for freedom requires new approaches to education for responsible action in the social context of freedom.

This perspective was developed most ardently by drafting participants from various Latin American countries, and the Brazilian delegate provided a kind of keynote statement on the importance of value-based education. He said the new Declaration must find a way to recognize that education provides the individual with the wherewithal "to develop his personality, which was the aim of human life and the most solid foundation of society."[20] An Argentine proposal quickly put substance on these abstractions mimicking Article 12 of the American Declaration of the Rights and Duties of Man. That language from the 12-month-old Declaration of Bogotá said: "Every person has the right to an education that will prepare him to lead a decent life, to raise his standard of living, and to be a useful member of society."[21] Calling for greater conciseness, Mrs. Roosevelt cautioned against language that would overload the right to education. And in this spirit, Cuba suggested that the message the Argentines wanted Article 26 to carry could be put in alternative simpler language—"education shall be directed to the full development of the human personality."[22] The Chilean delegate (Mr. Santa Cruz) supported the Cuban language to ensure a "logical and harmonious structure for the declaration."[23]

In his review of the origins of the Universal Declaration, Johannes Morsink says that the notion of the "full development of the human personality" emerged in relation to several articles, including those on civil equality and culture. It was intended as a linkage concept—"seen by most delegates as a way of summarizing all the social, economic, and cultural rights in the Declaration."[24]

The goal of "full development of the human personality" was evidently intended to capture the enabling qualities of the right to education, and of education about human rights to capacitate people to develop to their potential the faculties and talents necessary to ensure human dignity supported by effective self-management, security, and satisfaction. It seems significant that the key phrase—"full development of the human personality"—is immediately followed without so much as a comma by the phrase "and to the strengthening of human rights and fundamental freedoms." Using a standard approach to statutory construction, we might fairly assume that the joining of the two elements was deliberate and meaningful, especially in view of Mrs. Roosevelt's injunction to seek conciseness.

The logic of the two ideas in combination suggests that education promoting the full development of the human personality and the dignity it entails also promotes human rights. And for such full development, education for dignity should take into account the total menu of human rights, personal rights like privacy, political rights like participation, and the right to seek and disseminate information; civil rights like equality and nondiscrimination; economic rights like a decent standard of living, and the right to participate in the community's cultural life. If this analysis can be inferred from the Declaration's language, then it appears to prefigure the Brazilian Paulo Freire views advocated in his book, *The Pedagogy of the Oppressed*.[25] Freire emphasizes the connections between popular empowerment and self-realization as the consequence of people learning and exercising their human rights.

The second goal calls for education to *"promote understanding, tolerance and friendship among all nations, racial or religious groups...."* This idea started out under the guise of a different language. Professor René Cassin, the influential French delegate and Vice President of the Human Rights Commission drew support for stipulating that one goal of education should involve "combating the spirit of intolerance and hatred against other nations and against racial and religious groups everywhere."[26] But again, the Latin American delegations had the last word, showing their voting strength in supporting a Mexican substitute resolution. Mr. Campos Ortiz of Mexico, with a prompt endorsement from the Brazilian delegation, rose to criticize Cassin's formulation as excessively negative. Educational goals, he said, should be framed in positive terms instead of negative goals such as "combating hatred." He said that Article 26 should link the right to education with education for "the promotion of understanding, tolerance and friendship among all nations and racial and religious groups."[27]

Mrs. Roosevelt, who had been hectored repeatedly by the Soviets because of racial segregation in American schools, readily associated herself with the Mexican proposal because it promoted racial tolerance and understanding and "gave positive expression to the otherwise negative provisions suggested by the French" for Article 26. She went on to say that she would vote against the U.S.S.R. effort to condemn racial discrimination in education as that issue was already sufficiently covered by Article 2, saying "Everyone is entitled to all the rights and freedoms set forth in this Declaration, without distinction of any kind, such as race, color, sex, language, religion..." etc.[28] The Soviet amendment was defeated 22 to 7 with 4 abstentions, and then the Mexican proposal was accepted 35-0.[29]

The third goal says education should *"further the activities of the United Nations for the maintenance of peace."* In the final consideration of the Declaration before the General Assembly, the Mexicans also said that the right to education should be anchored in support of the peaceful objectives of U.N. activities. Mr. Watt from Australia promptly objected and urged support for a broader reference to all the "purposes and principles of the United Nations."[30] Again, Mrs.

Roosevelt expressed distaste for any formulation lacking conciseness and specificity and said for that reason she associated herself with the simpler Mexican proposition. She thought that for *educational purposes*, U.N. activities for the maintenance of peace should be recognized as "the chief goal of the United Nations."[31] True to pattern, other Latin American voices chimed in supporting the Mexican initiative. Mr. Carrera Andrade of Ecuador lyrically concluded that when the world's youth became imbued with "the guiding principles of the United Nations, then the future [would promise]...greater hope for all nations living in peace."[32]

Finally, the reference to U.N. peace activities was adopted by a vote of 34–2 with 1 abstention, and thereafter, all dissent was swept away with the final version of Article 26 winning a unanimous 36 votes with 2 abstentions. As a result, Article 26, with three separate sections, now reads:

1. Everyone has the right to education. Education shall be free, at least in the elementary and fundamental stages. Elementary education shall be compulsory. Technical and professional education shall be made generally available and higher education shall be equally accessible to all on the basis of merit.
2. Education shall be directed to the full development of the human personality and to the strengthening of respect for human rights and fundamental freedoms. It shall promote understanding, tolerance and friendship among all nations, racial or religious groups, and shall further the activities of the United Nations for the maintenance of peace.
3. Parents have a prior right to choose the kind of education that shall be given to their children.

On December 10, 1948, the General Assembly solemnly adopted and proclaimed the Universal Declaration of Human Rights. That body showed it realized that such a document could have little effect unless people everywhere knew about it and appreciated its significance for every human being. Therefore, the Assembly also passed Resolution No. 217 urging that the widest possible publicity be given to the Declaration and inviting the Secretary General and U.N. specialized agencies and nongovernmental organizations to do their utmost to bring the Declaration to the attention of their members.

Human Rights Education Today

The right to education was not a vague initiative in the minds of the framers of the Universal Declaration but is substantively imbued with educational goals drawing from internationally defined human rights values. Thus human rights education is not now and should not be a passing teaching fad. It is an international obligation with a half-century history. But if this is the case, then why does the term "human rights education" have such a new and even trendy ring to it? Where has it been since 1948? While the obligation for states, schools, and all of us to promote human rights through education is a 50-year-old internationally defined duty, it has only recently become more lively, more widely accepted, and more "people centered." Among several reasons for this, perhaps none is more important than the end of the Cold War, which made more realistic than heretofore the announcement of the U.N. Decade for Human Rights Education.

With the end of the Cold War, human rights education's day has come. That wasteful ideological conflict between superpowers played an important role in suppressing international efforts to promote human rights education. Today, the winds are blowing in new directions. From Southern Africa to Eastern Europe, from Southeast Asia to the Southern Cone of Latin America, a kind of global sea change has left political tyrannies discarded and isolated like seafarers at low tide. During the 1990s, a large array of states in every hemisphere has moved into the categories of emerging and reemerging democracies and proclaimed support for international human rights.

Many regimes newly engaged in institution building and the construction of democracies have gone on record calling for human rights education as a preventive measure against the recurrence of human rights abuses. First in line was the Philippines in 1987. Previously a dictatorship, it now has a ten-year-old Constitution that explicitly requires human rights education in all fields and at all levels.[33] "People power," as the Philippine and then international media began to call it, caught on again elsewhere in 1989. That year, when democratic forces began to assert themselves in Eastern Europe, the Helsinki Committee in Poland announced that "issues of ideology, removed from the school curricula, must now be replaced by the values of human dignity"—dropping *The Communist Manifesto* in favor of the UDHR in its public programs of education.[34] Argentina, Chile, and Paraguay, not long ago Latin American dictatorships, these days encourage teachers to design ways to infuse human rights topics into daily classes.[35] Thus, freedom of the press is examined in writing classes, the rights of the child in social studies, and so on, often with the technical assistance from the Inter-American Institute of Human Rights in Costa Rica. In Africa, Ethiopia—previously a Marxist-Leninist regime—has a new government, and its Ministry of Education designed human rights curriculum for public schools which began in 1999.[36] Indeed, the African Charter on Human and Peoples' Rights says signatory states are obliged not only to promote human rights education but also "to see to it that these freedoms and rights as well as corresponding obligations and duties are understood."[37] With all of these developments, it's time we recognize that we are at an important historical juncture. We must recognize that we have a rare "window of opportunity" to turn away from the sterile debates and values associated with the Cold War and to respond to an international "values gap" by building a global human rights culture.

When and where did this post–Cold War process begin by relying on education infused with human rights standards to bring about social change? Something new under the educational sun dawned in the Philippines in 1987. When the Marcos dictatorship in the Philippines was overthrown in 1986 by a peaceful revolution, the democratically elected government of President Corazon Aquino sponsored the writing of a new Constitution, the first in the world to require the teaching of human rights in all educational institutions, public and private, and at all levels of education, and to include human rights training for the police and military. The constitutional framer who proposed the requirement, Edmundo Garcia, said it would prevent human rights violations, first, when we have a citizenry that is convinced it must uphold its basic rights because it knows what they are, and second, when law enforcement officials are trained to respect human rights.[38] In this spirit, the President ordered that no military officer should be promoted who did not pass the human rights examinations. The Constitution of 1987 encourages nongovernmental organizations to undertake human rights education as well, and over the past ten years, such very creative programs have developed all over the country. In fact, by 1998, every village and community in the Philippines with a *barangay* captain—the equivalent of a sheriff—has or is scheduled to have a human rights office, and every school incorporates human rights lessons in its curriculum.

Another important development facilitating the spread of human rights education is based on the program of the United Nations Decade of Human Rights Education. More obviously than ever before, given international travel and communications technologies, we have become a global village. Hooked up by satellite communications to other regional conferences, the 1993 Bangkok-based Human Rights Conference of Asian NGOs was among the first of several regional conferences to endorse a campaign for a ten-year project of human rights education. This led to the World Conference on Human Rights held in Vienna asking the U.N. for action to accelerate the promotion of human rights. As a result, the United Nations General Assembly proclaimed the years 1995-2004 as the World Decade for Human Rights Education. The U.N. proclamation says the decade has as its aim "the full development of the human personality in a spirit of peace, mutual understanding and respect for democracy and the rule of law." Issues of methodology are important and as such, human rights education should be developed in all U.N. member states as a life-long process which includes formal education at all levels, informal education through trade unions, religious, civic, and similar organizations, favoring interactive, participatory, and culturally relevant learning methods, as well as nonformal education through families and the media.[39]

Building on these methodological objectives, let's turn now to some actual examples of new human rights education initiatives and profile a few programs, which embody some of the goals of the Universal Declaration and guidelines for the decade. Because I have tracked the Article 26 human rights education goals of (1) full personal development, (2) the promotion of tolerance, and (3) advancement of U.N. peace objectives, I will use them as my organizing principles and sketch a couple of programs fitting each of these Declaration goals. My thumbnail profiles will draw from both formal education (the conventional schooling system) and nonformal education where human rights groups target specialized constituencies.

Full Personal Development and Respect for Human Rights

The Rural Poor in Thailand
I had the pleasure four years ago of visiting the Thongbai Thongpao Foundation in Southeast Asia to observe how it brings legal assistance to Thailand's rural people, conducting training on basic human rights and the law for daily life.[40] In the weekend "Law to the Villages" program, rural residents learn about constitutional law, human rights, marriage, loans and mortgages, labor law, and other practical legal issues that concern them. The program concludes by setting up a local paralegal committee to deal with participants' complaints of exploitation by moneylenders, police, and landowners who assume peasants have no access to law. The weekend educators provide participants with a personalized photo identification card including their own Bangkok lawyer's name. The identification card also lists the rights of suspects: the right to

silence and to legal assistance, etc. While these programs have not been formally evaluated, witnessing them I have been struck by the palpable sense of pride and restored human dignity that is evident among Thai peasants when they feel armed with the tools of human rights information as well as contacts for resource people they can call upon to defend their rights if threatened by loan sharks, thugs hired by agribusinesses to drive them off the land, etc. Based on the theory that the people have the right to know their rights, Thongbai Thongpao's program has been emulated elsewhere in Asia and was given the Magsaysay Award sometimes described as Asia's equivalent of the Nobel Peace Prize. The award announcement said it was given in recognition of grassroots education for the poor and for "using their legal skills and pen to defend those who have 'less in life and thus need more in law.'"

Women's Rights in Ethiopia
Referring again to education for full personal development and respect for human rights, I turn now to an education program for African women and a project in Ethiopia initiated by a group called "Action Professionals for the People."[41] The Action Professionals were looking for a teaching program to promote women's rights, taking into account that Ethiopia has ratified the U.N. Convention on the Elimination of All Forms of Discrimination Against Women (CEDAW). I worked two years ago with that group observing them setting up community-based programs of human rights including one called "Bringing CEDAW Home." Let me highlight their procedure. First, the curriculum design team agreed on the objective of promoting women's empowerment through community-based nonformal education to break the old curse of domination by one gender over the other and to take action to eliminate discrimination. Next, they designed simple ways and simple language to introduce CEDAW—article by article, explaining that the Government has promised to abide by its provisions. Then, people were asked to speak from experience about any specific provision of CEDAW, such as Article 5, saying customary practices that are based on the idea of the inferiority of the sexes should be eliminated. Most important, using a problem-solving approach, participants designed programs of action and selected the one action plan, among several they designed, that they all would actually be willing to put into effect. For example, I witnessed women agreeing to stop using coercion and even force to back up arranged marriages among their preteenage daughters; all this to abide by Article 16 of the Universal Declaration saying everyone has a right freely to choose a spouse.

Before leaving this topic, I should point out that no group-specific educational program has attracted more organizing activity than women's rights. I'm thinking, for example, of "Sisterhood is Global," an impressive program for the human rights education of women in Muslim societies, with two texts, "Claiming our Rights," and "Safe and Secure," on violence against women.[42] In the United States, an excellent text is entitled, *Women's Human Rights: Step by Step*, published by two collaborating groups: Women, Law and Development International, and the Women's Rights Project of the Human Rights Watch.[43] Their book uses plain language to describe the content of human rights law, enforcement mechanisms, and implementation strategies useful to women seeking social change. I turn now to a couple of examples of human rights education promoting tolerance and international friendship.

Promoting Tolerance Among Groups and International Friendship

Real Estate Agents in Japan

In 1994, an Osaka real estate agent tried to trace the boundaries of an isolated and shunned neighborhood occupied by the Burakumin minority. They are Japanese who suffer prejudice because their disfavored status links them to an earlier period of caste-like social stratification. A complaint was filed that the agent's queries reflected discriminatory business practices—we would call it "redlining" in the United States. The Osaka complaint resulted in an administrative order "to study the Buraku issue" under guidance of the Buraku Liberation League. League educators eventually concluded that both the agent and company officials completed the course including its strong human rights content and demonstrated changed attitudes and modified behavior.[44] This incident shows how Japanese laws against discrimination, carrying no penalties against offenders, nevertheless can informally remedy transgressions through privately conducted "enlightenment education" when administratively ordered. Through experience with such nonformal education, the Buraku Liberation League has greatly expanded its activities and devised a systematic and wide-ranging curriculum program for children in primary schools, including the distribution of its book, *NINGEN (Human)*. It includes poems, songs, short stories, and articles to introduce children to the topic of human rights and discrimination against the Burakumin, Koreans in Japan, women, disabled persons, etc. It teaches that human rights are in accord with Asian values.

The Japanese government has associated itself with various U.N. human rights programs, announcing in 1996 that it regards private initiatives and the activities of NGOs as essential to achieving the aims of the U.N. Decade for Human Rights Education. Because of Japan's famous constitutional Article 9 renouncing war, they have little difficulty making the educational connection between education and support for U.N. activities on behalf of international peace.

Human Rights U.S.A.
Human Rights U.S.A. is an experimental new program in the United States designed to mobilize activity and social change and to promote human rights education nationally and in four pilot city programs. Organized in 1997, Human Rights U.S.A. has been working with school systems, community-based organizations, and the media to promote human rights in Atlanta, Minneapolis-St. Paul, St. Louis, and San Antonio. To launch test programs in each site, training materials used include: exercises called Universal Declaration *"passports," Human Rights Here and Now,* and *Human Rights for All*—a textbook having among other goals the promotion of friendship among nations because it is coauthored through collaboration by South Africans and Americans.[45] Participants in the four U.S. locales draw on the resources and expertise of Human Rights U.S.A.'s four partner organizations: the Human Rights Educators' Network of Amnesty International U.S.A., the Center for Human Rights Education, Partners in Human Rights Education (a joint project of the University of Minnesota Human Rights Center and Minnesota Advocates for Human Rights), and Street Law Inc. Participants can communicate through a common interactive Internet web site [http://www.hrusa.org], which, among other items, carries a lively and continuously updated forum on "Community Action Ideas." For example, in Atlanta, a few months ago, the "Georgia Citizens' Coalition on Hunger" held educational workshops at the Georgia State Capitol focusing on "Knowing and Claiming Our Rights." Participants met with state legislators, held a press conference, conducted a public hearing, and organized a rally focusing on racial discrimination and human rights violations leading to hunger and homelessness in Georgia. Without the Internet connection, grassroots organizers of these programs would not have been able to share their experience with the other three human rights cities. The hope, of course, is that new cities will be added to Human Rights U.S.A. in future years, partly attracted by the ease of access to the web site describing and promoting the program. Human Rights U.S.A. is a promising new program designed to bring

human rights concepts and principles to the grassroots level with cooperation and support from local schools, and to construct an innovative model to connect understanding with action.

Furthering Activities of the United Nations for the Maintenance of Peace

Diplomacy Training for Asia-Pacific NGOs

Human rights education has evolved in the 1990s to the stage that there is widespread recognition of the need for systematic programs of skills training for NGOs and teacher training. One such program is called "Diplomacy Training for NGOs," organized by the University of New South Wales, Australia.[46] It serves Asia-Pacific human rights activists and members of nongovernmental organizations. The program was organized by Australian law faculty in recognition of the worldwide maldistribution of NGOs, which puts such groups in the South at a disadvantage. Training sessions promote NGO familiarity and competence in using the U.N. human rights system, including the development of reports to the U.N. human rights treaty committees. Inasmuch as training is directed toward the development of skills, the New South Wales program relies on small group exercises, simulations, role-playing, rigorous coaching, and presentation/discussions. Asian and Pacific NGO members can develop expertise and confidence in using U.N. procedures and standards without undertaking expensive travel to Geneva or New York.

Also of regional importance in Asia this year is the initiative of members of the Hong Kong University Law Faculty headed by Professor Yash Ghai. They are designing a plan for teaching human rights to the police that relies on police training materials developed by the U.N. emphasizing the protection of human rights as a priority police objective.[47] The Hong Kong program will be open to participants throughout the Asia-Pacific region. In recently talking to Professor Yash Ghai about the program, he told me that he and his colleagues see no evidence of concern coming from Beijing. Along the same lines, the Canadian Human Rights Foundation has been helping Asia-Pacific government officials to develop human rights training programs, including the new Indonesian Human Rights Commission, which currently designs human rights training for the military, security, and police officials.[48]

Philippine Teachers University

The Republic of the Philippines is the only country in the world in which teachers are constitutionally bound to teach human rights. Since 1987 when the new Constitution mandated the teaching of human rights, teacher training in the island nation has been essential to implement the requirement within the framework of formal education. Educating future teachers at the Philippine Normal University in the 1990s involves serious efforts to prepare them with creative approaches to human rights.[49] They rely on UNICEF-developed materials, such as the "Meena Series" on girls' human rights, and they use the United Nations *Human Rights Trainers Guide* as an important resource. The latter stresses the need to develop participatory pedagogies and critical skills among teachers and students. In fact, teachers and students in a sense, exchange roles because the *Guide* says the choice of human rights issues should always take into account the students' own experiences. The Philippine Normal University's curriculum development combines human rights education with issues connected to global peace, international solidarity and development issues among Third World Countries. Their work in teacher training will be replicated as Mahidol University in Bangkok launches a masters' degree program on human rights and human rights education for teachers throughout the Asia-Pacific area. Putting teacher-training first in a national program of human rights education means educators have a strategic perspective on human rights and see it not simply as a new course to add to the school curriculum but rather as underlying the teaching of all school subjects and permeating every aspect of school life. Reliance on local and regional teacher training also has the advantage of presenting human rights standards mediated by cultural diversity. On this point, a 1993 Declaration by 110 Asia-Pacific NGOs said human rights education must respect the cultural setting within which they are taught, but significantly, it added "those cultural practices which derogate from universally accepted human rights, including women's rights, must not be tolerated."[50]

Supporting the new developments in human rights education is an important new resource developed by the United Nations and only very recently made available worldwide on the Internet. The *U.N. Cyber School Bus* is an attractive United Nations web site designed to facilitate infusing classroom activities with human rights information and materials. The U.N. Cyber School Bus includes an interactive UDHR, a "plain language version of the Universal Declaration," a Question and Answer site, definitions of human rights terms appropriate for primary and secondary school classes, and an ingenious "Global Atlas of Student Activities."[51]

Conclusion

In conclusion, many observers, activists, and educators now perceive the beginnings of an international movement here in support of human rights education. It is more viable for having globally available U.N. resources in combination with burgeoning international networking to promote creative and innovative human rights education initiatives under the sponsorship of the U.N. Decade. The vision shared by those who are involved is directed toward constructing a "universal culture of human rights." I have tried to suggest that this vision is no longer utopian, and that the challenge is no longer beyond the horizon. We are faced with the obligation at the international, national, local, and personal levels to implement effective programs of human rights education and to employ methodologies that will ensure the task is well done, consistent with the goals of world peace and respect for human rights everywhere.

To reinforce our responsibilities, let's finally recall that the UDHR has now been with us for more than fifty years. I close with this poignant comment by Eleanor Roosevelt. As if talking to us today, she said in 1948:

> It will be a long time before history will make its judgment on the value of the Universal Declaration of Human Rights, and the judgment will depend, I think, on what the people of different nations do to make this document familiar to everyone. If they know it well enough, they will strive to attain some of the rights and freedoms set forth in it, and that effort on their part is what will make it of value in clarifying what was meant in the Charter in the references to human rights and fundamental freedoms.

Notes

* The author wishes to express appreciation to Nancy Flores, Coordinator for the Educator's Network of Amnesty International U.S.A., for her constructive comments on this text.

1 Article 55. The United Nations shall promote [*inter alia*]: "universal respect for and observance of human rights and fundamental freedoms for all without distinction as to race, sex, language or religion. Article 56. All Members pledge themselves to take joint and separate action in cooperation with the Organization for the achievement of the purposes set forth in Article 55." *United Nations Charter*, signed at San Francisco, 26 June 1945; entered into force on 24 October 1945.

2   ECOSOC Resolution 1/5 of 16 February 1946.

3   *Universal Declaration of Human Rights,* United Nations General Assembly Resolution 217A (III) 3(1) U.N. GAOR Res.71, U.N. Doc. A/810 (1948).

4   Other members represented Australia, Belgium, the Byelorussian S.S.R., Chile, Egypt, India, Iran, Panama, the Philippines, the Union of Soviet Socialist Republics, the United Kingdom, Uruguay, and Yugoslavia.

5   Charles Malik, *These Rights and Freedoms* (United Nations: Department of Public Information, 1950), pp. 4-5.

6   *"Secretariat Draft"* (separate articles): Everyone has the right to education. Each State has the duty to require that every child within its territory receive a primary education. The State shall maintain adequate and free facilities for such education. It shall also promote facilities for higher education without distinction as to the race, sex, language, religion, class or wealth of the persons entitled to benefit there from. Everyone has the right to establish educational institutions in conformity with conditions laid down by the law.

7   *Drafting Committee* (First Session): Everyone has the right to education. Primary education shall be free and compulsory. There shall be equal access for all to such facilities for technical, cultural and higher education as can be provided by the State or community on the basis of merit and without distinction as to race, sex, language, religion, social standing, political affiliation or financial means.

8   *Commission on Human Rights, Second Session* (2 separate articles): Everyone has the right to education. Fundamental education shall be free and compulsory. There shall be equal access for higher education as can be provided by the State or community on the basis of merit and without distinction as to race, sex, language, religion, social standing, financial means, or political affiliation.

9   *Final Text, General Assembly, Third Committee, Article* 26: (1) Everyone has the right to education. Education shall be free, at least in the elementary and fundamental stages. Elementary education shall be compulsory. Technical and professional education shall be made generally available and higher education shall be equally accessible to all on the basis of merit. (2) Education shall be directed to the full development of the human personality and to the strengthening of respect for human rights and fundamental freedoms. It shall promote understanding, tolerance and friendship among all nations, racial or religious groups, and shall further the activities of the United Nations for the maintenance of peace. (3). Parents have a prior right to choose the kind of education that shall be given to their children.

10 U.N. Document E/CN/AC.1/3.

11 John P. Humphrey, *Human Rights and the United Nations, A Great Adventure* (Dobbs Ferry,

NY: Transnational Publishers, Inc., 1984), p. 37.

12 Johannes Morsink, *The Universal Declaration of Human Rights, Origins, Drafting and Intent* (Philadelphia: University of Pennsylvania Press, 1999), pp. 130-134.

13 *Official Record of the 3d Session of the General Assembly*, Part I, "Social Humanitarian and Cultural Questions," 3d Committee, Summary Records of Meeting, 21 September-8 December 1948, (reporting the 147th Meeting of the Commission, held at the Palais de Chaillot, Paris, 19 November 1948), pp. 586.

14 *Ibid.*, p. 592.

15 *Ibid.*, p. 582.

16 E/CN.4/SR.67. Commission on Human Rights, Third Session, *Summary Record of the 69th Meeting* (Lake Success), 11 June 1948, p. 6.

17 *Ibid.*, p. 13.

18 *Ibid.*

19 Isaac L. Kandel, "Education and Human Rights," in UNESCO, *Human Rights, Comments and Interpretations"* (Westport, CT: Greenwood Press, 1973), pp. 223-225.

20 *Official Record of the 3d Session*, p. 597.

21 Argentine Amendment (A/C.3/251), supra note 13, p. 597.

22 Cuban Amendment (A/C.3/261).

23 *Official Record., supra note 13*, p. 588.

24 Johannes Morsink, supra note 12, p. 212.

25 Paulo Freire, *Pedagogy of the Oppressed* (New York: Seabury Press, 1973).

26 *Official Record., supra note 13*, p. 587.

27 *Ibid.*, p. 584.

28 *Ibid.*, p. 590.

29 *Ibid.*, p. 603.

30 Ibid., p. 594.

31 Ibid.

32 Ibid., p. 589.

33 Richard Pierre Claude, *Educating for Human Rights, The Philippines and Beyond,* (Manila: University of Philippines Press; and Honolulu: University of Hawaii Press, 1996), pp. 21-24.

34 Helsinki Committee in Poland, *Human Rights in Poland, 1989* (Warsaw: International Helsinki Federation for Human Rights, Report No. 8, 1990), p. 2.

35 Abraham K. Magendzo, *Curriculum, escuela y derechos humanos* (Santiago: Programa Interdisciplinario de Investigación en Educación, 1989).

36 Richard P. Claude, *Education for Human Rights and Democratic Citizenship: The Ethiopia Experience* (Atlanta: The Carter Center, 1998).

37 African Charter on Human and Peoples' Rights (Banjul), O.A.U. Doc. CAB/LEG/67/3 rev. 5:21 I.L.M. 58 (1982), entered into force Oct. 21, 1986.

38 Richard P. Claude, *Educating for Human Rights,* supra note 33, chapter 2, "From Misrule to Re-emerging Constitutional Democracy," pp. 17-30.

39 U.N. General Assembly, Res. 48/127 and Res. 49/184.

40 Richard Pierre Claude, "Enhancing Legal Literacy Among Thailand's Rural Poor," in George Andreopoulos and Richard Pierre Claude, eds., *Human Rights Education for the Twenty-First Century* (Philadelphia: University of Pennsylvania Press, 1998), pp. 272-274.

41 Action Professionals Association for the People (APAP), *The Bells of Freedom* (Addis Ababa: APAP, 1995), available at <http://www.umn.edu/humanrts/education/belfry.pdf.

42 Mahnaz Afkhami and Haleh Vaziri, *Claiming Our Rights: A Manual for Women's Human Rights Education in Moslem Countries* (Bethesda, MD: Sisterhood Is Global Institute, 1998).

43 Women, Law and Development International/Women's Rights Project of Human Rights Watch, *Women's Human Rights Step by Step* (777 U.N. Plaza, NY: Women, Inc., 1997).

44 "Discriminatory Case, (2) Real Estate Agent Inquiry about Seat of Buraku, Hyogo Prefecture," *Buraku Liberation News* (Osaka: Buraku Liberation Research Institute, September, 1994), pp. 11-12.

45 Edward L. O'Brien, Eleanor Greene, and David McQuoid-Mason, *Human Rights for All*

(Minneapolis/St.Paul, MN: West Publishing Co., 1996).

46   Described in Richard P. Claude, *Educating for Human Rights,* supra note 33, p. 130.

47   Yash Ghai, "Human Rights and Governance: The Asia Debate" (The Asia Foundation: Occasional Paper No. 4, 1994).

48   *National Human Rights Institutions at Work, Regional Training Manual, Tagaytay City, Philippines* (Montreal: Canadian Human Rights Foundation; and Quezon City: Philippine Commission on Human Rights, 1999).

49   Richard P. Claude, *Educating for Human Rights,* supra note 33, pp. 109-111.

50   "Our Common Humanity: Asian Human Rights Charter," *The Netherlands Quarterly of Human Rights,* vol. 16 (4) (December, 1998), pp. 539-552.

51   [http://www.un.org/Pubs/CyberSchoolBus/humanrights].

CHAPTER EIGHT

A Strategy for Human Rights: Five Internet Projects That Can Change the World

Lloyd S. Etheredge

Most movements that are self-described as radical are highly urbanistic, or nationalistic, or oriented to obsolete class structures, or to central bureaucratic planning. The changes that we can see on the horizon are much more drastic than that. They reflect the ease with which communication can operate over global distances, and the abundance of bandwidth that can now be made available to all, without producing any exhaustion of the earth's resources....People who think about social change in traditional political terms cannot begin to imagine the changes that lie ahead. Conventional reformers cast their programs in terms of national policies, or in terms of laws and central planning. But in the end, what will shape the future is a creative potential that inheres in the new technologies [of freedom].

—Ithiel de Sola Pool [1]

The emerging global Internet brings remarkably good news for human rights. Today, as has often occurred in the past, institutions lag in taking advantage of new technologies. But if we recalibrate our imagination, there are new capabilities for political acceleration and problem-solving that would have seemed a miracle, beyond imagining, to earlier generations of statesmen.

First, I will draw four lessons from social science to predict how new communication technologies will partly shape our future. Then I will use this framework to explain five projects—beginning with the partial redesignation of the former United States Information Agency's (USIA) global satellite net—to accelerate international progress. These initiatives are not conventional political and human rights projects *per se*—i.e., they do not target the behavior of governments directly, and they are not databases or lectures. Rather, they are intended as system-level rewirings—complementary initiatives—that use new and unique technology to create a world order that naturally generates more rapid progress for human rights. Our foundation has been laying the groundwork for these five innovations. They are projects that institutions with a commitment to human rights can help make possible.

Four Lessons and the Road Ahead

There is a growing awareness of the continuing good news of rapid improvement in communications and computing technology and reductions in cost. These benefits will rapidly become available on a global scale: Today, the Internet has footholds in almost every country, and—breaking free of the earthbound economics of telephone wires, especially for the underdeveloped world—we are in a five-year period when we will launch more communication satellites into earth orbit than all of the satellites launched in the previous 40 years since *Sputnik*.[2]

Until now communication across large distances and to many people has been relatively expensive, accessible only to a few actors, and used technologies that could be regulated easily by governments. These constraints will continue to be mitigated by the forces of technology, by deregulation, and the growth of competition in the developed and Third World.[3]

Four lessons about where these changes will take us are:

- Increased Capabilities for Political Accelaration and Vision-Created Futures
- New Communication Technologies Promote Cosmopolitan Identities and Universal Norms
- The Prediction of Mixed Blessings
- The Prediction of Counterlearning

Increased Capabilities for Political Acceleration and Vision-Created Futures

The first lesson is that we will receive a windfall of increased capabilities for vision-created futures.

This lesson builds upon the work of my former colleague, Ithiel de Sola Pool, who called the new technologies, "technologies of freedom."[4] By this description, he meant that the world is entering a new era. From the first era of traditional methods of communications, humankind moved to mass communications, especially mass-circulation newspapers in countries with growing literacy, radio, and television; to today, a new era of computer-based high-capacity networks, of increasingly global scale, user-initiated and user-controlled, interactive, low cost, and widely available.

A Strategy for Human Rights

Thus, the story of our new global communications order is *not* primarily 500 or more mass communication television channels on each television set. As the new era slowly dawns, the more powerful story that will emerge is the possibility for hundreds of millions of individuals and institutions to create global links, moving from the old e-mail lists to do-it-yourself global television channels on desktop PCs, which can routinely reach audiences of hundreds or thousands. Yale Medical School, for example, has prototyped a regularly-scheduled Global Grand Rounds colloquium series (http://info.med.yale.edu/EIINet) that links weekly with audio and slides to several thousand health professionals in 140+ countries.[5] Continuous "streaming" audio and video also will be increasingly available to global audiences without government regulation (e.g., www.broadcast.com—an application that is well established for teen-age music events).

I think that Ithiel Pool's political forecast, in the quotation at the beginning of this paper, is correct. Applying this new type of technology, the traditional language and categories for political activism can be limiting anachronisms (e.g., "People who think about social change in traditional political terms cannot begin to imagine the changes that lie ahead. Conventional reformers cast their programs in terms of national policies, or in terms of laws and central planning. But in the end, what will shape the future is a creative potential that inheres in the new technologies [of freedom]").

The phrase "technologies of freedom" is a social science designation, based upon Pool's analysis of the impact of the telephone, the first of these new technologies.[6] The expansion of the telephone did not automatically force a future in a tightly coupled process. Rather, it empowered almost everybody. It gave people and institutions more options and made them more efficient at pursuing many goals: people could call friends or schedule voluntary activities in the new suburbs; businesses could serve customers quickly and coordinate activities at greater geographical distances; gamblers could call their bookmakers to place illegal bets; and local chapters of both the NAACP and the Ku Klux Klan could call their members. You cannot predict the full range of results from a technology of freedom until you know what people are drawn to do.

I will return to the implication of Pool's view—that, in the new era, progress in human rights can be shaped more effectively by the creative potential of the Internet than by programs cast in terms of laws or government policies—several times in this presentation.

New Communication Technologies Promote Cosmopolitan Identities and Universal Values

> *Without [the printing press], the Reformation would have been limited to a relatively minor theological dispute in a remote German province, and the Scientific Revolution, with its dependence on international communication among many scientists, would have been altogether impossible.*
>
> —Richard Tarnas[7]

Major improvements in communication technology typically widen identifications and the geographical range and scale of social, economic, and political organization. For the most part, they have been modernizing. An increasingly wired world may produce, some forecasters predict, the next step, a universal and cosmopolitan global village.[8]

Technically, since better communication technologies simply reduce the cost of a ubiquitous factor of production, all institutions and agendas can benefit. But some can benefit more than others: parochial, tribal, and xenophobic sensibilities can make less use of their widening potential. By contrast, institutions and groups that wish to learn what is going on, to reach out and link up, to build networks and accomplish wider projects, can do so at low cost. New networks of relationships—commerce, science, the arts, NGOs—can expand and be readily sustained.[9]

To be sure, as I will discuss below, there is always the possibility of regression: fragmentation, retribalization, and/or the option to use new technologies for political control and to reverse progress in human rights.[10] *1984* imagined the possibilities of perfecting telecommunication technologies for the mass manipulation, invasion of privacy, and totalitarian control that Fascist and Communist states have attempted. However, the road ahead is more likely to take us further in the direction first illustrated in the Renaissance. Then, moveable type, growing literacy, and a reliable postal system first produced a genuine community of scientists and scholars, a humanistic sensibility, and a degree of excitement and international cross-fertilization that stimulated spectacular progress in many fields.[11]

Politically, new communication technologies also are tools that support the increased size and scope of organization, including governments. Thus, even if there are tendencies to disband large organizations and bureaucracies—as some New Age prophets predict—another mode will, if history is our guide, be a major increase in international trade, transnational corporations and alliances, international linkages involving a wide range of institutions, the expanded formation of international regimes in specialized areas, further globalization of international financial markets, etc. And there may be crosscutting linkups among global cultures: *pace* Huntington, who sees a world of traditional ethnic/religious cultures and their anticipated clashes, we have seen the rise of a global teenage culture linked through music and MTV (which has become one of the first global television channels.)[12]

The Prediction of Mixed Blessings
As a counterpoint to excessive enthusiasm, the third lesson is a prediction of mixed blessings.

Advocates of new technologies—and even the public in opinion polls—often anticipate high-minded results. (Radio would bring opera and symphonies to the masses. The Internet will allow high school students across the country to access the transcripts of Presidential press conferences, download weather reports from Kenya, and browse the Library of Congress....) But freedom offers no guarantee except choice: the viewership of soap operas has grown more rapidly than of real operas; scientists use the Internet for scientific communication—and it is an invaluable resource—but a multibillion dollar/year international drug industry does not operate by smuggling paper currency across national boundaries and benefits enormously from the freedoms of new communication links. And people (or governments) who want to pry may find it easier to obtain private information about anybody. Any exercise in forecasting also should include a thoughtful reminder of the deep skepticism of mass democracy, and mankind's alleged susceptibility to demagoguery and skillful propaganda, which began with Greek observations of their own experience. By this scenario, the road ahead also might see the hyped use of mass communications and electronic technology to create a media circus of superficiality, dizzying overstimulation and norm-challenging sensationalism, image, misdirected priorities, and perhaps—depending upon who is drawn to use the new technologies—newly retribalized and impassioned societies.[13] Americans and the world have recently seen the potential effects of media competition for audiences on the attention that zealots can capture and the dramatization of scandal in the impeachment of President Clinton. We are in the uneasy position of hoping that the world's foreign newspapers and journalists, in dealing with international relations, will be more sober and responsible than our internal news organizations.[14] Other results probably will differ from the more idealistic expectations, a point made candidly by Larry Ellison (founder of Oracle), one of the multibillionaires of the new computer and telecommunications industry who will be bringing it to us. In a recent interview, he was asked about emerging strategies and plans for profits in national and global markets, including such "killer applications" as video (e.g., movies) on demand, home shopping channels, video games, direct-response advertising, and gambling:

> *[Gambling] is going to be huge. We are a bunch of sinners, as Pat Robertson might say. He will be able to come on and tell us about our sinning, and when we get tired of that we can go back to gambling. I don't think people are anxious to introduce this service right up front. I think we are all trying to be socially responsible and try to get the health care and education applications up before we get the pornography and gambling up.*[15]

New, inexpensive channels that, like small-circulation journals, can serve niche (rather than mass) markets also can empower political groups that were previously unorganized, marginalized, and ignored in mass markets. We have already seen this phenomenon under way: as new technology made possible the expanded capacity of cable television, the television evangelists of the political right emerged, with organized political followings and cash incomes provided by the new technology.

Thus my second lesson—of historical currents drawing us toward more homogenized, cosmopolitan, and tolerant cultures—is not a sole consequence of new telecommunications technology. As in an ocean, currents at different levels can move in different directions. Each direction will depend upon what different people want. Soon, if some people decide they really do not like one another or the homogenizing option of a mass culture, they can begin to retribalize and live within separate and fragmented realities and neighborhoods surrounded by electronic walls. Black channels, Jewish channels, Hispanic channels, Chinese/American channels, teenage channels (MTV), regional channels, etc., may grow. The new tribes may have an electronic (rather than geographic) organization. Political power within such electronic tribes may become more readily available to charismatic, demagogic personalities, now with ready and affordable access to global links unconstrained by licensing review. And some groups predictably will create web sites that engender paranoia and/or display hostility to anybody interested to visit them.

The Prediction of Counterlearning
My fourth lesson is the prediction of counterlearning.
Since the invention of movable type, there has been an early enthusiasm that each new communications technology will give greater voice, organiza-

tional resources, and power to the dispossessed; free citizens and society from traditional authority; and, thereby, provide a fundamental and permanent advance for human rights.[16]

However, especially when there are challenges to powerful institutions, reliable forecasting is seldom a matter of multiplying fixed coefficients in standard linear equations. Historically, initial enthusiasms are typically overoptimistic and ignore the (predictable, dialectical) phenomenon of counterlearning. After a lag, a counter-reformation begins: groups with opposing interests learn to adapt and organize to regain control and neutralize adversarial advantages. After the initial period of expanding freedom and enthusiasm, a period of greater regulation follows, and this in turn requires extraordinary and lengthy historical battles to regain the rights and progress that appeared, in the earliest days, to be secure.[17]

For example, Gutenberg invented movable type and the printing press in 1451 and in its early decades the technology was used relatively freely, often to publish Bibles and other established, respectable texts for those who could afford them. As printing became more widely used as a tool for political change, however, restrictions followed, although with a lag. In Germany, censorship of books was introduced in 1529; the legal restriction on the right to publish was introduced in England in 1557; in 1559, the Catholic Church introduced the *Index Expurgatorius*.

Two hundred years later, in the American colonies, the ownership of a printing press required a government license. The idea of allowing freedom of printing was considered as dangerous as permitting the unlicensed sale of explosives.

Similarly, radio was invented in 1895 and (at first) could be used freely. Beginning in the 1920s, after the U.S. Navy began to experience interference with its activities, the case for government regulation steadily grew.[18]

This fourth prediction, counterlearning, is also implied by the earlier lessons:

From Lesson 1: As new technologies empower more people and institutions to pursue their own visions, one result (in a world where discrimination and injustice remain ubiquitous) will be to accelerate progressive and humanitarian politics.

From Lesson 2: As genuinely cosmopolitan identities emerge, they can threaten adherents of more limited, parochial, or traditional values and loyalties.

From Lesson 3: As genuinely mixed blessings emerge, they will create motives and opportunities for restrictive coalitions linking *ad hoc* majorities who dislike or fear the erosion of boundaries (including empowered activities of numerous minorities, pornography, or gambling; indulgences in unrestrained sensationalism; invasions to privacy; subversions of copyright; loss of geographically based tax revenue or changing economic benefits; or other activities) that might be reinforced by general restrictions on the new technologies.

I will turn to a full discussion of implications of this lesson—of a unique window of opportunity that may begin to close—later in this paper. At this point, let me underscore one implication for human rights strategy: *Organize, move quickly, and take as much ground as possible.*

Five Internet Projects That Can Change the World

To draw implications for system-level innovations to promote human rights, I want to use a nonlegalistic, outcome-oriented framework developed by Lasswell and McDougal. This policy science tradition of jurisprudence sees the achievement of human rights as the realization of a world commonwealth of human dignity. And this is defined by better resources and outcomes for all human beings, indexed by eight categories of values: power, wealth, enlightenment, respect, rectitude, skill, affection, and well-being. It is a reasonably inclusive list (allied with the spirit of the Universal Declaration of Human Rights and the International Covenant on Economic, Social and Cultural Rights) and widely accepted across cultures and countries.[19]

By this conception, the achievement of human rights becomes a broad application of social science. And the new strategies for using new communication technologies to achieve human rights need *not* be framed in terms of laws or the language of legal rights.

Here, for example [Table 1] are five projects that rewire aspects of the international system so that progress in human rights can occur more quickly and naturally:

Table 1: Five Internet Projects That Can Change the World

1. A Global CSPAN, Using Internet Technology

2. **Preempt the Information Scarcity Gap**
   - Global CSPAN
   - 100,000 basic Internet terminals for UDCs ($15m - $20m)
   - Global purchasing cooperative for health, science, and education in UDCs

3. **Create Large-Scale Collaboration Systems**, e.g.:
   - Education—foreign languages
   - Education—conflict resolution & human rights education
   - "Inventions Wanted..." global Tuesday brownbag
   - Visual display systems for ending world hunger

4. **Organize Opportunities for Global Philanthropy**, e.g.:
   - International public health channel
   - International cultural affairs channel
   - International studies channel (cooperative)
   - Spiritual inquiry channel
   - Education research channel—all school subjects

5. **Organize Global Stakeholder Financing for Scientific Communication and Economic Growth**

Project 1. A global CSPAN, using Internet Technology

The first project is a partial conversion of the former USIA's (one-way, outbound) global satellite capacity [http://www.ibb.gov/worldnet/satmap.html] to create a Global Affairs Channel, using Internet technology.[20] This channel, by analogy to our domestic CSPAN, would acquire discussions of international interest from many sites internationally and make them available on desktop PCs in all countries.[21]

[The Internet technology for a Global Affairs Channel can improve upon our domestic CSPAN in three ways: (1) Programming can be archived on local servers and retrieved at a user's convenience; (2) It will be possible to skim presentations and use time efficiently; (3) The presentations will be linked to Web sites that support discussions with presenters, retrieval of printed texts—perhaps in several languages, linkups of viewers who discover shared interests, etc.]

The Global Affairs Channel would send the right messages and build the right norms. Respect is important, in domestic and world politics, and it can convey enormous respect to have policy conferences in Beijing or Moscow available to a global audience.[22]

The Channel will also create a new degree of international due process. It should quickly become the world's most prominent forum, and it can be used by individuals and organizations to make claims and proposals and to link up government and NGO professionals, foundations, scientists, and others with an engaged interest to respond or address urgent global issues. And it will extend the potential reach of every speaker and NGO conference to the desktop of every Foreign Ministry in the world. By contrast today when the Rockefeller Foundation organizes a conference, the audience typically is limited to those who have the economic resources to attend physically at a specific place and time. And there are the familiar anxieties of conference organizers about attendance and if a foundation report is issued, whether it will receive any visibility in the press and whether it will sell. (And, even if it sells, there is the deeper anxiety about how many policy-influencing people will have the time to read the report, or skim it, or even to skim the Executive Summary.) A Tuesday brownbag in international public health on a Global Affairs Channel, presenting high-quality programming that nobody would miss, may only achieve an audience of 2,400 government and NGO professionals, but a presenter could have a professional audience of the key people, worldwide, who need to be linked in a common discussion (and to know that their counterparts are linked) to move agendas.

Obviously, the selection of program material is critical. In an earlier iteration, the governments of the world created the United Nations General Assembly as a forum for public discussion of humanity's agenda, and we have inherited a venue for speeches conveying the official positions of governments that is almost universally ignored by every newspaper and has become an obligatory bore even for the members.[23] Better, I think, is a plan that uses a framework of value outcomes (such as the policy science list) and bloc grants global airtime to a wide range of NGOs, universities, and think-tanks in all countries who adopt a policy-analysis, problem-solving approach rather than the traditional (implicit) U.N. categories of nation-state interests and/or nation-state personae announcing their positions.[24] Thus, the Human Rights Program at Harvard Law School might receive a bloc grant for seven hours in 2001-2002 for its distinguished lecture series in human rights—a grant that would not involve any prior review of speakers or topics. The lecture series and conferences at the National Institutes of Health, a crossroads of the best and latest ideas in basic research, clinical applications, and areas of American

A Strategy for Human Rights

international leadership (e.g., malaria and polio eradication, women's health, environmental health, emerging infectious diseases), could begin a Global Grand Rounds initiative that, overnight, will enrich the curriculum at every medical school, research university, and four-year college in the world. The National Committee for U.S.-China Relations could receive a bloc grant to extend invitations to universities and international policy institutes in China.

In reviewing the emerging architecture of the Channel as a result of these bloc grants, a governing Board could, in the interests of fairness, *add* (but not censor) programming.[25]

Within the list of shared goals the Channel would seek, with journalistic integrity, to represent the views of actors sharing the commitment to progress and to support innovative projects intended for global audiences.[26]

Project 2. Pre-empt the Information Scarcity Gap

The second project, building upon the Global Affairs Channel, is to preempt the information scarcity gap, thereby, avoiding an unproductive use of traditional political categories that can require idealistic people to struggle (unnecessarily) for decades to solve the problem.

The international development community has already started to gear up for a major effort to frame issues in this traditional way, and mobilize reformist concern about the alarming and growing gap between haves and have-nots in the information age.

However, this is unnecessary. As far as information is concerned, the partial conversion of the unused capacity on USIA's global satellite nets will make possible, overnight, a daily flood of digitized data that could almost surely be greater than anybody could want.[27]

To preempt the gap fully, two remaining pieces are needed. First, it would be helpful to provide a critical mass of 100,000 basic Internet terminals for health, science, and education—basic public access—for the poorest countries. And it would be useful to have a global purchasing cooperative for bandwidth, equipment, and software to assure that the lowest available prices for a rapid growth of Internet-based global applications are available to UDCs.

In principle, the acquisition of 100,000 terminals is easy and perhaps especially so because the value of the American stock market has quadrupled over the past decade. The new (i.e., in the fall of 1999) Alcatel Internet screenphone is an example of emerging "Internet appliance" technology that can soon be purchased, in quantities of 100,000, for $150 to $200. Alternatively, $15 million is within the roundoff error of the personal wealth of a rapidly growing number of first-generation multibillionaires of the new information age—people who might enjoy the chance to make a critical, catalytic investment and revolutionize the world of international health, economic development, and other human rights by contributing to a historical startup package that (already) includes the global satellite time and a core of high-quality programming.[28]

Concerning a global purchasing cooperative for health, science, and education in UDCs: The character of new technology makes cooperative purchasing an attractive option: The new low-earth-orbit (LEO) satellite nets are not in geosynchronous orbits, and they are often designed so that two satellites are overhead at any location on the planet. They also are designed to handle peak loads in the markets of the advanced countries of the Northern Hemisphere. But the consequence is that as these multibillion-dollar investments rotate across the underdeveloped world, they generate no revenue. If you are an individual in the Third World, you may need to pay $3/minute, and there would be few sales. But an organization that could segment the nonprofit market and make bulk purchases for nonprofit institutions in health, education, and science in UDCs probably could make a deal.

We already have a good model for this type of cooperative in Telecommunications Cooperative Network (TCN), a joint venture of the Ford, Carnegie, and Benton Foundations in the U.S. at a time when there was monopoly pricing for long-distance telephone services. Today, the cooperative has expanded to 5,000 nonprofit members, many with international programs. It is a good jumping-off point and if the World Bank is prepared to be the 800-pound gorilla at the bargaining table on behalf, for example, of its 43 Global Knowledge Partners (organizations who expect to be major players in information technology and development), there could be extraordinary purchasing power leveraged for the poorest countries. And these Global Knowledge Partners could make the prices available to their projects and affiliates in the Third World. If the World Health Organization wished to sponsor them and serve as an agent, for example, every hospital, medical school, and clinic in the Third World could participate. As a start, it would be easy for the cooperative to obtain for everybody the types of lowest available price guarantees that very large purchasers in advanced industrial countries, like the U.S. government in its procurement contracts require and receive.[29] (The technology for large-scale, on-line global purchasing cooperatives, managed through a web site, became

A Strategy for Human Rights 197

available early in 2000.) [30]

The new global Internet technology also would permit a global purchasing cooperative to operate efficiently via a web site. Any company prepared to offer lowest available price guarantees and meet other conditions (e.g., international 800 numbers and multilingual support for technical assistance) could advertise today's price. Institutional purchasers (e.g., the World Bank, UNDP, etc.) could purchase directly, a model which Dell Computer has used to become the world's largest single supplier of computers. Small startup companies in UDCs, using older-generation chips and less-expensive operating systems (e.g., LINUX) for Internet terminals could find growing national or regional markets.

Project 3. Create Large-Scale Collaboration Systems

In addition to sending compressed multimedia files to local servers in all countries, the Global Affairs Channel satellite network can mirror high-use web sites in all countries and routinely transmit overnight updates of high-use data bases. From the Global CSPAN analogy, the range of global projects can expand to include support for large-scale collaboration systems. For example:

Educational Research
One example of a large-scale collaboration system has been proposed by MIT to accelerate applications of computers to foreign language instruction for seven languages, including English as a foreign language. They would create a global colloquia series by drawing upon the lectures at MIT's Center for Educational Computing Initiatives and two partner universities (in Europe and Latin America). The best and latest ideas could be transmitted at soon as possible to the desktops of researchers and teachers in all countries. Educational resources from all countries could be pooled and available to everybody in the world with a mouse click. Experimental materials, which now are almost impossible to evaluate with a large N of users, could be posted for use by, and feedback from, interested teachers worldwide.[31] For the first time, it may be possible to test the intuition that different students learn best by different methods and to have first-rate materials for each method available. The shared commitment to education—and to learning one another's language—would be a good step in realizing a human right (education) and conveying another value (respect).

Conflict Resolution and Human Rights Education
The creative opportunity to use these catalytic investments (the Global Affairs satellite net, the critical mass of terminals for health, education, and science in UDCs, and the purchasing cooperative) to support teachers and curriculum development in foreign language education (MIT's proposed project) brings me to a parallel strategic recommendation for a global colloquium series and large-scale collaboration system to build curriculum for human rights and conflict resolution, especially in public schools, and especially with a psychological component. Today, we can post material on local web sites and, in the global scavenger hunts of Internet searching, people may eventually find it. But if we begin with a high-visibility Global Affairs Channel and a regularly scheduled global colloquium series to discuss issues and current projects in human rights education drawn from many international sites, we can organize and support a global education movement.

I emphasize the inclusion of conflict resolution (and a psychological orientation) in human rights education because young people, in the teenage years, become interested in other people and relationships. To engage young people and to create the empathy for conflict resolution and principled settlements, the language of psychology can be more helpful than the traditional language of law.

Social science research has begun to illuminate how much of the world's violence, in teenage gangs, tribal and ethnic violence, and armies, involves recruiting young males with a wide range of appeals to discipline, self-sacrifice for a group, ideals of honor and loyalty, strategic calculation, and other traits....[32] If we view the extraordinarily youthful age structures in the developing world, especially in areas that may be highly prone to tribal warfare and violence, it would be timely to use these new technologies to get there first. For teenagers in the world's public schools, if we can build a curriculum that links to their interpersonal interests—and conveys a message that people engaged in human rights advocacy and conflict resolution have admirable qualities of honesty, strength of character, astute insight, maturity, moral reasoning, and idealism that are called forth by this work—the human rights movement can enroll young people in a good cause. If there are local public school teachers, anywhere, who want to develop such courses, a large-scale collaboration system for sharing curriculum materials, supporting them, and affording global peer recognition for contributions, might be an extraordinarily beneficial long-term investment.[33]

A Tuesday Global Brownbag: "Inventions Wanted…"
A related proposal for a large-scale collaboration system: an "Inventions Wanted…" series, a global Tuesday brownbag for the international scientific community. The purpose would be to discuss breakthroughs that scientists and engineers are trying to achieve and where they are stuck. It would be an invitation to think about a new problem and to work together in a creative process, across disciplines and national boundaries. For example, it would be attractive to gene-splice seaweed and cash crops, thereby being able to plant crops in the desert, irrigate with salt water, remove the salt biologically and make the deserts bloom. A few people are trying to do this, but everything they have invented tastes terrible…and thereby begins a global process of scientific engagement and creative potential.

Another example: It is typical to discuss soil chemistry by reference to inorganic chemicals e.g., this soil needs more nitrogen or phosphates and the application of chemical fertilizers to affect the change. But scientific analysis of highly fertile soils now shows that a wide range of microbes make a contribution. And one research project has recommended that a selection of 27 different microbes now might be packaged together in a nutrient solution, sprayed onto soil, multiply, enjoy a life in ecological balance, vastly enhance soil fertility, and reduce the need for commercial fertilizers to 1/3 or less.[34] And the excitement of a high-visibility global colloquium as any scientist will recognize is that the mixture, SC27, is only a first draft…and research scientists and undergraduates around the world can immediately begin to use SC27 as a jumping-off point, testing how it could be improved for different initial soil and climate conditions, crops, etc. An "Inventions Wanted…" global collaboration project can orchestrate new lines of global work, for amateur and professional inventors, for the common good.[35]

Visual Display Systems for Ending World Hunger
Shared visual display systems also can help NGOs to organize resources. In seeking to end world hunger, for example, it would be helpful to create and regularly update an on-line map with each village in Africa, where infant mortality exceeds a threshold value (an index of malnutrition) marked in red. Like fund-raising for local charities, donors could watch the map slowly change color as a result of their activities and perhaps use the challenge, visually displayed, to mobilize new resources to speed the process.

Each of these projects and perhaps especially the large-scale collaboration systems embody an early lesson from the development of Radio Free Europe/Radio Liberty and Voice of America. Their original belief was that programs of rock-and-roll and jazz entertainment would enroll audiences, who then would stay tuned for the news shows, which would be the pro-democracy, pro-human rights, political messages. But, over time, it became clear that rock-and-roll *was* a political argument. It conveyed the case for freedom, individual self-expression, and democracy effectively for generations of young people. Likewise, global Internet projects can be a political argument if they are linked to a global satellite distribution network that assures universal access, supports exciting and effective projects for global collaboration, and, with high visibility, expands the space of imaginative possibilities.

Project 4. Organize Opportunities for Global Philanthropy

The final two projects address the problem of financing. Many good causes already compete for the limited funds of foundations. Unless new sources of revenue can be organized, the future of well-intentioned and idealistic people may be to struggle for years to secure even the modest funds needed to build creative Internet applications for the common good. And it will help the cause of human rights if these decades of struggle can be bypassed.

Domestically, we have expected large communication carriers (who use such public resources as radio frequency spectrum and satellite parking orbits without charge) to contribute to the public good. Our domestic CSPAN is an example: It is supported by annual donations from the cable industry, provided in lieu of regulatory requirements or otherwise needing to alter the programming of individual members.

At this point, we are in an unusual historical period where the United States government has pressed passionately for global deregulation of the communications industry. And yet it has, at the same time, remained silent about the global civic obligations of the new multibillion dollar global communications oligopolies.

There has been a logic to this silence. First, American foreign policy has sought to secure the great and overriding advantages of deregulation and business opportunities for American companies to compete in global markets without permitting other political issues to interfere with a broader pro-market swing in public policy. Second, there has been a legitimate fear that any public

A Strategy for Human Rights 201

discussion of international public service obligations would open the door to political abuse, as hundreds of local claimants step forward in 180+ countries (including, in addition to legitimate causes, profit-seekers waving idealistic banners, suspect advocates of political fairness and other mischief from the earlier days of UNESCO's history, etc.) and threaten to reinstate government regulation.

My suggestion is that we end the silence about public service obligations, and simultaneously address the concerns that erected these barriers, by creating global vehicles for corporate and private philanthropy in the common good. For the global communications industry it would be an opportunity—like our domestic CSPAN—to write checks that would preempt inevitable political difficulty and a growing resentment of extraordinary profits (and the free use of public resources) without a civic conscience.

The creation of these philanthropic vehicles follows, in sequence, from the startup of the original Global Affairs Channel and prototype large-scale collaboration systems. They could evolve into a core of other global CSPANs that support both global colloquia and other large-scale, Internet-based collaboration systems. Each could be spun off to have a life of its own with philanthropic support from corporations, foundations, and other actors. For example:

An International Public Health Channel
Perhaps the most dramatic project to accelerate the achievement of a world commonwealth of human dignity would be in public health, a visible commitment to the physical well-being of each person on the planet. An International Public Health Channel could include: Global Grand Rounds from the world's leading medical schools available on the desktop PCs of medical professionals in all countries; overnight transfer of changes in the *Index Medicus* and other high-use medical databases and web sites. A series of "best practices" reports about projects to address public health problems at the local level in UDCs; a core group of on-line teaching resources to train nurse practitioners; research colloquia on malaria and polio eradication, emerging infectious diseases, and women's health; planning conferences and experiments for the development of telemedicine; a research colloquium series on applications of new technology to assist the disabled, etc.

An International Cultural Affairs Channel
A consortium of multinational corporations could, through support for an In-

ternational Cultural Affairs Channel, provide core grants to one or more leading national museums in each country (e.g., the Smithsonian Institute). These grants could be used to develop a web site of key holdings and also to digitize (for their own citizens and distribution to worldwide audiences) 15 hours/year (x 180 countries) of current lectures, symposia, and exhibits concerning their national history, cultural heritage, visual and performing arts, etc. Web sites for each national museum could include museum reproductions and add revenues derived from global audiences.

An International Studies Channel
The U.S. Department of Education provides grants for international and area studies to American research universities—often, grants to 10-15 universities for each major area of the world. The grants include funds for speakers' programs and outreach. It would be a simple step to bring these American lectures and research conferences, for each area of the world (e.g., Chinese studies) into a global Channel. And the next step—because it is rather limiting to have American academics talking to American academics about China—would be to provide basic startup authoring-technology grants of $15,000, plus $5,000 for annual costs, to leading universities worldwide (including Chinese universities) to contribute to a Chinese Studies Channel cooperative. Each university would contribute its own best materials, x hours per year, and receive, in return, many times its own contribution. And everybody worldwide—not just the university members—would benefit.[36]

We also have many scholarly societies who might be willing to get these projects under way. Especially so if the project could be organized with a global boldness and visibility to appeal to corporate philanthropy and to convey genuine respect for all cultures.

A Spiritual Inquiry Channel
I suggest the option of a Spiritual Inquiry Channel (in our secular Western age) because we may neglect, to our peril, the origin of much of human rights progress in religious traditions, at least in their more universal expressions of spiritual growth. It might be wise to nourish this. And also to recognize that intergroup conflicts are often intensified and become more violent from the linkups of the political/ethnic right and the religious right.

As a scientist, my intuition is that there is a common core of spiritual growth across religious traditions—independent of the contents of beliefs or dogma—and it would be an interesting inquiry to linkup.[37] The Channel could

A Strategy for Human Rights 203

begin with a selection of the best sermons and spiritual teachers each week from around the world, and in many areas of the world that are less cosmopolitan and pluralist it might come as a revelation that there are common sensibilities about spiritual growth. Even specialized topics (such as forgiveness—why should you forgive those who have wronged you?) which are especially relevant to the difficult processes of resolving prolonged conflicts, might be addressed in ways that become useful to curriculum development in conflict resolution.

An Education Research Channel
It would be easy to expand the large-scale collaboration system that MIT has proposed (above) across a wide range of school subjects that are generic in all countries: reading (including the latest research ideas and aides for diagnosis and treatment of learning disabilities), algebra, geometry, high school biology, calculus, computer programming, technical skills. Research discussions and conferences could be linked to global audiences of educators to stimulate the creative process, and updates of new teaching resources could be transmitted to local servers overnight. Once these vehicles are established, a comparatively modest boost from corporate philanthropy ought to make it possible for any student or teacher, anywhere, to have on-line access to the best education resources in the world.

Project 5. Organize Global Stakeholder Financing for Scientific Communication and Economic Growth

A final project of system-level innovation to enhance revenue, unleash a creative potential for global collaboration, and accelerate scientific innovation and economic growth is the development of stakeholder financing for scientific communication along the lines of the Industrial Liaison Program at MIT. Under MIT's program, corporate sponsors make annual donations and receive, in return, access to preprints and briefings of state-of-the-art research 1–2 years before print publication. Revenue is shared and, in return for their participation, individual lecturers and research centers receive financial credits.[38]

In most scientific fields, it would be possible to generalize the MIT model to a global scale. The best and latest ideas concerning renewable energy research, for example, could be acquired from all sources and arrive on desktop PCs of academic researchers and corporations as quickly as possible.[39] A Renewable Energy Channel could be financed solely as a cooperative, with each leading university, for example, spending $5,000/year to put its 10 best lectures on the channel, with the expectation that every other leading university and scientific society would put lectures worthy of international attention into the channel and receive many times its own investment. But it also would be interesting—and revenue-generating—to ask leaders in R&D-oriented industries what technologies they believe to be crucial for the future of their industry and to use this list to inform priorities and organize stakeholder contributions.

Thus, for example, the international automobile industry might identify key technologies related to environmentally sustainable development to be photovoltaics, battery design, efficient manufacturing, plastics, and synthetic fuels. And from this list, the programming and donations could flow.

In each case, of course, corporate supporters will be agreeing to compete on the basis of their ability to recognize and use good ideas, the efficiency of capital markets, the alertness of management, etc., rather than on proprietary and exclusive access to information.

Several years ago, the Sloan Foundation sponsored an interesting study that suggests that advertising revenues from global scientific channels might become substantial. (In addition to products, companies also could advertise for new employees—5-minute multimedia recruiting ads, carried on several weekday evenings in the early fall, with job opportunities for petroleum engineers, etc.) Perhaps it is not surprising to learn that a 4-color, 2-page ad in *Scientific American* sells for $70,000+ and that the information recall of a 1-minute television ad, compared with such a magazine ad, has been estimated at a 3:1 advantage.[40] For a mere academic, however, even the thought of selling 100 minutes/year of global advertising at these rates starts to exceed the amount of money that might be needed. Perhaps (and readily) there can be money for programming, and a great deal more, besides.

Today, nobody knows how much advertising revenues for Internet channels, or sponsorships, could secure. But it might be attractive to develop limited partnerships of stakeholders, all of whom agree that the revenue streams they seek are in the flow of creative and usable new ideas to desktop PCs and perhaps the growth of scientific capacity in a field alongside any immediate monetary return.

Conclusion

In conclusion, we have a windfall of new technologies to accelerate political progress and build a world that begins to work for everybody, across a wide range of outcomes [e.g., Table 2]. New technology also makes available a wider range of strategies than traditional political advocacy. And the new options are available at a surprisingly affordable cost that does not exhaust any of the world's resources. A strategy of five system-level innovations, adopted now, can accelerate progress.

Table 2
The Internet and World Politics: New Global Outcomes for Human Rights

Value	Examples
Power	High visibility Global Affairs Channel with due process for non-U.S. & NGO actors; creates a more open and improved global democratic policy process.
Enlightenment	Large-scale collaboration systems accelerate educational research, share educational resources across all fields globally; new channels (e.g., Global Affairs, cooperatives in International Studies, International Cultural Affairs, scientific research and health) enrich the curriculum of all educational institutions.
Wealth	"Inventions Wanted..." series and stakeholder-financed global scientific channels to accelerate scientific innovation, incl. key environmental technologies. Preempting information scarcity for UDCs. Global Affairs Channel supports NGOs concerned with sustainable development.
Well-Being	Best and latest ideas from NIH and other medical capture points available globally. Regularly scheduled colloquia on global health issues (polio, malaria, emerging infectious diseases, etc.) from CDC, Yale Medical School.
Skill	Building empathy & democratic skills via youth-oriented conflict resolution/human rights education.

Affection	Spiritual Inquiry Channel. Widening networks of mutually beneficial relationships.
Respect	Making global public access and international public goods a high-priority norm in the emerging world order. Opportunities for input (e.g., International Cultural Affairs) from all countries and cultures.
Rectitude	Global public commitment to advance widely shared values. Establish norms of global civic contributions from multinational corporations.

Notes

1 Ithiel de Sola Pool, "Four Unnatural Institutions and the Road Ahead (1983)," in *Politics in Wired Nations: Selected Writings of Ithiel De Sola Pool*, ed. Lloyd S. Etheredge (New Brunswick, NJ: Transaction Publishers, 1998), p. 237.

2 John Montgomery, "Fiber in the Sky," *Byte*, November 1997, p. 64.

3 E.g., What will be the price of this magical universal service? Surprisingly, on a per-bit basis, every company I talked to said it will be probably not much more than what you're paying for your land line services. That may seem like a pretty amazing statement, considering the investment required to get some of these systems running—Teledesic, for example, is forecasting a $9 billion start-up charge.... But Teledesic president Daggatt thinks it's reasonable. "It's a very high-capacity system. And unlike a wire-line network, where all the capacity of the infrastructure is rigidly dedicated to locations and users regardless of whether they are actually using it at a given moment, Teledesic offers 'bandwidth on demand,' where the system capacity used is limited to that required by a particular user and a particular application at a particular moment...." Other system operators agree. Savatiel [Karl Savatiel, Vice President for Broadband Systems at Lockheed and President of Astrolink] says, "The price can compete with underutilized T1s, like 25 percent utilized T1s.... [Ron Maehl, President of Cyberstar]...sees Cyberstar's service coming in at about $20 per month for basic service" Montgomery, Ibid., p. 70, and p. 72. However these are wholesale prices and the charges to individual end-users (i.e., without a purchasing cooperative, discussed below) could be much higher.

4 For a historical overview with informed discussions of deregulation, see Ithiel de Sola Pool, *Technologies Without Boundaries: On Telecommunications in a Global Age*, ed. Eli Noam (Cambridge, MA: Harvard University Press, 1990); Harvey Sapolsky et al., *The Telecomunications Revolution: Past, Present, and Future* (New York, NY: Routledge, 1992). Recent devel-

opments are summarized by Frances Cairncross, *The Death of Distance: How the Communications Revolution Will Change Our Lives* (Boston, MA: Harvard Business School Press, 1997).

5   Ithiel de Sola Pool, *Technologies of Freedom* (Cambridge, MA: Belknap Press, 1983).

6   The technical steps are routine and require about 1.5 hours to edit lightly, digitize, and compress the audio component of a 1-hour presentation, and 30 minutes to digitize and compress 20-30 slides. Including the original recording (by conventional means) and later uploading to a web site, universities report that about 3-4 hours of a technician's time is involved to make a 1-hour presentation available on the web for global distribution, with charges ranging from $20/hour to $65/hour. This is a relatively small additional cost, given the expense of a major conference or distinguished lectures series, and it also makes presentations available to alumni and to campus viewers who were not able to attend at the time of the original presentation.

7   For an overview of Pool's work, see Lloyd S. Etheredge, ed., supra note 1.

8   Richard Tarnas, *The Passion of the Western Mind : Understanding the Ideas That Have Shaped Our World View* (New York, NY: Harmony Books, 1991), 226. Tarnas *(ibid.)* continues, *"Moreover, the spread of the printed word and growing literacy contributed to a new cultural ethos marked by increasingly individual and private, noncommunal forms of communication and experience, thereby encouraging the growth of individualism. Silent reading and solitary reflection helped free the individual from traditional ways of thinking, and from collective control of thinking, with individual readers now having private access to a multiplicity of other perspectives and forms of experience."*

9   See, for example, the works of Marshall McLuhan, e.g. Marshall McLuhan and Quentin Fiore, *War and Peace in the Global Village; An Inventory of Some of the Current Spastic Situations That Could Be Eliminated by More Feedforward* (New York, NY: McGraw-Hill, 1968).

10   The historical shift toward a more modern, cosmopolitan, and enlightened sensibility is suggested by the human baseline observed by the economic historian Charles Kindleberger: *"Man in his elemental state is a peasant with a possessive love of his own turf; a mercantilist who favors exports over imports; a Populist who distrusts banks, especially foreign banks; a monopolist who abhors competition; a xenophobe who feels threatened by strangers and foreigners...."* Charles Kindleberger, "International Public Goods Without International Government," *American Economic Review*, vol. 76(1), (1986), p. 4.

11   Retribalization does occur. Latin (once, a universal language that eased the tasks of communication and commerce) surrendered its status to the new forces of group identity and the appeals of the vernacular.

12   John Rigby Hale, *The Civilization of Europe in the Renaissance*, 1st American edition ed. (New York, NY: Atheneum, 1994).

13 E.g., contrast Samuel P. Huntington, *The Clash of Civilizations and the Remaking of World Order* (New York, NY: Simon and Schuster, 1996); with Timothy Dean Taylor, *Global Pop: World Music, World Markets* (New York, NY: Routledge, 1997); and Robert Burnett, *The Global Jukebox: The International Music Industry* (New York, NY: Routledge, 1996). For an example from cuisine, see William Grimes, "The French Learn to Speak Fusion," *The New York Times*, April 14, 1999.

14 For a comprehensive historical overview, see Harold D. Lasswell, Daniel Lerner, and Hans Speier, eds. *Propaganda and Communication in World History* (Honolulu: University Press of Hawaii, 1979); Harold D. Lasswell, Daniel Lerner, and Hans Speier, eds. *The Symbolic Instrument in Early Times*, vol. 1 (Honolulu: University Press of Hawaii, 1979); Harold D. Lasswell, Daniel Lerner, and Hans Speier, eds. *A Pluralizing World in Formation* (Honolulu: University Press of Hawaii, 1980); and Harold Dwight Lasswell, Daniel Lerner, and Hans Speier, eds. *Emergence of Public Opinion in the West* (Honolulu: University Press of Hawaii, 1980).

15 See Lloyd S. Etheredge, "Human Rights Education and the New Telecommunications Technology," in George J. Andreopoulos and Richard Pierre Claude (eds.), *Human Rights Education for the Twenty-First Century*, (Philadelphia, PA: University of Pennsylvania Press, 1997), esp. pp. 547-554 and pp. 559-564 for a cautionary discussion.

16 Larry Ellison, "Interview with Larry Ellison," *Broadcasting and Cable*, January 17, 1994, p. 84.

17 There is truth to these claims: the development of popular democracy can be seen as a political history of a free press and literacy.

18 Similarly, when the language of human rights comes to define progressive politics, all groups will be drawn to recast their claims into such language. With only modest casuistry, the claims of both group integration *and* group separatism can promote themselves for inclusion in human rights education. The claims for respect of traditional cultures and native peoples will be an especial challenge: various myths of national or tribal virtue notwithstanding, traditional practices have, almost universally, been partially egregious; worldwide, discrimination remains ubiquitous.

19 Ithiel de Sola Pool, *Technologies of Freedom*, supra note 5.

20 The Lasswell-McDougal approach also has an advantage that it is unnecessary to derive (or argue about) justifications from constitutions or other traditional sources of legal justification: Harold D. Lasswell and Myres S. McDougal, *Jurisprudence for a Free Society: Studies in Law, Science and Policy*, 2 vols., (Boston, MA: M. Nijhoff, 1991). Similar non-legalistic approaches to human rights are reflected in Johan Galtung, *Human Rights in a New Key* (Cambridge, MA: Polity Press, 1994); and Amartya Kumar Sen, *Development as Freedom* (New York, NY: Knopf, 1999). The U.N. Declaration and International Covenant are reprinted in Walter Laqueur and Barry Rubin, eds. *The Human Rights Reader*, Revised edition

A Strategy for Human Rights 209

ed. (New York, NY: Penguin Books, 1989).

21 If the Global Affairs Channel begins with a rudimentary, public domain technology a one-hour presentation (audio + slides every 2-3 minutes) can be compressed to about 6-8 megabytes, that can be reconstituted by the PC at the other end. This can be transmitted globally in about 1 second over the USIA's global satellite networks that were built for commercial radio and television during the Cold War. And, thus, each 10 minutes per week of the global satellite capacity would support 600 hours (60 seconds/minute x 10) of shared programming. The technology is good enough to begin, and steady improvement can be anticipated. Since all INTELSAT satellites are regulated by intergovernmental agreements, another route would be to create such a global multimedia satellite backbone, to be available without charge for global projects, via inter-governmental agreement. But it will be easier if the U.S. government begins the project by converting its underused Cold War assets.

22 This project has been proposed in Richard Burt, Olin Robison, and Barry Fulton, *Reinventing Diplomacy in the Information Age: A Report of the CSIS Advisory Panel on Diplomacy in the Information Age*, CSIS Panel Reports, 0899-0352 (Washington, D.C.: Center for Strategic and International Studies, 1998). This report by an advisory group of 63 people represented a wide range of American institutions (including former government officials from both parties). The traditional practices of diplomacy were created for a world of absolute monarchs who conducted international relations by the court protocols of the age of the Congress of Vienna (1814-1815).

23 It also can express respect for people in all countries to assure that the highest quality material concerning a wide range of global issues is universally available: A distinguished lecture series that is an international crossroads in women's health at the National Institutes of Health, for example, will no longer be restricted to people who can attend in Bethesda, Maryland. Any discussion of international interest can be available to all peoples.

24 Every user of on-line discussion forums and chat rooms recognizes how quickly these idealistic innovations can alienate users and kill themselves.

25 There is a list similar to the policy science list, developed by former Vice President Gore's Reinvention process at the Department of State. The list includes such goals as: security and peaceful settlement of disputes; human rights and democracy; economic growth with well-functioning global markets; health; effective assistance in humanitarian emergencies, and environmentally sustainable development. The list is bipartisan and based on wide consultation in America. It omits several goals (e.g., education/enlightenment) but it is a good beginning.

26 It also could issue invitations to countries (e.g., China) with a greater cultural distance where institutions would not necessarily apply but linkups and dialogue about global issues would be desirable.

27 The partial conversion of USIA's global satellite net (and 300 downlink sites, at all embassies and legations) will provide a large, prepaid pipeline for Internet multimedia, a capacity that is especially helpful for links to UDCs. The support of the U.S. government also will give high visibility to the project, dramatize the opportunity for creative global applications (with free global transmission) and should help to secure matching investments from other major players (e.g., the discussion below of 100,000 basic Internet terminals).

28 In addition to multimedia programming, the satellite net can be used to transmit databases such as the *Index Medicus*.

29 I can attest to being an alumni of a university that recently raised $1.7 billion from its alumni, almost none of whom knew, with much precision, how the money would be used.

30 Direct contracts with global communication companies are not the only option. The world's most extensive private data network, SITA, supports the world's international airlines reservations system and has dedicated links and substantial unused capacity throughout the Third World. Ted Turner's CNN satellite net and downlink sites might add global Internet capacity at a marginal cost. The world's leading hotel chains are securing their own private telecommunications links, and it would be straightforward for a cooperative to negotiate an umbrella contract with good prices for (e.g.) an AAAS meeting in a Hilton hotel to include, in the price of the convention, linkups to Hilton hotel meeting rooms in Moscow, Nairobi, and Beijing. A more detailed discussion is Lloyd S. Etheredge, *A Purchasing Cooperative for Health, Science, and Education: A Preliminary Report to the World Bank's Global Knowledge Sponsor's Group* (New Haven, CT: Policy Sciences Center, Inc., 1997) (on file with the author).

31 Justin Hyde, "Automakers to Merge Internet Buying," *AP Wire Service*, 3:09 AM, ET, February 26 2000; Gregory L. White, "How GM, Ford Think Web Can Make Splash on the Factory Floor," *The Wall Street Journal*, December 3, 1999.

32 Steven Lerman, *Internet Colloquium: Technology in Language Instruction* (Cambridge, MA: MIT Center for Educational Computing Initiatives, 1996) (on file with the author). Because of an institutional interest to improve its own undergraduate curriculum, MIT has offered to start the project for $15,000 seed money (to expand its lecture series), donate faculty time, and raise the rest of the money from a wide range of sources. Among those might be international textbook publishers who currently consider language-training texts a limited market because they do not become obsolete quickly enough. But if you generate new and better approaches, then you create marketing opportunities to induce the school systems of the world to scrap their earlier generations of textbooks.

33 E.g., Michael Ignatieff, *The Warrior's Honor: Ethnic War and the Modern Conscience* (New York, NY: Henry Holt & Co., 1997); Robert Alan LeVine and Donald T. Campbell, *Ethnocentrism: Theories of Conflict, Ethnic Attitudes, and Group Behavior* (New York, NY: Wiley, 1972).

34 A wide range of worthwhile topics is suggested in George J. Andreopoulos and Richard

Pierre Claude, (eds.) *Human Rights Education*, supra note 15.

35 The product is being manufactured in the U.S. by Martin Marietta Technologies Corporation: Martin Marietta Technologies Corp. Optimum Yield Inc., *SC27: A Live Microbial Product* (n.d.), Pamphlet.

36 The National Research Council has a project under way to identify potential scientific contributions to the goals of American foreign policy, which could be one source of ideas.

37 It might be revealing to learn, from an American Studies Channel, what universities in other parts of the world are teaching about us.

38 E.g., Ken Wilber, *The Marriage of Sense and Soul: Integrating Science and Religion* (New York, NY: Random House, 1998) takes a different angle on the same question.

39 While these cannot be taken as personal income, they can be used to pay for professional travel, to purchase books and additional equipment, and other research expenses.

40 A good model, alongside MIT's, is the Technology Transfer Institute of Japan which routinely interviews American NSF grantees and other researchers and produces a 20-minute daily satellite television program for corporate viewers through Japan.

41 Gary Welz, *SETN: Information for Advertisers* (New York, NY: Association for Computing Machinery, 1993), (on file with the author.) The business plan for a Science and Engineering Television Network study was developed in both non-profit and for-profit versions. The advertising rates are from the early 1990s.

APPENDIX

Selective Overview of Major Developments in Human Rights—1948 to today

Promoting Human Rights

Since the adoption of the Universal Declaration of Human Rights, the corpus of international human rights law has grown exponentially. A series of human rights instruments have entered into force addressing key issue areas relating to civil and political rights and economic, social, and cultural rights. More specifically, the principal international human rights treaties (International Covenant on Civil and Political Rights, International Covenant on Economic, Social and Cultural Rights, the International Convention on the Elimination of All Forms of Racial Discrimination, the Convention on the Elimination of All Forms of Discrimination Against Women, the Convention Against Torture and Other Cruel, Inhuman or Degrading Treatment or Punishment, and the Convention on the Rights of the Child), which include monitoring mechanisms (often described as treaty bodies), have been ratified by the majority of member states. In addition, the United Nations Commission on Human Rights, by investigating patterns of gross and systematic violations of human rights, has focused world attention on cases of torture, disappearance, and arbitrary detention and has generated international pressure to be brought upon governments to improve their human rights records. The first world conference on human rights took place in Teheran in 1968. In 1989, the General Assembly called for another world meeting that would review and assess progress made in the field of human rights and identify obstacles and ways to overcome them. As a result, a second world conference took place in Vienna in 1993. This conference issued The Vienna Declaration and Programme of Action, which took new steps to promote and protect the rights of women, children, and indigenous peoples. Among other things, the Declaration called for the creation of a Special Rapporteur on Violence against Women, for the universal ratification of the Convention on the Rights of the Child by the year 1995, and recommended the proclamation by the General Assembly of an international decade of the world's indigenous peoples. Consequently, this recommendation was carried out by the General Assembly. The Vienna Declaration also called for the establishment of the Office of the High Commissioner for Human Rights. This recommendation was made in an effort to strengthen and harmonize the monitoring capacity of the United Nations system. The post was created on December 20, 1993, with General Assembly resolution 48/141.

Promoting Self-determination and Independence

The United Nations has played a role in bringing about independence to former colonial territories. The first major step was taken through the adoption by the General Assembly of the Declaration on the Granting of Independence to Colonial Countries and Peoples in December 1960. This declaration established that "[a]ll peoples have the right to self-determination; by virtue of that right they freely determine their political status and freely pursue their economic, social and cultural development." One of the major challenges in this area was the existence of the apartheid regime in South Africa. By imposing measures ranging from an arms embargo to a convention against segregated sporting events, the United Nations was a factor in bringing about the downfall of the apartheid system, which the General Assembly called "a crime against humanity." Elections were held in April 1994 in which all South Africans were allowed to participate on an equal basis, followed by the establishment of a majority government. The antiapartheid campaign in South Africa demonstrates the success of the politics of human rights in this region. This success was primarily achieved as a result of the coalition between governments and NGOs, and it challenged the prevailing view that apartheid could only be defeated by violent means. The positive results of the antiapartheid campaign demonstrate that human rights are an important factor in achieving justice and peace.

Providing Humanitarian Aid to Victims of Conflict

There are more than 19 million refugees, mostly women and children, who are receiving food, shelter, and medical aid, education, and repatriation assistance. Moreover, there is a growing number of internally displaced persons as a result of the numerous internal armed conflicts that have been taking place over the last decade. An estimated 20 to 25 million people are suffering the catastrophic effects of these conflicts. Since 1951 the UN High Commissioner for Refugees, in a continuing effort coordinated by the United Nations and other agencies, has assisted more than 30 million refugees fleeing war, famine, or persecution. The UN Office for the Coordination of Humanitarian Affairs (OCHA) addresses all humanitarian issues, and it coordinates humanitarian emergency response. In the 2001 report of the Secretary-General to the Security Council on the protection of civilians in armed conflict (S/2001/331), the Secretary-General affirms that international efforts to protect civilians can only be complementary to those of governments. Governments have the primary responsibility for the protection of civilians; in cases where governments lack the resources to ensure such protection, "it is incumbent on them to invoke the support of the international system." In order to achieve the latter, the Secretary-General provides several recommendations. These recommendations address primarily the need for better flow of information, the building of new partnerships, and effective coordination of the varied entities addressing the different needs of the victims. Furthermore, to deal with the problem of internally displaced persons, the Secretary-General stresses the importance of separating armed elements from those displaced populations. Failure to do so may result in negative effects on neighboring countries not involved in the conflict. Consequently, the Secretary-General urges the Security Council to further develop the concept of regional approaches to regional conflicts and to support the efforts of the separation of armed elements in situations of population displacement.

Promoting Women's Rights

A long-term objective of the United Nations has been to improve the lives of women and to empower women to have greater control over their lives. Several conferences during the U.N.-sponsored International Women's Decade set an agenda for the advancement of women and women's rights. In addition, there were also several conventions reaffirming the importance of the norm of nondiscrimination. Most important in this context is the Convention on the Elimination of All Forms of Discrimination Against

Women (the Women's Convention). Other relevant treaties include: the International Convention on the Elimination of All Forms of Racial Discrimination, the European Convention for the Protection of Human Rights and Fundamental Freedoms, the American Convention on Human Rights, and the African Charter on Human and Peoples' Rights. The Women's Convention, concluded in 1979 and entered into force in 1981, is the greatest accomplishment of the U.N. system regarding human rights of women. It is often described as a Bill of Rights for women. In 1995, the Fourth World Conference on Women, which took place in Beijing, finalized the Declaration and Platform for Action. This conference called for a five-year action plan to enhance the social, economic, and political empowerment of women, improve their health, advance their education and promote their marital and sexual rights. Moreover, in June 2000, the General Assembly held a special session, "Women 2000: Gender Equality, Development and Peace for the Twenty-first Century," also known as Beijing +5. The objective of this special session was to review the progress made since the Beijing Conference. It focused on examples of good practices, positive actions, lessons learned, and the obstacles and key challenges remaining since the 1995 Conference. It also considered further actions and initiatives for achieving gender equality in the new millennium.

Promoting Worker Rights

The International Labour Organization (ILO) has promoted the right to freedom of association and other worker-related rights. Moreover, it has consistently campaigned against discriminatory and child labor practices. Last but not least, ILO's standard-setting work has contributed to the reduction of work-related accidents. The UN has adopted numerous international labor conventions. Among these conventions, ten of them are basic human rights conventions, which establish standards on freedom of association, against forced labor, and nondiscrimination in employment. The latter were adopted by the General Assembly and by regional organizations. They include: Freedom of Association and Protection of the Right to Organize Convention, 1948; The Right to Organize and Collective Bargaining Convention, 1949; Labour Relations (Public Service) Convention, 1978; Forced Labour Convention, 1930; Abolition of Forced Labour Convention, 1957; and Discrimination (Employment and Occupational) Convention,

1958. Another example of the growing attention to human rights issues is the North American Agreement on Labor Cooperation (NAALC). This agreement is also known as NAFTA's Labor Side Agreement. NAALC's proponents argue that the agreement provides a framework for international labor solidarity. This agreement was negotiated by the governments of Canada, Mexico, and the United States, and it can act as a vehicle for the transnational mobilization of labor rights advocates among the different countries to fight for their rights.

Empowering the Voiceless

As affirmed by the United Nations Charter, the Universal Declaration of Human Rights, the International Covenants, and related human rights instruments, every person is entitled to exercise their civil, political, social, and cultural rights equally. U.N.–sponsored international years and conferences have caused governments to recognize the needs and contributions of groups usually excluded from decision-making, such as the aging, children, youth, women, homeless, indigenous and disabled people. The empowerment of these groups is of paramount importance given that it would maximize their chance to contribute to a nation's economic, social and cultural advancement. Some of the recent conferences that dealt with the empowerment of the voiceless include: the United Nations Conference on the Environment held in 1992, the World Conference on Human Rights held in 1993, the International Conference on Population and Development held in 1994, the World Summit for Social Development held in 1995, the Fourth World Conference on Women held in 1995, and Habitat II held in 1996. United Nations subsidiary bodies and specialized agencies also contribute to the advancement of the well-being of members of these groups. Examples include the United Nations Educational, Scientific and Cultural Organization (UNESCO), which provides special education for persons with disabilities; the World Health Organization (WHO), which provides technical assistance in health and prevention; the United Nations Children's Fund (UNICEF), which supports various programs and provides technical assistance in collaboration with Rehabilitation International (a non-governmental organization); and the International Labour Organization (ILO), which is committed to improving access to the labor market and increasing economic integration through international labour standards and technical cooperation activities.

Human Rights Education

Education is a right, not a benefit. As stated in Section 1 of Article 26 of the UDHR, "Everyone has the right to education. Education shall be free, at least in the elementary and fundamental stages. Elementary education shall be compulsory." During the 1990s a large range of states have supported human rights education as a way to fight human rights abuses. Some countries, such as the Philippines in 1987, have created constitutions that require the teaching of human rights in all educational institutions. Moreover, the General Assembly proclaimed the years 1995-2004 as the U.N. Decade for Human Rights Education. Consequently various programs have been created in order to accomplish its objectives. Some of these programs concentrate on the training of select groups of professionals who can influence public debate on accountability and governance. Several examples include: the Human Dignity and Policing course offered by the John Jay College of Criminal Justice of the City University of New York, which uses role-playing exercises to help police officers understand the importance of human dignity; another example is the program at the Philippine National University which makes use of the United Nations Human Rights Trainers Guide to teach its students the importance of incorporating students' experiences in the choice of the pertinent human rights issues; a third example is the program led by the Association Mondiale pour l' Ecole Instrument de Paix (EIP) which created the International Training Centre on Human Rights and Peace Teaching (CIFEDHOP). Every year, CIFEDHOP organizes an international training seminar in Geneva for specialists and teachers on human rights education and peace. As a direct result of the efforts of U.N. agencies, in conjunction with intergovernmental and NGO initiatives, a greater number of adults in developing countries can now read and write, and more children in these countries can attend school.

Promoting Democracy

Human rights cannot be fully realized in the absence of a commitment to the rule of law and democratic governance. Article 21 section 3 of the Universal Declaration of Human Rights declares that "the will of the people shall be the basis of the authority of government; this will shall be expressed in periodic and genuine elections which shall be by universal and equal suffrage and shall be held by secret vote or by equivalent free voting procedure." Since its adoption, there has been a steady movement toward democratic governance. The United Nations has enabled people in over 45 countries to participate in free and fair elections, including those held in Cambodia, Namibia, El Salvador, Eritrea, Mozambique, Nicaragua, and South Africa. It has provided electoral advice, assistance, and monitoring of results. Moreover, the Universal Declaration of the Rights of People adopted in July 1976 sets forth the right for every person to have a democratic government representing all the citizens regardless of race, sex or beliefs. Another beneficial aspect of promoting democracy is that it also allows for the promotion of peace. As stated by the Secretary-General in the Millennium Report: "We the People," the increasing number of democratic states has contributed to the decline of inter-state warfare. For a variety of reasons, established democratic states "rarely fight each other militarily."

CONTRIBUTORS

George J. Andreopoulos is Associate Professor of Government at the John Jay College of Criminal Justice and at the Graduate Center, CUNY, Director of the Center for International Human Rights at John Jay College, and lecturer at Yale University. Before coming to CUNY, he taught for several years at Yale University, where he was also the Founding Associate Director of the Orville Schell Center for International Human Rights. His publications include *The Laws of War: Constraints on Warfare in the Western World* (with Sir Michael Howard and Mark Shulman, Yale University Press, 1994), and *Human Rights Education for the Twenty-First Century* (with Richard Pierre Claude, University of Pennsylvania Press, 1997). He is currently working on a book on *Humanitarian Intervention* for Yale University Press.

Richard Pierre Claude is Professor Emeritus of Government and Politics at the University of Maryland, College Park, and the Founding Editor of *Human Rights Quarterly*. Twice a Fulbright Research Scholar in Asia, Claude has written extensively about human rights education, including his books: *Educating for Human Rights: The Philippines and Beyond* (University of Hawaii Press, 1997), co-edited (with George Andreopoulos) *Human Rights Education for the 21st Century* (University of Pennsylvania Press, 1997). He has conducted human rights education workshops in Ethiopia, the Philippines, Cambodia, Portugal and elsewhere. Claude's *Popular Education for Human Rights* is available on line at: <hrea.org>. Based on a course he initiated for science majors at Princeton University in 1996, Claude is completing a college textbook, *Righting Science. Human Rights Links to Science, Technology and Health*.

Lance Compa is a Senior Lecturer at Cornell University's School of Industrial and Labor Relations in Ithaca, New York, where he teaches U.S. labor law and international labor rights. He is the author of the 2000 Human Rights Watch report *Unfair Advantage: Workers' Freedom of Association in the United States Under International Human Rights Standards*, and he is co-editor of the book *Human Rights, Labor Rights, and International Trade* (University of Pennsylvania Press, 1996).

Lloyd S. Etheredge received his B.A. degree from Oberlin College (1968) and his M.A. (International Relations, 1970) and Ph.D. (Political Science, 1974) from Yale University, where he was trained in the policy science tradition of Harold Lasswell and Myres McDougal. Dr. Etheredge was a faculty member at MIT for eight years (where he received a teaching award from graduate students) and, for two years, Director of Graduate Studies for International Relations at Yale. He has held fellowships or visiting positions at the Center for Advance Study in the Behavioral Science, Swarthmore, Duke, Oberlin, UC Berkeley, the University of Toronto, and other institutions. He is currently working in the Washington, D.C., area and completing a book, *The Internet and the 21st Century: Unprepared Institutions and the Road Ahead*.

Richard Falk is Albert G. Milbank Professor Emeritus of International Law and Practice at Princeton, where he has been a member of the faculty since 1961. His most recent books are *Law in an Emerging Global Village* (1998), *Predatory Globalization: A Critique* (1999), and *Human Rights Horizons* (2000). He is currently a member of the Independent International Commission on Kosovo and the U.N. Commission of Inquiry on Human Rights Violations on Palestine.

Tom Farer, former President of the Inter-American Commission on Human Rights of the Organization of American States and also of the University of New Mexico, is Dean of the Graduate School of International Studies at the University of Denver and Director of its Center for China-United States Cooperation. He has served in the State and Defense departments, edited and written 11 books and monographs and close to 100 articles and book chapters on international law, foreign policy and human rights issues. In 1993, he served as legal advisor to the U.N. intervention force in Somalia.

Susan Waltz is Professor of Public Policy at the Gerald R. Ford School of Public Policy, University of Michigan. From 1993 to 1999 she was a member of Amnesty International's International Executive Committee and from 1996 to 1998 was chairperson of that governing board. She is the author of *Human Rights and Reform: Changing the Face of North African Politics* and numerous articles on politics in North Africa and human rights issues.

INDEX

"Action Professionals for the People," 14, 175
Africa, 39, 44, 58, 61, 80, 172, 199
  Charter on Human and Peoples' Rights, 173
  East, 73
  Saharan, 46, 63
  Southeast, 38, 43, 174
  Sub-Saharan, 41, 84
  West, 83
African National Congress (ANC), 30
Ahtisaari, Marti, 15
Aideed, Mohammed Farah, 73, 85, 87, 88–89, 92
Algeria, 63, 104
Algerian League of Human Rights (Ligue Algerien des Droits de l'Homme, LADH), 62–63
American Declaration of the Rights and Duties of Man, 169
American Friends Fund, 144
American Revolution, 27
Amin, Idi, 94
Amnesty International, 8, 28, 61
  Human Rights Educators' Network, 177
  Nigerian section, 65
Amuedo, Rosa Naire, 65
An Agenda for Peace, 98–99, 101, 106, 121
Andrade, Carrera, 170
Andreopoulos, George J., 11, 13, 19, 97–137, 221
Angola, 74, 83
Annan, Kofi, 98, 100, 109, 112, 121
apartheid, 21, 30, 53, 214
Aquino, Corazon, 173
Argentina, 58, 65, 169, 172
arms,
  antipersonnel landmines, 46, 80
  compounds, 89
  destruction of, 83, 104
  recovery, 111
  sales, 79–80
Arusha Peace Agreement, 109
Asia, 60, 67–68, 80, 172
  financial crisis, 45
  human rights training, 178–190
  southeast, 38, 43, 174
Asian Development Bank (ADB), 5, 11
Asociación Nacional de Abogados Democráticos (ANAD), 144, 146
Australia, 14, 171
Autotrim/Breed Technologies, 149–150

Balkans, 46
Barre, Siad, 85, 89
Baruka Liberation League, 176–177
Belgium, 52, 88, 110, 112, 166
Bernadino, Minerva, 52, 58
Bogotá, 58, 169
Booth, Ken, 40
Bosnia, 74, 76, 78, 94, 116, 119, 120
Boutros-Ghali, Boutros, 86, 88–89, 115
Brazil, 52, 159, 169, 170,
Bricker, John, 55
"Bringing CEDAW Home," 14, 175
Britain, 2, 52, 90, 151, 191
Bush, George (Sr.), 7, 87, 104, 140
Byelorussia, 53

Cambodia, 74, 219
Canada, 36, 93, 115, 139–141, 150, 165, 178
  NAO cases, 147–148, 157, 158
  workers' rights violations, 153
Canadian Human Rights Foundation, 178
Cassin, Rene, 51, 165–166, 170
Chang, Peng-chen, 52, 57–58
cease-fire, 73–74, 82, 87
  monitoring, 73, 75
censorship, 191

Charter of the International Military
    Tribunal (Nuremberg), 1, 2–3,
    107
Chile, 2, 46–47, 53, 58, 94, 169, 172
China, 11, 23, 30, 46, 52, 57, 83
Cisneros, Guy Perez, 58
civil rights, 30, 52, 59, 165, 170, 174
civil society, 5, 30, 42–43, 66–67
    fostering, 82
    rebuilding, 83–90
civil war, 30, 74, 80–83, 87–88
civilians
    protection, 8, 12, 73, 107
    targeting of, 13, 63, 91, 118
civilizational identities, 24, 44
Claude, Richard Pierre, 14, 163–184, 221
Clinton, Bill, 88, 140–141, 189
Coalition for Justice in the Maquiladoras,
    144, 149
Cold War, 6, 7, 25, 26, 57, 93, 100, 101,
    172, 173
    post-, 13, 41, 74–76, 83–90, 98
Colombia, 52
Colonization, 53
Columbia University, 57, 150
Commonwealth, 37
Communication Workers of America
    (CWA), 146, 150, 151, 157
Communism, 30, 55, 172, 188
Compa, Lance, 13–14, 139–161, 221
"compassionate regionalism," 45–46
Convention Against Torture and Other
    Cruel, Inhuman or Degrading
    Treatment or Punishment, 213
Convention on the Elimination of All
    Forms of Discrimination of
    Women (CEDAW), 175, 213,
    215–216
Convention on the Rights of the Child, 213
Copenhagen, 45
Costa Rica, 52
counterlearning, 190–192
cross-border labor action, 139–161
Cuba, 39, 52, 58, 169
"Culture of prevention," 99

cultural rights, 21, 39, 167–168, 170, 179
    practices, 44–45, 54, 64, 68
    values, 30, 35, 44–45
Cyprus, 74
Czechoslovakia, 30, 53

Dallaire, General, 110–112
De Cuellar, Javier Perez, 98
death squads, 39, 64
Declaration of the Rights of Indigenous
    Peoples, 36
Declaration on the Granting of
    Independence to Colonial
    Countries and Peoples, 214
decolonization, 21, 59
democracy, 6, 42, 43, 172
    promoting, 218–219
    restoration of, 76
development of human personality, 168–
    169, 174, 175–176
dignity, 169
    education for, 169, 174–175
    universal standards of, 44
"Diplomacy-Training for NGOs," 14, 28,
    178–179
"disappearances," 39, 64, 65
disarmament, demobilization, and
    reintegration (DDR), 82, 83, 104,
    105, 106, 109
displaced persons, 75
Dominican Republic, 52, 58
Donnelly, Jack, 62
Duke, Charles, 57

East Timor, 22, 97
Echlin/ITAPSA, 147–148
Economic and Social Council, 3, 4
Ecuador, 170
education, 58, 174, 197–203
    compulsory, 166, 171
    for freedom, 168–169
    goals, 167, 170–172
    parental rights bearing on, 166–167
    right to, 163–184
    technical/professional, 166, 171

Egypt, 53, 85
Eisenhower, 56
El Salvador, 74, 76, 219
Electronic tribes, 190
Ellison, Larry, 189–190
Etheredge, Lloyd, 14–15, 185–211, 221
Ethiopia, 14, 85, 172–173, 175
Europe, 45–46, 59, 76
    Eastern, 11, 43, 61, 80, 172
    boundaries in, 30
emancipation, 30–31
    Western, 80
European Convention for the Protection of Human Rights and Fundamental Freedoms, 216
European Enlightenment, 32, 44, 53

fascism, 166, 167, 188
Falk, Richard, 11, 21–50, 221
Farer, Tom, 11, 12, 73–95, 221
Fathellah, Youssef, 62–63
Finland, 15
France, 27, 51, 60, 88, 91, 112, 170
free elections, 52, 63, 67, 75, 83–84, 219
Free Trade Agreement of the Americas (FTAA), 159
freedom of expression, 44, 59, 67, 164, 172, 200
Freire, Paulo, 170
Frente Auténtico del Trabajo (FAT), 143, 147–148, 152, 157
Frente Democratico Campesino (FDC), 152

Gai, Yash, 178
Gandhi, 33
Garcia, Edmundo, 173
gender discrimination, 39, 52, 64, 68, 147, 175–176, 191
General Electric, 143–144, 157
Geneva Conventions, 8–9
Genocide, 1, 13, 53, 163
    "ethnic cleansing," 46, 91
    prevention of, 97–137
    Rwanda, 46

Genocide Convention, 56, 107, 108, 115
Germany, 27, 45, 63, 80, 85, 91, 151, 188, 191
Giddens, Anthony, 45
global community, 5, 30, 41, 42, 45, 46, 173
global market, 45, 189, 190
global South, 51–71, 61, 63, 65, 67
globalization, 30, 41–42, 45, 47
    advantages of, 46
    economic, 41, 43, 46
    negative impact of, 42
    people-oriented, 42
    responding to, 43
    responsible, 45
Gorbachev, Mikhail, 6–7, 30
Gossendi, Bob, 89, 90
grassroots activism, 5, 28, 29, 75, 175, 177–178
Greece, 52
Guatemala, 74, 76
Gulf War, 22, 113–114

Haiti, 52, 59, 76, 94
Helsinki Committee, 11, 30, 172
Henkin, Louis, 23–24
Herzegovina, 119
Higgott, 5
High Readiness Brigade (HRB), 114
Hitler, Adolph, 27
Holland, 166
Holman, Frank, 55
Honduras, 53
Honeywell, 143–144, 157
Howe, Jonathan, 89, 90
Human Development Report, 41
human rights
    activism, 7–8, 60–62, 62, 198, 202
    "autonomy dilemma," 66
    critics of, 10
    local, 64, 66–68
    networking, 11
    partisan politics, 66–67, 101
    defense of, 13, 62–64, 185
    defining, 164
    discourse, 11, 15, 24, 54

enforcement action in defense of, 2–3, 46
   mechanisms, 9, 60
failure to implement, 21
international, 8, 9, 28, 30–31, 42, 43, 46, 56, 57, 59–61, 64, 68, 172
language of, 4, 44
major developments in, 213–217
movement, 51–71
norms/standards, 2, 3, 7, 9, 10, 24, 26, 30, 36, 38, 42, 44, 51–71, 107, 172
   implementation of, 23, 59
rescuing, 74–95
respecting, 173, 174–176
tradition, 30, 43–44
violations/abuses of, 5, 7, 35–36, 63, 99, 113, 173
   accountability, 7, 46
   culturally sanctioned, 39, 64
   dissemination of information about, 8, 164
   governmental, 38–39, 62
   root causes of, 15
   selective attention to, 38–39, 47
   war crimes, 63, 107, 113, 121
"human rights culture," 43, 180
human rights education (HRE), 11, 14, 153–184, 197, 205, 218
   today, 171–174
Human Rights U.S.A., 177–178
Human Rights Watch, 28, 145, 147
   Women's Rights Project, 176
humane governance, 21–50
   challenges of, 21–50
   global, 46–47
   promise of, 39–43
   quest for, 45–47
humanitarian considerations, 100
humanitarian emergencies, 100, 116
humanitarian intervention, 11, 12, 23, 27, 46, 47, 74–95, 86, 87, 88, 91, 97–137,
   assistance, 81, 102, 214–215
   consensual, 101
   forcible, 118, 121
   language of, 118–119
   policies, 98
   politicization of, 102–103
   responsibilities of, 116
Humphrey, John, 57, 165–166

India, 33, 44, 59, 88
indigenous peoples, 34–37, 44, 68, 88, 214
Indonesia, 22, 30, 178
Indonesian Human Rights Commission, 178
International Brotherhood of Teamsters, 143, 152, 157
International Committee of the Red Cross (ICRC), 8, 101
International community, 9, 11, 26, 64, 73–74, 80, 100, 108, 115
International Convention on the Elimination of All Forms of Racial Discrimination, 213, 216
International Covenant on Economic, Social, and Cultural Rights, 37, 192, 213
International Covenant on Civil and Political Rights, 56
International Court of Justice (ICJ), 119
International Criminal Court for the former Yugoslavia (ICTY), 108
international criminal justice system, 15
   establishing, 46, 107
International Criminal Tribunal for the former Yugoslavia (ICTY), 108
International Criminal Tribunal for Rwanda (ICTR), 108
International Federation of Human Rights, 61
International human rights law (IHRL), 7, 9, 11, 121, 213
International humanitarian law (IHL), 9, 118
International Labor Rights Fund, 144, 145, 146, 153
International Labour Organization (ILO), 146, 155, 216

international labor solidarity, 156–159
international law, 1, 21, 24, 27, 61
International Monetary Fund, 45, 79
international peace, 7, 100, 177, 179
International Union of Catholic Women's Leagues, 166
International Women's Decade, 215
Iran, 22
Iraq, 22, 52, 58
Ireland, 30
    Northern, 84
Israel, 22, 39
Italy, 85, 88, 112
Japan, 53, 57, 90, 176–177
Jilani, Hina, 64
Junta de Conciliación y Arbitraje, 145–146
Kandel, Isaac L., 168
Kenya, 85
Khomeini, Ayatollah, 44
Kigali, 109–111
Kosovo, 91, 94, 97, 117–118, 119, 120
Kosovar Liberation Army (KLA), 119
Kuwait, 22
labor rights, 174, 216
    activism, 10, 139–161
    business/government abuse, 139–155
Lasswell-McDougal, 192–204
Latin America, 12, 25, 40, 53, 57, 58, 61, 164, 165, 169–171, 172
"dirty wars," 64, 67
LaFontaine, Oskar, 45
"Law to the Villages" program, 14, 174
Lebanon, 12, 51, 57, 166
Liberia, 74, 83, 117

Malik, Charles, 52, 57–58, 164
"Magna Carta of Mankind," 53
Magsaysay Award, 175
Mandela, Nelson, 30
Market-oriented constitutionalism, 41–42
Marriage rights, 58, 64, 174, 175–176
Material sustenance, 39, 40, 58
Maxi-Switch, 146, 156
McCarthy, Joseph, 55
McDonald's, 153

Médecins Sans Frontières (MSF), 101
Media coverage, 143, 154, 157, 174
Memorandum of Understanding (MOU), 114
Mexico, 58, 139, 140–141, 154, 158, 170–171
    Conciliation and Arbitration Boards (CABs), 144, 148
    NAO cases, 143, 150–153, 157
    Supreme Court, 145
    workers' rights violations, 143–150
Military operations, 8
Milosevic, 119
Mogadishu, 86, 87–90, 92–93, 104, 109
Moore, Jonathan, 79
Morsink, Johannes, 40, 165, 169
Moscow Trust Group, 30
Mozambique, 74, 219
Mulroney, Brian, 140
Multinational corporations, 140
Myanmar, 30

Namibia, 219
National Institutes of Health, 194–195
National liberation movements, 9
National Union for the Total Independence of Angola (UNITA), 83
Nazi movement, 27, 31, 53, 166,
    Hitler Youth, 166
neoliberalism, 42
    economics, 45, 47
"new humanitarian order," 13, 98
"new internationalism," 12, 46
Nicaragua, 219
    Sandinistas, 39
Nicholls, Lord, 1
Nigeria, 65
    Lagos, 65
Nobel Peace Prize, 175
Non-Governmental Organizations (NGOs), 4, 11, 39, 42, 57, 61, 62, 67, 99, 101, 142, 144, 154, 166, 173, 199, 205
    dialogue with, 10
    leaders, 93

relief organizations, 81, 86, 92
North America,
    Labor standards, 14
North American Agreement on
    Environmental Cooporation
    (NAAEC), 141
North American Agreement on Labor
    Cooperation (NAALC), 10, 13,
    139–161, 217
    11 Labor Principles, 139–140, 142,
    155
    Article 29, 142
    background, 140–141
    critics of, 154
    institutions, 141–143, 148–149
        Arbitral Panel, 142
        Commission for Labor
        Cooperation, 141
        Complaint Procedures, 139, 142–
        143, 155–156
        Evaluation Committee of
        Experts (ECE), 142
        National Administration Offices
        (NAOs), 141–143
North American Free Trade Agreement
    (NAFTA), 6, 141, 154–156, 217
    Committee of the Industrial Relations
    Research Association, 154155
    critics of, 13
    Labor Agreement, 13, 139–161
North Atlantic Treaty Organization
    (NATO), 22, 76, 78, 91, 97, 116,
    117,118, 119
    War against Serbia, 22

Oakley, Robert, 87, 89
Operation Allied Force, 117–118, 119
Operation Restore Hope, 7, 103, 104, 105
Operation Turquoise-France, 116
Organization for Economic Cooperation
    and Development (OECD), 154
Organization of American States, 76
organized labor, 42, 139, 140
    weakening of, 42
Ortiz, Campos, 170

Pakistan, 58, 63–64, 88, 89–90, 104
Palestine,
    Displacement, 53
Paraguay, 172
peace building, 99, 106, 177
peace operations, 12, 73, 75, 82, 83, 86, 87,
    106, 114
    enforcement, 76, 88, 90–94, 119–120
    air cover, 88, 91, 117
    maintaining, 101, 103, 116, 178–180
    multidimensional/multifunctional,
    75–76, 99
    obstacles to success of, 73–83
    rehabilitation facet, 13, 79, 81–82
        agencies, 80, 92
        funding for, 80
        training for, 86–87, 93, 173
Pesca Union, 145–146, 156
Philippines, 30, 43, 52, 58, 172, 173
    Teachers University, 179
Pinochet, Augusto, 1, 2, 46–47, 53, 94
Plant Closings and Labor Rights, 151, 156
Poland, 30, 53, 81, 172
Political acceleration, 186–189
political considerations, 100–107
political rights, 30, 59, 165, 169
Pool, Ithiel De Sola, 185, 186, 187
Poverty, 5, 39, 40, 64, 174–176
    eradicating, 41, 42, 43
Powell, Colin, 86
Protection of Civilians in Armed Conflict,
    106–107

Quebec Federation of Labor, 153
racial discrimination, 30, 33, 36, 55, 170,
    176–178, 187, 191
refugees, 75, 214
relief-to-development continuum, 13, 99,
    100
religion, 37, 44, 63–64, 174, 202–203, 206
    as a political force, 32, 37–38, 119
    Christianity, 32
    Hinduism, 33
    Islam, 22, 32, 35, 37–38, 58, 63, 84,
    176

Judaism, 32
Rights of Indigenous Peoples, The, 35
Romulo, Carlos, 58
Roosevelt, Eleanor, 27–28, 34, 54–56, 58, 164, 165, 169, 170–171, 180
Roosevelt, Franklin, 54, 55
Rorty, Richard, 43
Rosenau, James, 66
Rushdie, Salman, 44
Russia, 23, 90
Rustow, Dankwart, 65
Rwanda, 13, 46, 74, 94, 108, 109, 110, 111, 114, 116, 120
Rwandan Government Forces (RGF), 111
Rwandan Patriotic Front (RPF), 109, 112–113

Sahnoun, Mohamed, 104
Salinas, Carlos, 140
Santa Cruz, Hernan, 58, 169
Sarwar, Samia, 63–64
Saudi Arabia, 52, 53, 58, 83, 85
Savimbi, Jonah, 83
Schroeder, 45
"secularism," 31, 44
security, 7, 47, 52, 62, 109, 114, 121
 collective, 98
self-determination, 21, 36–37
Serbia, 22, 91, 94, 118
Sierra Leone, 83
Sinai, 74
Sindicato de Telefonistas de la República Mexicana (STRM), 146, 150, 151, 157
slavery, 59, 64
social activism, 6, 38
social democracy, 40, 45
social inequity, 39, 41, 62
social justice, 58, 61
socialism, 40, 42
 scientific, 85
socioeconomic rights, 21, 39, 41, 43, 55, 58, 59, 165, 170
 promotion and protection of, 13

Somalia, 7, 12, 73, 74, 76, 84–90, 92, 103, 104, 105, 106, 111, 116, 120
 economy, 85
 Habr Gedir, 85, 92
 nationalism, 85
Sony, 144–145
Soros, George, 45
South Africa, 30, 53, 56, 58, 100, 214
sovereignty, 26, 27, 40, 68, 99, 107, 154
 evolution of, 97–98
 limitations of, 59
 rights of, 26
 territorial, 46–47
Soviet Union (U.S.S.R.), 11, 22, 25–26, 31, 52, 53, 54–57, 59, 60, 73, 84–85, 167, 170
 Collapse of, 29–30
 Moscow, 25, 30, 53
 Reformers, 6
Spain, 1, 46
Sprint, 150–151, 156, 157
Stalin, Joseph, 25
Sweden, 52, 73
Switzerland, 52

TAESA, 148–149, 158
Tarnas, Richard, 188
technology, 47
 communications, 94, 185, 186, 188–190
 deregulation of, 200
 global, 187
 satellites, 186, 195–196
 government regulation of, 186, 187
 information, 41, 186
 Internet, 11, 14–15, 177, 189
 projects, 185–211
  conflict resolutions, 198, 205
  world hunger, 199–200
  Create Large-scale collaboration systems, 193, 197–200
  Education Research channel, 203

foreign language education, 198
Global Affairs channel, 195, 197, 198, 205
Global CSPAN, 192–195, 197, 201
Global Grand Rounds, 195, 201
global village, 188
International Cultural Affairs channel, 201–202, 205, 206
International Public Health channel, 201, 205
International Studies channel, 202, 205
organize global stakeholder financing, 193, 203–204
organize opportunities for global philanthropy, 193, 200–203, 206
preempt the information scarcity gap, 193, 195–197
Renewable Energy channel, 204
Spiritual Inquiry channel, 202–203, 206
Tuesday Global Brownbag: "Inventions Wanted," 199, 205
  screen phone, 195–196
 printing press, 188, 191
 radio, 191, 200
Teheran, 59, 213
Telecommunications Cooperative Network (TCN), 196
Thailand, 14
Thant, U, 53
Third World, 58, 59, 88, 179,196
Thongbai Thongpao Foundation, 14, 174-175
tolerance, 32–33,
 promoting, 170–171, 176, 176–178

religious, 32
torture, 1, 39, 64
trade unions, 143–154, 155–158, 174
traditional peacekeeping, 73–75
transnational activism, 4–7, 28, 42, 46–47
Truman, Harry, 55, 56
Turkey, 39
Ukraine, 53
Unified Task Force (UNITAF), 7, 103, 105, 116
United Electrical Workers, 143
Unión Nacional de Trabajadores (UNT), 152
United Electrical (UE) Workers Union, 156–157
United Farm Workers Union, 152
United Kingdom, 30, 46–47
United Nations (U.N.), 21–22, 25–26, 37, 58–61, 64, 77–94, 106, 108, 165, 170, 173–174, 178–180
 architects of, 22
 Assistance Mission in Rwanda (UNAMIR), 109–112
   Rules of Engagement (ROE), 109
 authority of, 25–26, 56
 budget, 77
 credibility of, 114
 Department of Humanitarian Affairs (DHA), 78
 Development Program (UNDP), 41, 78
 Director of Human Rights, 52
 Committee on Social, Humanitarian, and Cultural Questions (Third Committee), 51–53, 56–58, 165, 166
 Economic and Social Council, 79, 164
 Educational, Scientific, and cultural Organization (UNESCO), 166, 168, 201, 217
 Food and Agricultural Organization (FAO)
   founding of, 163–164

Index

General Assembly (GA), 12, 14, 23, 30, 35, 36, 55, 56, 77, 78, 163, 164, 165, 170–171, 174, 194, 213, 214
  1948, 51, 68
  1999, 13, 98–99
High Commissioner for Human Rights (UNHCHR), 118
High Commissioner for Refugees (UNHCR), 78, 81
Human Rights Commission, 3, 36, 57–58, 164–165, 168, 170, 213
Informal Working Group of Indigenous Population, 36
International Children's Emergency Fund (UNICEF), 78, 81, 179, 217
Intervention Force
  UNOSOM I, 103, 104
  UNOSOM II, 73, 101, 103, 105
Office for the Coordination of Humanitarian Affairs (OCHA), 78
responsibilities, 121
role of, 73–95, 97–137
Security Council, 8, 12, 22, 77, 80–81, 102, 106, 111, 115, 117, 121
  President, 107
  Resolutions, 78, 101
    688, 98
    770, 102
    794, 103, 105
    872, 109, 111
    925, 111–112
    1244, 117
Secretary-General, 8, 9, 13, 77–78, 80, 82, 87, 92, 97–98, 102, 104–106, 112–114, 120–121, 165
  Millennium Report, 97, 219
  Special Representative, 81, 89, 120
Soviet resistance to, 25
Standby Arrangements System (UNSAS), 114, 115, 121
Volunteer Force, 115, 116

web site, 179
World Food Program (WFP), 78, 81
World Health Organization (WHO), 79, 196, 217
United Nations (U.N.) Charter, 2–3, 4, 24, 108, 163, 164, 167, 217
  adoption, 113–114
  Article 2 (7), 26
  Chapter VI, 101, 114
  Chapter VII, 102, 104, 108, 110, 113, 114, 117, 121
  creation of, 22
  Inter-Agency Standing Committee (ISAC), 9
  language of, 3, 163–164
  shortfalls of, 22
United Nations Decade for Human Rights Education, 14, 163, 172–174, 177, 180, 218
United States (U.S.), 6, 22, 30, 38, 40, 41–42, 44, 46, 53–56, 64, 73, 75, 80, 91, 112, 139, 196, 200, 205
  Council for International Business (CIB), 154
  foreign policy, 59, 74
  global leadership, 23
  Information Agency (USIA), 185
  McCarthyism, 52
  NAO cases, 143–146, 153, 157, 158
  National Labor Relations Board (NLRB), 151, 157
  Senate, 56
  Somalia, 86–90, 103–105, 116
  State Department, 55–56, 57
  worker's rights violations, 150–153
Universal Declaration of Human Rights (UDHR), 1, 3–4, 23–39, 51–71, 192
  adoption, 4, 11, 213
  Article 1, 58
  Article 2, 59
  Article 9, 177
  Article 13 (2), 34
  Article 17, 34
  Article 20, 58

Article 21, 51–53, 54, 218–219
Article 22, 167
Article 25, 34, 40, 42, 43, 45
Article 26, 163, 166, 167, 170, 176
Article 27, 167–168
Article 28, 40, 42, 43, 45, 167
Article 29, 168
critics of, 12, 39
drafting of, 27–28, 34, 51, 53–55, 163–171
emergence of, 23–33
flexibility, 4
goals of, 175
hearings, 58
language of, 34, 168–170
origins of, 12
ownership of, 12, 53–60
Preamble, 164
right to education, 163–171
weaknesses of, 11, 33–39
"universality," 35, 59, 61
University of New South Wales, 14
Uruguay, 53

Venezuela, 52, 166
Vienna, 59, 67, 213–214
    Declaration and Programme of Action, 213
    Special Rapporteur on Violence Against Women, 213
vision-created futures, 186–189
Waltz, Susan, 12, 51–71, 221
Washington State Apple Industry, 143, 152–153, 154
Western values and norms, 12, 35–36, 37, 38, 39, 44, 45, 54, 57, 58, 59, 60, 61, 90
Westphalian world order, 6, 26, 40
    post-, 45
Women, Law and Development International, 176
World Bank, 45, 79, 196–197
    World Knowledge Partners, 196
World Conference on Human Rights 1993, 59, 67, 173–174

World Economic Forum, 45
World Jewish Congress, 167
World War II, 2, 21, 28, 30, 60, 94, 107, 163

Yale Medical School,
    Global Grand Rounds web site, 187
Yalta, 30
Yemen, 53
Yugoslavia, 22, 30, 46, 53, 59, 97, 101, 102, 108, 117, 119

Zimbabwe (Southern Rhodesia), 100